AFRICA

Tony Brown Jones

/ ISBN 534-3522

HLAKANYANA'S SHIELD

[See p. 169]

Photo A. M. Duggan-Cronin. By permission of the McGregor Museum, Kimberley

Fr.

AFRICA

ALICE WERNER

SENATE

Africa – Myths & Legends

First published in 1933 by
George G. Harrap & Co. Ltd, London

This edition published in 1995 by Senate, an imprint of
Studio Editions Ltd, Princess House, 50 Eastcastle Street,
London W1N 7AP, England

Copyright © this edition Studio Editions Ltd 1995

Reprinted 1995

ISBN 1 85958 154 4

Printed and bound in Guernsey by
The Guernsey Press Co. Ltd

PREFACE

THERE is at the present day a widespread and growing interest in the customs, institutions, and folklore of more or less 'primitive' peoples, even among persons who are still a little shy of the word 'anthropology.' This interest is of comparatively recent growth; but when one looks back over the nineteenth century it seems almost incredible that Moffat could write, in 1842, that "a description of the manners and customs of the Bechuanas would be neither very instructive nor very edifying." Twenty years earlier James Campbell, whom one suspects of a secret and shamefaced interest in the subject, apologizes for presenting to the notice of his readers the " absurd and ridiculous fictions " of the same tribe.

The apology is certainly not needed to-day—witness the collections of folk-tales pouring in from every quarter of what used to be called the Dark Continent, contributed by grave divines, respectable Government officials, and all sorts and conditions of observers. In fact, so much new matter has appeared since I first took the present work in hand that it has proved impossible to keep pace with it. But I have endeavoured to present to the notice of the reader fairly typical specimens of myth and legend from as many as possible of the various Bantu-speaking tribes, confident that the result will not be (if I may again quote Campbell) to "exhibit the puerile and degraded state of intellect" among the said tribes.

I have been obliged, however, to my great regret, to omit some very striking legends of the Baganda, less known than that of Kintu (familiar from several other works, and, moreover, told at length in my own *African Mythology*). But it would have been easy, given sufficient time, to expand this book to twice the covenanted length.

A word as to the pronunciation of African names. No attempt has been made to render them phonetically, beyond the rough-and-ready rule that vowels are to be pronounced as in German or Italian, consonants as in English, every syllable as ending in a vowel, and every vowel to be pronounced. Thus it has not been considered necessary to put an acute accent over the *e* in Shire (which, by the by, ought to be *Chiri*) and Pare. Where *ng* is followed by an apostrophe, as in ' Ryang'ombe ' (but not in ' Kalunga-ngombe '), it is sounded as in 'sing,' not as in 'finger.'

African experts may discover some inconsistency in the rendering of tribal names. One ought, I suppose, either to use the vernacular plural in every case, as in Basuto, Amandebele, Anyanja, or to discard the prefix and add an English plural, as in Zulus (too familiar a form to be dropped); but it did not seem possible to attain consistency throughout. At any rate, one has avoided the barbarism of 'Basutos,' though sanctioned by no less an authority than Sir Godfrey Lagden. Moffat, as will have been noticed, was guilty of 'Bechuanas,' and I have not ventured to correct his text.

It may not be superfluous to point out that the person-class in the Bantu languages has, in the singular, the prefix *mu-* (sometimes *umu-* or *omu-*, and sometimes shortened into *m-*) and, in the plural, *ba-* (*aba-*, *va-*, *ova-*, *a-*). The prefix *ama-* or *ma-*, sometimes found with tribal names, belongs to a different class. It is probably a plural of multitude (or ' collective plural '), which has displaced the ordinary form.

The titles of works cited in the footnotes have been abbreviated in most instances. The full titles of such works, together with other details, will be found in the Bibliography.

It is a pleasant task to convey my sincere thanks to those who have kindly permitted me to make use of their published work : the Revs. E. W. Smith and T. Cullen Young; Mr Frederick Johnson (Dar-es-Salaam), for his Makonde and Iramba tales, published in a form not readily accessible to the general reader; Captain R. S. Rattray, who is better known nowadays in connexion with the Gold Coast, but once upon a time did very good work in Nyasaland; Dr C. M. Doke (University of the Witwatersrand); M. Henri

PREFACE

A. Junod; the Rev. Father Schmidt, editor of *Anthropos*, for permission to use P. Arnoux's articles on Ruanda; Professor Meinhof, for matter appearing in his *Zeitschrift für Eingeborenensprachen* (Hamburg), and his contributor, the Rev. C. Hoffmann (another contributor, the Rev. M. Klamroth, is, unfortunately, no longer living); the Rev. J. Raum (and Dr Mittwoch, editor of the series in which his *Chaga Grammar* appeared), for the story of Murile; the Rev. Dr Gutmann, for some delightful Chaga tales; the Rev. D. R. Mackenzie and the late Rev. Donald Fraser, for some very interesting quotations from their respective works. If any others have been inadvertently omitted I can only crave their indulgence.

A. W.

CONTENTS

ILLUSTRATIONS

MYTHS AND LEGENDS OF THE BANTU

ILLUSTRATIONS

CHAPTER I: INTRODUCTORY

Who are the Bantu?

BANTU is now the generally accepted name for those natives of South Africa (the great majority) who are neither Hottentots nor Bushmen—that is to say, mainly, the Zulus, Xosas (Kafirs), Basuto, and Bechuana —to whom may be added the Thongas (Shangaans) of the Delagoa Bay region and the people of Southern Rhodesia, commonly, though incorrectly, called Mashona.

Abantu is the Zulu word for 'people' (in Sesuto *batho*, and in Herero *ovandu*) which was adopted by Bleek, at the suggestion of Sir George Grey, as the name for the great family of languages now known to cover practically the whole southern half of Africa. It had already been ascertained, by more than one scholar, that there was a remarkable resemblance between the speech of these South African peoples and that of the Congo natives on the one hand and of the Mozambique natives on the other. It was left for Bleek—who spent the last twenty years of his life at the Cape—to study these languages from a scientific point of view and systematize what was already known about them. His *Comparative Grammar of South African Languages*, though left unfinished when he died, in 1875, is the foundation of all later work done in this subject.

The Bantu languages possess a remarkable degree of uniformity. They may differ considerably in vocabulary, and to a certain extent in pronunciation, but their grammatical structure is, in its main outlines, everywhere the same. But to speak of a 'Bantu race' is misleading. The Bantu-speaking peoples vary greatly in physical type: some of them hardly differ from some of the ' Sudanic '-speaking [1] Negroes of West Africa (who, again, are by no means all of one pattern), while others show a type which has been

---

[1] Most of these languages, which had long seemed to be a hopeless chaos, have been found to belong to one family, called by Professor Westermann the ' Sudanic.' Typical members of this family are Twi (spoken in the Gold Coast Colony), Ewe, and Yoruba.

accounted for by a probable 'Hamitic' invasion from the north.

But on questions connected with 'race' and racial characteristics ethnologists themselves are by no means agreed, and in any case we need not discuss them in this book.

The Bantu-speaking peoples, then, include such widely separated tribes as the Duala, adjoining the Gulf of Cameroons, in the north-west; the Pokomo of the Tana valley, in the north-east; the Zulus in the south-east; and the Hereros in the south-west. Some are tall and strongly built, like the Zulus; some as tall or taller, but more slender, though equally well formed, like the Basuto—or even over-tall and too thin for their height, like the Hereros; others short and sturdy, like the Pokomo canoe-men, or small, active, and wiry, like some of the Anyanja. They vary greatly in colour, from a very dark brown (none, I think, are quite black) to different shades of bronze or copper. Colour may not be uniform within the same tribe: the Zulus themselves, for instance, distinguish between 'black'—that is, dark brown—and 'red'—or lighter brown—Zulus.[1]

It does not seem likely, then, that all these various tribes ever formed parts of one family, as their languages may be said to do. But it may be assumed that a considerable body, speaking the same language, set out (perhaps two or three thousand years ago) from somewhere in the region of the Great Lakes towards the south and east. Whether they came into Africa across the Isthmus of Suez, bringing their language with them, or—as seems more likely—developed it in that continent need not concern us here. As they moved on, separating in different directions (as our Teutonic ancestors did when they moved into Europe), their several languages grew up.

---

[1] The expression 'Red Kafirs,' however, so often heard in South Africa, does not refer to skin colour, but to the custom of painting the body with red ochre or some similar mineral—a custom not without hygienic justification, under the given conditions.

BUSHMAN PAINTINGS
In a rock-shelter near Salisbury, South Rhodesia.
Photo Strachan and Co., Salisbury

INTRODUCTORY

The Bushmen

They did not find an empty continent awaiting them. The only previous inhabitants of whom we have any certain knowledge are the Bushmen, the Pygmies of the Congo forests (and some scattered remnants of similar tribes in other parts), and perhaps the Hottentots.[1] The present-day Bushmen, most of whom are to be found in the Kalahari Desert, are small (often under four feet in height), light-complexioned (Miss Bleek says " about putty-colour "), and in various other respects differ markedly from the Bantu. They live by hunting, trapping, and collecting whatever small animals, insects, fruits, and roots are regarded as edible. They were driven into the more inhospitable regions and partially exterminated, first by the invading Bantu and then by Europeans—whose treatment of them is a very black page in our history. The Bantu, however, in some cases killed the men only, and married the women, which accounts for unusual types met with here and there among the South African Bantu.[2] And sometimes (as G. W. Stow thought was the case with the earliest Bechuana immigrants) the newcomers may have settled down more or less peaceably with the old inhabitants. This I think not unlikely to have happened in the district west of the Shire, in Nyasaland, where the local Nyanja-speaking population (calling themselves, not quite correctly, 'Angoni') are small, dark, and wiry, and seem to have absorbed a strong Bushman element. This fact, if true, may explain some of their notions about the origin of mankind, as we shall see later on.

The Bantu Languages

The Bantu languages, on the whole, are beautiful and harmonious. None of them differ from each other much

[1] I say 'perhaps' because, though we know that the Hottentots were in the Cape Peninsula long before the first Bantu reached the Fish river, we do not know the relative times of their earlier migrations.

[2] Indeed, tradition records that a certain Xosa chief chose a Bushwoman for his principal wife, so impressed was he by her skill in preparing a certain kind of food to his taste.

more than French does from Spanish or English from Danish. No two, for instance, would be as far apart as English and French, or French and Welsh, though all these belong to the same Indo-European family. The words used are often quite different (we know that English and American people, both speaking English, may use different words for the same thing); but the grammar is everywhere, in its main outlines, the same. It is scarcely necessary, at this time of day, to say that an unwritten language may have a grammar,[1] and even a very complicated one.

It is not often that a speaker of one Bantu language can understand another without previously learning it; but most natives pick up each other's speech with surprising quickness. An East African who has travelled any considerable distance from his home will probably speak three or four dialects with ease.

Customs and Beliefs: The Spirit World

Besides this relationship in language, all the Bantu have many customs and beliefs in common. All of them have, more or less vaguely, the idea of one God, though some of them do not clearly distinguish him from the sky or the sun, or even, as we shall see, from the first ancestor of the tribe. They believe in survival after death, and think that the ghosts of the dead can interfere to almost any extent in the affairs of the living. They do not seem to have any idea of immortality as we understand it; in fact, some distinctly say that the ghosts go on living only as long as people remember them (which is very much what Maeterlinck says in *The Blue Bird* !). Ordinary people have no memory or

---

[1] This is not the place to give details of Bantu grammar; but it may be explained that nouns are divided into classes, distinguished by prefixes, which also serve to differentiate the singular and plural. The class which consists of nouns denoting persons has, in the singular, the prefix *Mu* or *M*, in the plural *Ba*, or some modification of the same; thus Mu-ila is one individual of the Ila tribe, Ba-ila more than one. Sometimes the plural prefix *Ama* is used, as in Ama-ndebele. Other prefixes (*Ki, Chi, Si,* or *Se*—sometimes *Lu*) are used with the same stem to indicate the language, as Ki-swahili, Chi-nyanja, Se-suto, Lu-ganda. But it is often more convenient to use the stem without the prefix.

tradition of anyone beyond their great-grandparents, so that, except for great chiefs and heroes, there would never be more than three generations of ghosts in existence. But, however that may be, the influence of the dead is seen in every department of life. A man gets directions from his father's spirit before starting on any undertaking—either in a dream, or by consulting a diviner, or through all sorts of omens. For instance, a Yao,[1] when thinking of going on a journey, would go to his chief, who would then take a handful of flour and drop it slowly and carefully on the ground. If it fell in the shape of a regular cone the omen would, so far, be good. They would then cover up the cone with a pot, and leave it till the next morning. If it was found to be quite undisturbed the man could go on his journey with an easy mind; but if any of the flour had fallen down he would give it up at once. Either the spirits did not, for some reason of their own, wish him to go, or they knew that some danger awaited him, and this was their warning.

If anyone is ill it is supposed that some ancestral ghost is offended and has sent the sickness, or else that some human enemy has bewitched the patient. In either case the diviner has to consult the spirits to find out who is responsible and what is the remedy. Drought, floods, a plague of locusts, or any other natural calamity may be due to the anger of the spirits.

In short, one may say that this belief in the power and influence of the dead is the basic fact in Bantu religion. We hear, rather doubtfully, of other spirits, some of which may be personified nature powers, but many of these (such as the Mwenembago, 'Lord of the Forest,' of the Wazaramo, in Tanganyika Territory) seem to have been human ghosts to begin with.

The dead are supposed to go on living for an indefinite time underground, very much as they have done on the upper earth. There are many stories describing the

---

[1] The home of the Yao tribe is in the Lujenda valley, in Portuguese East Africa, whence they have spread into Tanganyika Territory and Nyasaland.

19

adventures of people who have accidentally reached this country (called by the Swahili *kuzimu* [1]), usually through following a porcupine, or some other burrowing animal, into its hole. This happened, in Uganda, to Mpobe the hunter, to the Zulu Uncama, and to an unnamed man of the Wairamba (in Eastern Unyamwezi). The story is found in so many different places that the idea seems to be held wherever a Bantu language is spoken.

One does not hear very much of ghosts appearing to survivors " in their habit as they lived " ; though it is a common occurrence (as I suppose it is everywhere) for people to see and talk with their dead friends in dreams. But they often come back in other shapes—mostly as snakes, and very often as birds—sometimes in the form of that uncanny insect the mantis, which some people call " the spirits' fowl." Later on we shall find some very striking tales, in which the ghost of a murdered man or woman haunts the murderer in the shape of a bird and calls on the kinsmen to avenge the slain.

The High God

The High God, when thought of as having a definite dwelling-place at all—for usually they are rather vague about him—is supposed to live above the sky, which, of course, is believed to be a solid roof, meeting the earth at the point which no one can travel far enough to reach. People have got into this country by climbing trees, or, in some unexplained way, by a rope thrown up or let down; and, like Jack after climbing the beanstalk, find a country not so very different from the one they have left. In a Yao tale a poor woman, who had been tricked into drowning her

[1] The Swahili are a Bantu-speaking people, descended partly from Arab traders and colonists, and partly from the different African tribes with whom these Arabs intermarried. Their home is the strip of coast from Warsheikh to Cape Delgado, but they have travelled far and wide as traders, carriers, and Europeans' servants, and spread their language over a great part of the continent. The root -*zimu*, with different prefixes, is found in many Bantu languages, and sometimes means a mere ghost, sometimes a kind of monster or cannibal ogre.

20

baby, climbed a tree into the Heaven country and appealed to Mulungu,[1] who gave her child back to her.

The High God is not always—perhaps not often—connected with creation. The earth is usually taken for granted, as having existed before all things. Human beings and animals are sometimes spoken of as made by him, but elsewhere as if they had originated quite independently. The Yaos say, "In the beginning man was not, only Mulungu and the beasts." But they do not say that God made the beasts, though they speak of them as "his people." The curious thing is that they think Mulungu in the beginning lived on earth, but went up into the sky because men[2] had taken to setting the bush on fire and killing "his people." The same or a similar idea (that God ceased to dwell on earth because of men's misconduct) is found to be held by other Bantu-speaking tribes, and also by the Ashanti people in West Africa and the 'Hamitic' Masai in the east. It may be connected with the older and cruder notion (still to be traced here and there) that the sky and the earth, which between them produced all living things, were once in contact, and only became separated later.

Whatever may once have been the case, prayers and sacrifices are addressed to the ancestral spirits far more frequently than to Mulungu or Leza. The High God is not, as a rule, thought of as interfering directly with the course of this world; but this must not be taken too absolutely. Mr C. W. Hobley, among the Akamba, and the Rev. D. R. Mackenzie, among the people of North Nyasaland,

---

[1] This word, which in some languages means 'the sky,' is used for 'God' by the Yaos, the Anyanja, the Swahili (who shorten it into Muungu), the Giryama, and some others. Other names are Chiuta, Leza, Kalunga (in Angola), Nzambe (on the Congo; American Negroes have made this into *jumbi*, mostly used in the plural, meaning ghosts or bogies of some sort), Katonda (in Uganda), and Unkulunkulu (among the Zulus). This last (which is not, as some have thought, the same word as Mulungu) has sometimes been taken to mean the High God, sometimes the first ancestor of the tribe, who lived so long ago that no one can trace his descent from him.

[2] For whom Mulungu was in no way responsible. The first human pair were found by the chameleon (a prominent character in African mythology) in his fish-trap! See Duff Macdonald, *Africana*, vol. i, p. 295.

have recorded instances of direct prayer to the High God in times of distress or difficulty.

The Origin of Mankind

As to the way in which mankind came into being, there are different accounts. The Zulus and the Thongas (Delagoa Bay people) used to believe that the first man came out of a reed; some say a reed-bed, but the more unlikely-sounding alternative is probably the true one, as some native authorities distinctly mention the exploding of the reed to let him out. Besides, it is a custom of the Basuto to stick a reed in the ground beside the door of a hut in which a baby has been born. The Hereros think their ancestors came out of a certain tree called Omumborombonga. This identical tree (I understand that ordinary members of the species are not uncommon) is believed to exist somewhere in the Kaoko veld, north of the Ugab river, in the South-western Territory. The Hereros, who are great stock-breeders (or were till the tribe fell on evil days), said that their cattle came out of Omumborombonga along with them, but the small stock, sheep and goats (*kleinvee* in Dutch), came out of a hole in the ground, along with the Bushmen and, presumably, the game on which the Bushmen lived. The mention of sheep and goats in this connexion is curious, as the Bushmen never kept any domestic animals, except dogs. The Bechuana did not attempt to account for the origin of the Bushmen: they had been in the country, along with the game, from time immemorial, before the Bechuana came into it.

The hole in the ground is interesting, because the Anyanja of Nyasaland used to say that the first people came out of a hole or cave somewhere to the west of Lake Nyasa: the place, which is called Kapirimtiya, has even been pointed out to Europeans. The footprints of the first man and of the animals which came out with him are said to be impressed on a rock in this place.

The Bantu never seem to have regarded death as an inevitable process of nature. Everywhere we find stories

22

explaining how it began, and usually blaming the chameleon. I shall tell some of these in a later chapter. People who do not accept the chameleon story sometimes speak of Death as a person, and call him Walumbe, or Lirufu, or Kalunga-ngombe.

We hear now and then about people who live in the sky, though it is not very clear who they are. In the legends of the Baganda Heaven (Gulu), his sons, and his daughter Nambi are very much like an ordinary human family; but Heaven is less personal in the thought of the Bathonga, who call it Tilo, and speak of its sending rain, lightning, locusts, and—twins! M. Junod says it " is sometimes looked on as a real being, sometimes as an impersonal power "; and the ' rain-doctor,' when facing the approaching thunderstorm, shouts, " You, Heaven, go further! I have nothing against you! I do not fight against you! "—addressing it as a person. Besides Tilo himself, the sky is inhabited by little people called Balungwana, who have sometimes been seen to fall from the clouds when some disaster was about to befall the country. Twins, too, are called the " children of Heaven." [1] Elsewhere the Heaven-dwellers are, strangely enough, described as having tails; but it is difficult to learn much about them.

There is in the legends of some South African tribes a mysterious being called Hobyana (Huveane) or Khudjana, sometimes said to be " the creator of heaven and earth and the first ancestor of the race," and sometimes the son of the creator (Rivimbi, Luvimbi, or Levivi, by others vaguely identified with a famous rain-maker of old times). But at the same time he is represented as a tricksy being, some of whose exploits recall those of the European Till Eulenspiegel. He does not seem to be known beyond the Zambezi —indeed, I doubt whether his legend reaches as far as that; but parts of it coincide with incidents in the life of some very different heroes—Kachirambe and the boy who saved his people from the Swallowing Monster, as we shall see later on.

[1] Twins are in some parts of Africa considered very lucky, in others very unlucky—so much so that it has sometimes been the custom to kill one or both.

23

As a rule one does not go to fairy-tales for high moral teaching; they are the playground of irresponsible fancy, and we do not look too closely into the ethics of Jack the Giant-killer or Rumpelstilzchen. Legends, of a more or less religious character, are a different matter, and this story of the Swallowing Monster may be taken as coming under that description. There is another type of story embodying a deep feeling of right and wrong, in which the spirit of a murdered person haunts the slayer in the form of a bird, and at last brings him to justice, as in the stories of "Nyengebule" and "Masilo and Masilonyane."

Ogres (Amazimu)

The monster just mentioned links on to a class of beings variously described in English as 'cannibals,' 'ogres,' or merely 'monsters'—in Zulu *amazimu*; in other languages *madimo, marimu,* or *zimwi*. It is a little misleading to call them cannibals, as they are never merely human beings, though sometimes taking (temporarily, at least) human shape. Zulu folklore is full of them, but one meets them more or less everywhere, and one favourite story, about the girl who, in some versions, was swallowed, in others carried about in a bag, crops up in all sorts of unexpected places. The *irimu* of the Chaga people (on Kilimanjaro mountain) is sometimes spoken of as a leopard; but he is clearly not an ordinary leopard, and in a Nyanja story, which will be told in full later on, we shall find a hyena who can turn himself into a man when he pleases. It is everywhere thought possible for animals to change into human beings, or human beings into animals; there are even at the present day people who say they have known it to happen: it is a favourite trick of the most wicked kind of witch. Besides turning themselves into animals, witches and wizards have the power of sending particular creatures out on their horrid errands—the baboon, the hyena, the owl; sometimes the leopard and the wild cat. This is why Zulus do not (or did not till lately) like you to use the words *ingwe* (leopard) and *impaka* (wild cat; the domestic cat, *ikati*, does not

24

A Scene in Natal

The home of some typical South African Bantu.

Photo Mariannhill Mission

24

matter); you must call them by some other name. Another kind of familiar is the resuscitated and mutilated corpse (Zulu *umkovu*, Yao *ndondocha*), of which some account will be given in Chapter XVI.

Animal Stories

Many of the stories which I shall have to tell are entirely concerned with animals, who are shown speaking and acting just as if they were human beings. We all remember the "Uncle Remus" stories, which originally came from Africa, though naturally somewhat changed through being adapted to American surroundings: Uncle Remus felt called upon to explain that "de beastesses" were once upon a time like people; the original story-teller would not have thought it necessary, since, to his mind, there was no great difference. We do not hear animals talk, but that may be because we cannot understand their language—and why should we suppose that their minds work otherwise than ours?

It seems quite likely that our Æsop's Fables originated in Africa. Luqman, the Arab fabulist spoken of with approval by Muhammad, in the thirty-first chapter of the Koran, is said to have been an 'Ethiopian'—that is, a Negro—slave. His stories were passed on to Greece, where he was known as Aithiops, and this was taken to be his name and turned into Æsop.

The favourite animal in the Bantu stories is the Hare: there are no rabbits in Africa south of the Sahara, and it would seem that Europeans, warned by the calamities of Australia, have refrained from introducing them. Uncle Remus, knowing more about rabbits than hares, has turned him into Brer Rabbit, just as the hyena (who cheats and ill-treats the hare, and is finally 'bested' by him) has become Brer Wolf or Brer Fox. If Uncle Remus nearly always gives animals a title—'Brer Rabbit,' 'Mis' Cow,' and so on—this must be because his African forefathers did the same; we generally find them distinguished in some way when figuring in tales; sometimes, indeed, they are called by quite a different name. But the Bantu do not go as far as the Bushmen, who use different forms of words (with extra clicks) for the speeches of animals in the stories, and have a different tone of voice for each animal when reciting these speeches.

In some parts, as in the Congo forest country, where there are no hares, the same tales are told of a little antelope, the water chevrotain (*Dorcatherium*), called by the Congo natives *nseshi*. The reason why these two creatures, so small and weak, are made the principal heroes of African folklore seems to be a deep-seated, inarticulate feeling that the strong cannot always have things their own way and the under-dog must some time or other come into his own. The lion and the elephant stand for stupid, brutal force, though the hyena, on the whole, gets the worst character; the tortoise overcomes every one else in the end (even the hare) by quiet, dogged determination; but he sometimes (not always) shows a very unamiable side to his disposition.

These are the principal figures in the animal stories, though a good many others make their appearance incidentally.

The Zulu stories which have been collected (there must still be many others not published or even written down) are more or less like our own fairy-tales: about chiefs' sons and beautiful maidens, lost children, ogres, witches, enchanters, and so forth; but they also have their hare stories.

Much the same may be said of the Basuto, only they give some of the hare's most famous adventures to the jackal. This trait is probably borrowed from the Hottentots, who, like the Galla in North-eastern Africa (where the Hottentots came from, no one knows how long ago), have no opinion of the hare's intelligence, and tell you that it is the jackal who is the clever one. And some of the same incidents are told by the Zulus of a queer little being called Hlakanyana, a sort of Tom Thumb, apparently human, but by some people identified not with the hare, but with a kind of weasel.

INTRODUCTORY

The circumstances of his birth are peculiar, which is also the case with some very different personages: Kachirambe of the Nyanja, Galinkalanganye of the Hehe, and usually the boy-hero who slays the Swallowing Monster. Ryang'ombe, the hero of the Lake Regions, distinguished himself by eating a whole ox when only a few hours old—a feat in which he even surpassed Hlakanyana.

The Baganda and Banyaruanda have many tales or legends of a type similar to those mentioned above, while other Bantu tribes seem to have more animal stories and less of the other kind; but they probably exist side by side everywhere. In attempting, as I have done, to present the most attractive specimens of both I have sometimes found it necessary to combine two or more versions so as to get a more complete and coherent whole.

CHAPTER II : WHERE MAN CAME FROM, AND HOW DEATH CAME

NO one seems to know when the South African Bantu first came into the country now occupied by them. It is certain that the Bushmen, and in some places the Hottentots, were there before them. One proof of this is found in the names of places, and especially of rivers, which in the Cape Province often contain clicks (the Iqora, called by Europeans Bushman's River; the Inxuba, which is the Fish river; and many others); while in Natal and Zululand most of the river-names have a decided Bantu sound—Umgeni, Tugela, and so on. The Bantu came from the north-east, and reached the Kei river about the end of the seventeenth century, when they first came in contact with the Dutch colonists. But they must have been in Natal and the regions to the north-east long before that, for in 1498, when Vasco da Gama's fleet touched somewhere near the mouth of the Limpopo, one of his crew, Martin Affonso, found he could understand the talk of the natives, because it was very much like what he had picked up on the West Coast, probably in Angola or on the Congo. It is also known that the Makaranga, who are still living in Southern Rhodesia, were there in 1505, when the Portuguese first heard of them, and they must have settled there long before, as they had something like an organized kingdom, under a paramount chief, whom the Portuguese called Monomotapa.

Zulu Clan Tradition

These Makaranga are by some thought to be the ancestors of the Amalala, the first of the Bantu to take up their abode in the countries we know as Natal and Zululand. One of their tribes has a quaint story of the way in which their first ancestor brought his family to their new home. This was Malandela, son of Gumede, who came into the Umhlatuze valley, Father Bryant thinks, about 1670. It is said that when they had marched, day after day, for many

28

FILLING A BASKET WITH GRAIN

Photo A. M. Duggan-Cronin. By permission of the McGregor Museum, Kimberley

weary miles, and the old man found his strength failing, he made his wives and children get into an *isilulu*—" one of the huge globular baskets still used for storing grain." [1] He then, with one last effort, launched the basket on its way with one mighty kick, and fell back dead. It rolled on " over hill and dale, river and forest, till at last it stopped and steadied ; and when those within ventured to look out they found themselves in this country where we now live," so some of their descendants, " who are still nicknamed ' those belonging to the basket,' " told Miss Colenso.[2] But Father Bryant, who has made very careful inquiries into Zulu traditions, has unkindly spoilt this story. He says that the real meaning of " those belonging to the basket " is that Malandela's family, when driven by famine from their old homes, brought with them these grain-baskets, which were then a novelty to the people among whom they settled.

However that may be, Malandela was the father of Ntombela, the father of Zulu, and so the ancestor of the great Zulu kings. Solomon, son of Dinuzulu, who has recently died, was the twelfth in descent from him. The graves of these kings, from Malandela to Senzangakona, father of Tshaka, are pointed out near Babanango, in the valley of the White Imfolozi river. Dinuzulu too is buried near them, but his father lies in the Inkandhla forest, in Zululand, and his grandfather, Mpande, at Nodwengu.

Tribal Migrations

Zulus and Xosas alike trace their descent from a tribe called Nguni (Abenguni, a name still preserved by the Angoni of Nyasaland), who, after coming from the north, as well as the Basuto, Bechuana, and Hereros, settled somewhere in the Upper Limpopo valley. Father Bryant thinks that they must have made a long circuit to the west,

---

[1] Alas, the degenerate *izilulu* (plural) of the present day are not more than three or four feet across !

[2] Josiah Gumede, who came to England in 1919 to petition the Imperial Government for justice to the Zulus, claims to be a descendant of this family.

crossing the Zambezi near its source, or even going round its head-waters, as it would have been impassable to them " by any eastern or even central crossing." [1] Be that as it may, while some of the Nguni remained in the Limpopo valley part of the tribe set off about the year 1300 to the eastward, and these, again, two hundred years later, broke up into two sections, one of which continued its southward march, and ultimately gave rise to the Xosa and Tembu tribes. Zulu and Xosa may now be considered as dialects of the same language : they do not differ much more, if at all, than Lowland Scots and standard English, and originally, of course, they were one.

> As centuries progressed, old words and forms fell out here and new came in there, each section developing its speech along different lines, till to-day Ntungwa and Xosa are separated by a quite considerable extent of dialectical difference in speech. The Xosa language, it may be noted, has preserved for us the old-time term *ebu Nguni* (Nguniland—there whence they came) as signifying " in the West." [2]

The differences in vocabulary are considerable, just as we find that in different English counties the same things are not always called by the same names; the grammar is almost identical; but the Xosa intonation, rather than the pronunciation of individual sounds, is decidedly strange to an ear accustomed to Zulu. This being so, it is only to be expected that both sections of the South-eastern Bantu should have many tales and legends in common, and I shall not always try to distinguish between them.

The Reed and the Reed-bed

The Bantu, as a rule, do not try to account for the origin of the human race as a whole, or, rather, their legends seem to assume that the particular tribe in question *is* the human race; though, as we have seen, there are some who con-

---

[1] Yet we know that Zwangendaba's host crossed in 1835 near Zumbo in the height of the dry season, when the river was very low.

[2] Bryant, *Olden Times*, p. 9.

descend to recognize the Bushmen. They also frequently fail to distinguish between a non-human creator and the first human ancestor, which has led to a good deal of discussion as to the real meaning of the Zulu Unkulunkulu, who ' broke off ' mankind from Uhlanga. *Uhlanga* means ' a reed,' and there seems no reason to doubt that this at first was intended quite literally, for, as one native told Dr Callaway, " it was said that two people came out of a reed. There came out a man and a woman." Some have refused to believe that this was really meant, and take Callaway's view that *uhlanga* is a metaphorical expression for " a source of being." It certainly has come to be used in this sense, but I should be inclined to look on this as a later development and the reed as the original idea. The Baronga of Delagoa Bay [1] told M. Junod that " one man and one woman suddenly came out from a reed, which exploded, and there they were ! " Some native authorities say that the first pair came out of a reed-*bed* (*umhlanga*), but one is inclined to think that the cruder version is the more primitive, and is reminded of the Hereros and their Omumborombonga tree.

The Chameleon

Most, if not all, of the Bantu have the legend of the chameleon—everywhere much the same, though differing in some not unimportant details—explaining how death came into the world, or, rather, how it was not prevented from coming. I will give it first as it was told to Dr Callaway by Fulatela Sitole, and afterwards mention some of the variations.

It is said he (Unkulunkulu) sent a chameleon ; he said to it, " Go, chameleon (*lunwaba*), go and say, ' Let not men die ! ' " The chameleon set out ; it went slowly, it loitered in the way ; and as it went it ate of the fruit of a bush which is called

---

[1] The Baronga are a branch of the great Thonga nation (Amatonga). Father Bryant says that " the relationship between the Nguni (Zulu-Xosa), Sutu (Basuto), and Thonga Bantu families may be likened to that existing in Europe between the English, Germans, and Scandinavians of the Nordic race."

Ubukwebezane. At length Unkulunkulu sent a lizard [*intulo*, the blue-headed gecko] after the chameleon, when it had already set out for some time. The lizard went; it ran and made great haste, for Unkulunkulu had said, " Lizard, when you have arrived say, ' Let men die ! ' " So the lizard went, and said, " I tell you, it is said, ' Let men die ! ' " The lizard came back again to Unkulunkulu before the chameleon had reached his destination, the chameleon, which was sent first—which was sent and told to go and say, " Let not men die ! " At length it arrived and shouted, saying, " It is said, ' Let not men die ! ' " But men answered, " Oh, we have accepted the word of the lizard; it has told us the word, ' It is said " Let men die." ' We cannot hear your word. Through the word of the lizard men will die." [1]

Here no reason is given for Unkulunkulu's sending the second messenger. I do not think any genuine native version suggests that he changed his mind on account of men's wickedness. Where this is said one suspects it to be a moralizing afterthought, due perhaps to European influence.

The Luyi Legend

Some other versions assume that the creator had not made up his mind, and decided to let the issue depend on which messenger arrived first. The Luyi tribe of the Zambezi call the creator Nyambe, and give him a wife, Nasilele.[2] She wanted men to die for ever, but Nyambe wished them to live again. Nyambe had a dog of whom he was very fond. The dog died, and Nyambe wished to restore him to life, but Nasilele objected. " He is a thief, and I do not like him." Some time after this Nasilele's mother died. (Nyambe and his wife are stated to have been the first human couple; but the student of mythology must learn not to be surprised at contradictions of this sort.) She asked Nyambe to revive her mother, but he refused, because she had wanted his dog to stay dead. Some versions add that he gave in after a time, and set to work,

---

[1] Callaway, *Amazulu*, p. 3.
[2] Told in full by Jacottet, " Textes Louyi," No. XLV.

but when the process was nearly complete Nasilele ruined everything by her curiosity. Then came the question whether mankind in general should die for ever or live again, and they agreed to settle it by sending the chameleon and—not the lizard, but the hare, who, as might be expected, arrived first.

Elsewhere the lizard overhears the message, and, out of mere spiteful mischief, hastens to get in first with the (alleged) counter-order. It is not surprising that both these creatures should be held unlucky. No unsophisticated African will touch a chameleon if he can help it, or likes to see a European handling one; while for an *intulo* to enter a Zulu hut is the worst of evil omens. In some parts, indeed, the herd-boys, whenever they find a chameleon, will poison it by squirting tobacco-juice or sprinkling snuff into its open mouth.

The chameleon is the creature usually associated with this legend among Bantu-speaking peoples; the Hottentots, in a similar story, make the messenger the hare, who is sent out by the Moon to tell people, "As I die and, dying, live, so shall ye die and, dying, live." In some versions he reverses the message out of forgetfulness or stupidity; in one he does it wilfully, having taken the place of the insect who was to have carried the message.[1] It is to be noticed that the idea throughout is not that man should be exempt from death, but that he should return to life after it.

Legends current in Uganda

The Bantu must have brought this legend with them when they came from the north, for it is also known to the people of Uganda, as well as to others in between. But the Baganda have another story telling how Death came—Death, who, in this tale, is thought of as a person, and called Walumbe. This one belongs to the Bahima (or Batusi) cowherds, who came in from the north with their long-horned cattle, and made themselves chiefs in Uganda and Unyoro

[1] Bleek, *Reynard the Fox in South Africa*, pp. 69–73; Schultze, *Namaland und Kalahari*, p. 448.

and Ankole.[1] But it is the peasants, the original Bantu living in the country before the Bahima came, who have the chameleon story. The tale of Kintu, the first man, who married the daughter of Heaven (Gulu), has been told so often that it need not be repeated here. It may be read in Dr Roscoe's *The Baganda*, and in a charming little book by Mrs Baskerville, *The King of the Snakes*. There, too, can be found the story of Mpobe, the hunter, who wandered into the presence of Death, but was allowed to depart with a warning never to speak of what he had seen. He was able to resist all persuasion to do so, till at last his mother overcame his reluctance, and Death immediately came to claim him.

Such personifications of Death do not seem to be very common in Bantu mythology; but the Basumbwa of North-western Unyamwezi, in a somewhat similar legend, call him Lirufu, and one occasionally hears of a " chief of the ghosts," who may be identical with him.

Kalunga of the Ambundu

The Ambundu of Angola speak of Kalunga, a word which may mean either Death, the King of the Netherworld (usually called, why I do not know, Kalunga-ngombe, "Kalunga of the cattle "), or the sea. This is not strange when one remembers that, though living, many of them, on the coast, they are not a seagoing people, and to the sense of dread and mystery with which the ocean would naturally affect them would be added the memory of the thousands carried away on slave-ships, never to return. The Ndonga and Kwanyama, to the south of Angola, use this name for their High God, whom the Hereros too call Njambi Karunga.

Some Mbundu stories give us a glimpse of Kalunga and his kingdom. Here are two of them.[2]

[1] They are no longer a separate people in Uganda itself, as they are in Ankole and Ruanda, since even their kings and great chiefs married women of the country.

[2] Chatelain, *Folk-tales of Angola*, pp. 223 and 249.

The first is called " King Kitamba kia Shiba." Kitamba
was a chief who lived at Kasanji. He lost his head-wife,
Queen Muhongo, and mourned for her many days. Not
only did he mourn himself, but he insisted on his people
sharing his grief. " My village, too, no man shall do anything therein. The young people shall not shout; the
women shall not pound; no one shall speak in the village."
His headmen remonstrated with him, but Kitamba was
obdurate, and declared that he would neither speak nor eat
nor allow anyone else to do so till his queen was restored to
him. The headmen consulted together, and called in a
'doctor' (*kimbanda*). Having received his fee (first a gun,
and then a cow) and heard their statement of the case, he
said, " All right," and set off to gather herbs. These he
pounded in a ' medicine-mortar,' and, having prepared some
sort of decoction, ordered the king and all the people to
wash themselves with it. He next directed some men to
" dig a grave in my guest-hut at the fireplace," which they
did, and he entered it with his little boy, giving two last
instructions to his wife : to leave off her girdle (*i.e.*, to dress
negligently, as if in mourning) and to pour water every day
on the fireplace. Then the men filled in the grave. The
doctor saw a road open before him; he walked along it with
his boy till he came to a village, where he found Queen
Muhongo sitting, sewing a basket, She saw him approaching, and asked, " Whence comest thou? " He answered, in
the usual form demanded by native politeness, " Thou
thyself, I have sought thee. Since thou art dead King
Kitamba will not eat, will not drink, will not speak. In the
village they pound not; they speak not; he says, ' If I shall
talk, if I eat, go ye and fetch my head-wife.' That is what
brought me here. I have spoken." [1]

The queen then pointed out a man seated a little way off,
and asked the doctor who he was. As he could not say, she
told him, " He is Lord Kalunga-ngombe; he is always
consuming us, us all." Directing his attention to another
man, who was chained, she asked if he knew him, and he

[1] Chatelain's literal translation of his speech.

answered, "He looks like King Kitamba, whom I left where I came from." It was indeed Kitamba, and the queen further informed the messenger that her husband had not many years to live,[1] and also that "Here in Kalunga never comes one here to return again."[2] She gave him the armlet which had been buried with her, to show to Kitamba as a proof that he had really visited the abode of the dead, but enjoined on him not to tell the king that he had seen him there. And he must not eat anything in Kalunga; otherwise he would never be permitted to return to earth.

One is reminded of Persephone and the pomegranate seeds, but the idea is one which frequently recurs in Bantu legends of the Underworld, and there is no reason to suppose that it was borrowed, directly or indirectly, from the Greeks. It seems quite natural to think that the food of the dead would be fatal to the living.

Meanwhile the doctor's wife had kept pouring water on the grave. One day she saw the earth beginning to crack; the cracks opened wider, and, finally, her husband's head appeared. He gradually made his way out, and pulled his small son up after him. The child fainted when he came out into the sunlight, but his father washed him with some 'herb-medicine,' and soon brought him to.

Next day the doctor went to the headmen, presented his report, was repaid with two slaves,[3] and returned to his home. The headmen told Kitamba what he had said, and produced the token. The only comment he is recorded to have made, on looking at the armlet, is " Truth, it is the same." We do not hear whether he countermanded the official mourning, but it is to be presumed he did so, for he made no further difficulty about eating or drinking. Then, after a few years, he died, and the story concludes, " They wailed the funeral; they scattered."

---

[1] This seems to be shown by the appearance of his wraith in the Underworld, but the point is not further explained.

[2] Kalunga therefore denotes the place, as well as its ruler.

[3] Chatelain's informants in the eighteen-eighties treat this sort of thing quite as a matter of course.

WHERE MAN CAME FROM

How Ngunza defied Death

The other story is about two brothers. Ngunza Kilundu was away from home when a dream warned him that his younger brother Maka was dead. On his return he asked his mother, "What death was it that killed Maka?" She could only say that it was Lord Kalunga-ngombe who had killed him. "Then," said Ngunza, "I will go out and fight Kalunga-ngombe." He went at once to a blacksmith and ordered a strong iron trap. When it was ready he took it out into the bush and set it, hiding near by with his gun. Soon he heard a cry, as of some creature in distress, and, listening, made out words of human speech: "I am dying, dying." It was Kalunga-ngombe who was caught in the trap, and Ngunza took his gun and prepared to shoot. The voice cried out, "Do not shoot me! Come to free me!" Ngunza asked, "Who are you, that I should set you free?" The answer came: "I am Kalunga-ngombe." "Oh, you are Kalunga-ngombe, who killed my younger brother Maka!" Kalunga-ngombe understood the threat which was left unspoken, and went on to explain himself. "You accuse me of killing people. I do not do it wantonly, or for my own satisfaction; people are brought to me by their fellow-men, or through their own fault. You shall see this for yourself. Go away now and wait four days: on the fifth you may go and fetch your brother in my country."

Ngunza did as he was told, and went to Kalunga. It is not said how he got there—probably by some such means as the doctor in the other story. There he was received by Kalunga-ngombe, who invited him to take his place beside him. The new arrivals began to come in. Kalunga-ngombe asked the first man, "What killed you?" The man answered that on earth he had been very rich; his neighbours were envious and bewitched him, so that he died.[1] The next to arrive was a woman, who admitted that 'vanity' had been the cause of her death—that is, she had been

---

[1] A more likely occurrence—and one that has been known to take place—would have been that an accusation of witchcraft was trumped up, which led to his execution.

greedy of finery and admiration, had coquetted with men, and had in the end been killed by a jealous husband. So it went on : one after another came with more or less the same story, and at last Kalunga-Ngombe said, " You see how it is—I do not kill people; they are brought to me for one cause or another. It is very unfair to blame me. Now you may go to Milunga[1] and fetch your brother Maka."

Ngunza went as directed, and was overjoyed at finding Maka just as he had left him at their home, and, apparently, leading much the same sort of life as he had on earth. They greeted each other warmly, and then Ngunza said, " Now let us be off, for I have come to fetch you home." But, to his surprise, Maka did not want to go. " I won't go back ; I am much better off here than I ever was while I lived. If I come with you, shall I have as good a time ? " Ngunza did not know how to answer this, and, very unwillingly, had to leave his brother where he was. He turned away sadly, and went to take leave of Kalunga, who gave him, as a parting present, the seeds of all the useful plants now cultivated in Angola, and ended by saying, " In eight days I shall come to visit you at your home."

This part of the story grows very puzzling, as no reason is given for the visit, and it would almost seem, from what follows, as if some condition had been imposed which Ngunza did not keep.[2] Kalunga came to Ngunza's home on the eighth day, and found that he had fled eastward— that is, inland. He pursued him from place to place, and finally came up with him. Ngunza asked why Kalunga should have followed him, adding, " You cannot kill me, for I have done you no wrong. You have been insisting that you do not kill anyone—that people are brought to you through some fault of theirs." Kalunga, for all answer, threw his hatchet at Ngunza, and Ngunza " turned into a *kituta* spirit." This is not further explained, but we

---

[1] It is not clear what this place was. Chatelain could not even make out the word in the original manuscript.

[2] Chatelain seems to have had some difficulty in getting a connected narrative out of the " poorly written notes " left by a native helper who died.

find elsewhere that a *kituta* (or *kianda*) is " a spirit or demon
. . . who rules over the water and is fond of great trees
and of hill-tops." Such river-spirits figure in several other
stories from Angola.

In the story from Uganda already referred to Mpobe had
to die because he had, in spite of the warning received,
spoken about his visit to the kingdom of the dead. Something of the sort may have been said in the correct version
of the Mbundu story. Then, again, Ngunza is not said to
have been killed, but to have become a *kituta*—one does not
see why. In the ordinary course of things, one gathers,
those who depart this life go on living for an indefinite time
in Kalunga ; but after that they die again, and this time cease
to exist. We shall have to consider this point more fully
when speaking of the ancestral spirits.

It seems quite clear from all these legends that the African
does not, when he thinks about the matter at all, look upon
death as an essential fact in nature. It appears to be accepted
that, but for some unforeseen accident, or perhaps some piece
of carelessness or wilful disobedience, people need never
have died at all. To the same set of ideas belongs the
prevalent belief that any death whose cause is not understood (and the number of such deaths is now steadily
decreasing) must be due to witchcraft. Kalunga, if we are
to think of him as the High God, is exceptional in living
underground. Leza, Mulungu, Iruwa, and so on, if they
have a local habitation at all, are placed in the sky, as we
shall see in the next chapter.

CHAPTER III: LEGENDS OF THE HIGH GODS

THE Leza and Nyambe of the Upper and Middle Zambezi tribes exhibit the same confusion between the High God and the first man which we noticed in the case of the Zulu Unkulunkulu; and, further, they appear to be more or less identified with the sky and the rain. The Basubiya say that Leza once lived on earth. He was a very strong man, a great chief; when he was seated in his *khotla* (place of the chief's council) " it was as though the sun were sitting there." It was he who sent out the chameleon with the message that men should live again after death. Leza is said to send rain; the Baila use such expressions as " Leza will fall much water," " Leza throws down water."

The Rev. E. W. Smith obtained from these people a curious story,[1] the conclusion of which recalls the only comfort Gautama Buddha could give to the bereaved mother. It also indicates the belief that Leza causes death—at any rate, premature death.

The Woman's Search for God

An old woman, whose parents had died when she was a child, lost all her sons and daughters, one after another, and was left with no one belonging to her. When she was very old and weary she thought she must be about to follow them; but instead of that she found herself growing younger, and was seized with a strong desire to find Leza and ask him the meaning of it all. Thinking that he had his abode in the sky, she began to cut down trees and make a scaffolding by which she could climb up. A similar device is said to have been tried by the Baluyi, by the Wasu of Pare (East Africa), and by the ancestors of the Ashanti.

But when she had built it up to a considerable height the lower poles rotted away, and the whole fell down, she falling with it. She was not hurt, and tried again, but with no better success. At last she gave up in despair, and set out

---

[1] Smith and Dale, *The Ila-speaking Peoples*, vol. ii, p. 197.

A MAN OF THE BAKWENA

Photo A. M. Duggan-Cronin. By permission of the McGregor Museum, Kimberley

to re_ch the place where, as she believed, the sky joins the eartn. So she wandered through one country after another, and when the people asked her what she wanted she said, "I am seeking Leza." "What do you want of him?" "My brothers, you ask me? Here in the nations is there one who has suffered as I have suffered? . . . I am alone. As you see me, a solitary old woman, that is how I am!"

The people answered, "Yes, we see! That is how you are! Bereaved of friends and kindred? In what do you differ from others? Shikakunamo [1] sits on the back of every one of us, and we cannot shake him off!"

Prayer to the High God

It is often stated that Africans in general neither pray to the High God nor offer sacrifices to him, nor, in fact, notice him at all, beyond recognizing his existence. This is certainly not true in the case of the Baila, and we have evidence to the same effect from various quarters. The Bapedi (a branch of the Basuto living in the Transvaal) say that their High God (*Modimo o mogolo*) is called Huveane, and they pray to him for rain.[2] He made the sky and the earth, and when he had finished them he climbed up into the sky (conceived, of course, as a solid vault) by driving in pegs on which he set his feet, taking out each one as soon as he had stepped on the next, so that people should not be able to follow him. And in the sky he has lived ever since. This seems to be the original form of the incident, which, when the myth had degenerated into a comic folk-tale, appears as a trick played by the graceless Huveane on his father.

Mr Hobley distinctly states that the Akamba tribe, in Kenya Colony, pray to the God whom they call Engai,

[1] Shikakunamo is one of the names sometimes used by the Baila for Leza; it means 'the besetting one,' the one who will never let you alone—in this case sending one affliction after another. But in general he is described as compassionate and merciful, despite the unreasonableness of mankind, who beg him for boons, and then complain of what they get.

[2] We shall meet with a different Huveane—or with a very different conception of the same being—in a later chapter.

especially in seasons of distress. When sickness is rife among the people the headman prays first to Engai and then to the spirit (*imu*) supposed to have caused the sickness. "They first pray to Engai, because they believe the spirit has gone to Engai."

Gutmann speaks of sacrifices offered to God (Iruwa) by the Wachaga, which are clearly distinguished from offerings made to the ancestral spirits, and quotes old forms of prayer used on such occasions. The Ngonde (Konde) people, at the north end of Lake Nyasa, pray to Kyala (also known as Ndorombwike), and other instances might be cited. Thus the High God cannot in all cases be described as 'otiose,' dwelling apart and not concerning himself with mankind or his affairs.

Chungu's Prayer

The Ngonde, just mentioned, say as a rule that they do not pray directly to Kyala, but ask the spirits of their fore-fathers to intercede for them with him. Yet sometimes they pray directly: "Be gracious to us, O God, and hear the prayers of those whom we have named"—*i.e.*, the ancestral spirits. Mr Mackenzie tells of a chief called Chungu, known to his people as "the man who speaks with God," and relates a remarkable story [1] of this Chungu having been called in when the *Domira* steamer had run aground (near Karonga's, on Lake Nyasa) and could not be got off. Chungu came down to the shore and prayed, after sacrificing a white cock, and immediately the vessel floated. It is a pity that this incident does not seem to have been reported by any of the Europeans who must have been on board.

Legend of Ngeketo

These same Ngonde people have a strange legend about one Ngeketo, once a god of theirs, but now, as they say, wor-shipped only by the white men. He was the youngest of three, the others being Lyambilo (still worshipped by the Wakinga) and Mbasi, by some writers called 'the Devil,'

[1] *The Spirit-ridden Konde*, p. 23.

though that notion is wholly foreign to Bantu thought. These two became jealous of Ngeketo, because he was the first to plant maize in the country—the old home of the Ngonde, near what is now Mahenge. Together with " the elders of the people " (who usually, on principle, dislike innovations), they conspired to kill Ngeketo ; but after three days he came back to life in the form of a serpent. Thereupon they cut him in pieces, but the pieces joined together, and he revived once more. Again they killed him, and again he arose. Some people saw him, but he disappeared and went away to the coast, " where he became the god of the white men."

We are assured that this story cannot be due to missionary influence : it was known to the old men before the white men came, and they told Mr Mackenzie that it had not been changed in any way. It seems most likely that Ngeketo was not really a High God, but a human ancestor, though not honoured as such in the ordinary way, either because his family had died out or because the tribe had moved away from the place where he was buried and where only offerings could be made to his spirit. If he really introduced the maize plant (which, as we know, was brought from Brazil by the Portuguese) his legend must certainly be later than the sixteenth century ; but the mention of that grain may be a modernizing touch, in the usual manner of story-tellers, and, originally, he may have planted millet or beans, both of which seem to have been known from very early times. It is interesting to note, in passing, that where there is a tradition about millet the discovery is attributed to a woman, and, strangely enough, is usually associated with a discreditable motive.

Imana of the Ruanda

The people of Ruanda recognize a Supreme Being called Imana, clearly distinguished from the deified hero Ryang'ombe, whose legend will be given in another chapter, and from the *imandwa*, or ghosts. He is often spoken of as a helper in difficulty and distress, but is never prayed to direct: appeals to him are always expressed, one might say, as conditional wishes. Thus: "If Imana were with me he would help me." Imana is frequently referred to in Ruanda proverbs, such as: "Imana gives you—it is not a thing bought" (*i.e.*, his gifts are free); "He who has received a gift from Imana is not stripped of it by the wind"; "Imana has long arms"; "There is none equal to Imana"; "A cultivator who has not Imana on his side has [at any rate] his two arms." This last seems to mean that a man must depend on his own exertions, instead of waiting on Providence, and so might be held to run counter to the general trend of thought as expressed in the others. But it may be merely a counsel of despair; in any case, one has not sufficient information to see what lies at the back of this utterance.

Imana figures in various legends, which show him distinctly acting and speaking as a person, though, strangely enough, his name is not, grammatically, placed in the personal class, but in that containing the names of animals—a point which opens up avenues of speculation not to be entered on here.[1]

The Serpent the Enemy

One of these legends[2] suggests marked Hamitic influence, in the mention of the serpent. Imana, once upon a time, used to talk with men. One day he said to a man (whether this was the first man on earth does not appear), "Do not go to sleep to-night; I am coming to give you some good news." There was a serpent hidden in the hut, who overheard these words. The man kept awake till cockcrow, after which he was overpowered by sleep, and did not hear when Imana came and called him. The serpent was on the watch and answered the call. Imana (who is never assumed to be omniscient) thought the man was speaking, and said,

[1] Spirits, as a rule, are not placed in the personal class of nouns, but yet not in the same class as Imana. Mulungu would have the plural *mi*lungu (not *wa*lungu, as if personal), but I must say I have never come across it in the plural, except where there was reason to suspect European influence.

[2] Johanssen, *Ruanda*, p. 119.

" You will die, but you will rise again ; you will grow old, but you will get a new skin, you, your children, and your grandchildren." Next morning the man went to see Imana, and complained that he had not received any message. Imana asked, " It was not you, then, to whom I spoke in the night ? " " No." " Then it must have been the snake, who is for ever accursed. If a Tusi ever comes across that snake let him kill it—likewise the Hutu and the Twa. Let them kill one wherever they find it. But as for you, you will die, you and your children and your children's children."

Abarea, a local headman of the Galla, in the north-east of Kenya Colony, told me a somewhat similar story current among his people. In some respects it has a closer resemblance to the chameleon legend : here the messenger is a bird (as far as I could make out, a sort of hornbill) who is beguiled by the snake into reversing his message. As Abarea remarked in Swahili, "*Nyoka ni adui*—the snake is the enemy."

It seems to be assumed that Imana is unable to reverse the doom incurred through the serpent's treachery. Batusi, Bahutu, and Batwa are the three tribes who make up the population of Ruanda : the shepherd aristocracy, the Bantu cultivators, and the potter serfs, probably descended from the forest Pygmies.

The Story of the Glutton

Then we have the tale of Sebgugugu, the Greedy Man,[1] enforcing the homely old moral of the Goose who laid the Golden Eggs, through a quite extraordinary case of stupid and obstinate selfishness. Sebgugugu was a poor man whose sole wealth was a white cow with her calf. One day, while his wife was away, hoeing her garden-plot in the jungle, and he was sitting in the sun outside his hut, a bird came and perched on the gate-post. It began to sing, and as he listened he seemed to hear these words : " Sebgugugu, kill the White One (*Gitale*) ; kill the White One and get a

---

[1] Père Hurel, *La Poésie chez les primitifs*, p. 174. The story is also told, with variations, by Johanssen, *Ruanda*, p. 120.

hundred!" When his wife came home the bird was still singing, and he said, " Look here, wife! Do you hear what this bird says?" She answered, "Nonsense! It's only a bird singing." Again it sang the same words, and Sebgugugu said, " Don't you understand? Imana is telling me that if I kill Whitey I shall get a hundred cows. Isn't it so?" "What do you mean? I have to feed our children on her milk, and if you kill her they will die. Do you mean to say you are going to believe what a bird tells you?" But he would not listen; he took his axe and went and killed the cow. The family had beef for dinner, and lived for some time on the rest of the meat, but no cows appeared in place of the White One. Then the bird came again, and this time advised him to kill the calf, which he did, in spite of his wife's opposition. When the meat was finished and no cows were forthcoming they all began to be very hungry. (An African might ask, " What about the garden produce?" —but no doubt it was the wrong time of year for that.) Sebgugugu said to his wife, " Now the children are starving!" She answered, "Did I not tell you what would happen when you would kill Whitey?" Then, in despair, they decided to tramp in search of food.

He tied up some of the children in mats, and put the rest into a basket, which his wife carried on her head; he took up the bundles, and so they started. They went on till they were quite tired out, and sat down by the wayside, and Sebgugugu cried out in his despair, " What shall I do with my children?" Then Imana, who is the creator, came along and said, " Sebgugugu, what is your trouble?" The man told him, and Imana pointed to a distant hill, saying, " See, yonder is a cattle-kraal. Go there and drink the milk of the cows. They are being herded for me by a crow. You must always give him some of the milk, and be sure never to strike him or use bad words to him." So they went to the kraal. There was no one there, but they found vessels full of milk. When Sebgugugu had drunk as much as he wanted he gave his wife some, and she fed the children. Then they all sat down and waited to see what would happen.

46

When the sun was low they saw the cattle coming home; there was no man or boy with them, but a great white-necked crow kept flying to and fro above them, calling them and keeping them together. When they arrived Sebgugugu lit a fire at the kraal gate to drive away the mosquitoes, fetched a pail, and milked the cows, doing as he had been told and giving a bowl full of milk to the crow herdsman, before they all had their supper.

In this way all went well for some time, and then Sebgugugu began to be discontented. It is not clear what he had to complain of; but evidently he was " that sort of man." He said to his wife, " Now the children are old enough to herd the cattle for me I don't see what we want with that crow. I shall kill him." The wife protested in vain, and Sebgugugu, taking his bow and arrows, lay in wait for the return of the cattle when evening fell. When the crow came near enough he shot an arrow at him, missed, shot again—the crow flew away, and when he looked round there were no cattle to be seen—not so much as a stray calf! The family were once more reduced to destitution. Sebgugugu said, " What shall I do? " His wife, of course, could give him no comfort, so they picked up the children and set out on their travels. Worn out, as they sat by the wayside resting, he cried once more to Imana, and the long-suffering Imana directed him to a wonderful melon-vine growing in the bush, from which he could gather not only melons and gourds, but a variety of other fruits. Only he must not attempt to cultivate or prune the vine, or do anything but gather daily supplies from it. He found the vine, gathered gourds, and his wife cooked them. So again for a time all went well, till the man took it into his head that the vine would be more productive if its branches were cut, and it immediately withered away, like Jonah's gourd. Again he was in despair, but Imana gave him one more chance. Going into the bush to cut firewood, he came across a rock with several small clefts, from which oozed forth Guinea corn, milk, beans, and other kinds of food. He gathered up what he could carry and returned to his wife.

47

Next day he went back to the rock, taking with him a basket and a jar; but he grew impatient, because the corn, and so on, trickled out slowly, and he took a long time in filling his basket. He complained of this to his wife, but persevered for some days, and then told her that he was going to widen the cracks in the rock, so that they could get more abundant supplies. She tried to dissuade him, with the usual result: he went and cut some stout poles and hardened them in the fire. He went to the rock and tried to enlarge the clefts, using his poles as levers, but, with a crash like thunder, they closed up, and no more corn or milk came forth. He went back to the camping-place and found no one there; his wife and children had disappeared without leaving a trace, and he was alone in the forest. We are left to suppose that this was the end of him.

Another version gives one more incident, perhaps less dramatically effective, in which he is guilty of wilful disobedience, and is devoured by a monstrous wild beast. Both agree in showing that Imana's patience had its limits.

Imana and the Childless Woman

One more legend[1] about Imana suggests the idea of a wise and loving providence. A childless woman came to him with the petition made by such women in all ages. Imana, reader of hearts, said to her, " Go home, and if you find a little creature in your path take it up and be kind to it." She set out, pondering over these words, of which she could not see the sense, and as she drew near her sister's house she saw the latter's little children playing in the dirt. One of them getting in her way, she pushed it back, saying angrily, " Be off! You're all over mud!" The child's mother came out, picked it up, and washed it clean. Her sister went home and waited a year: nothing happened. She went again to Imana, who asked if she had not seen the little creature he told her of. She answered, " No." He said, " You saw it, but you would not touch it with your hands." She still denied it, and he explained, telling her

[1] Johanssen, *Ruanda*, p. 124.

that she was not fit to be a mother and should have no children.

Another story, in which Imana appears in a very human aspect, will be given in the next chapter.

It has been suggested that Imana may be the same as Kihanga, supposing this last name to be derived from *kuhanga* (in some languages *kupanga*), ' to form, construct, create.' But Kihanga is a different person, an ancient king of Ruanda, who, legend says, was the first to introduce cattle to that country. (Or, rather, it was his injured daughter Nyiraruchaba who was responsible, but " that's another story.")

Imana must also be distinguished from Ryang'ombe, who is supposed to be the chief of the *imandwa* (ghosts). His proper place is among the heroes, and we shall come to his legend later on, in Chapter VIII.

CHAPTER IV: THE HEAVEN COUNTRY AND THE HEAVEN PEOPLE

THE Zulus appear to have recognized a sky-god distinct from Unkulunkulu. This seems to strengthen the probability that the name Unkulunkulu is not, as Bleek thought, identical with Mulungu, since the latter name for the High God in some languages actually means 'sky.' "The king which is above," Umpengula Mbanda informed Dr Callaway, "we did not hear of him first from white men. In summer-time, when it thunders, we say, 'The king is playing.' And if there is one who is afraid the elder people say to him, 'It is nothing but fear. What thing belonging to the king have you eaten?'[1] This is why I say that the Lord of whom we hear through you we had already heard of before you came. But he is not like the Unkulunkulu, who, we say, made all things. But the former we call a king, for, we say, he is above; Unkulunkulu is beneath."[2]

They seem, however, to have been somewhat hazy on the subject, for another informant said that they were the same, Unkulunkulu being "the creator of all things," who is in heaven, though at first he was on earth; but "he went up to heaven afterwards." This would connect with the Yao legend, alluded to in our introductory chapter, that Mulungu used to live on the earth, but afterwards ascended to the sky by means of the spider's thread. The idea appears to be tolerably widespread, and is found outside the Bantu area. The Nandi myth of the Thunder leaving the earth and taking up his abode in the sky (impelled by the misconduct of the ancestral Dorobo) is perhaps an echo of it.

'Leza,' the name used for the High God by the Baila, Batonga, and several other tribes of Northern Rhodesia and the adjoining territories,[3] also, in one language at least, means

[1] *I.e.*, you must have committed some sin against him or you would not be afraid.
[2] Callaway, *Amazulu*, p. 19.
[3] Also, along with Mulungu, by the Anyanja.

'rain.' "But," says E. W. Smith, "it is not plain that they regard rain and God as one and the same"; rather they speak of Leza as "the rain-giver," "the giver of thunder and much rain," "the one who does what no other can do." So, too, the Wachaga, who call their God 'Iruwa,' use the same word for the sun, but insist that the sun is not the same thing as God. Yet it is possible that in the beginning it really was the material sun that was worshipped. A story, recorded by Bruno Gutmann,[1] seems to point this way.

The Man who would shoot Iruwa

A poor man, living somewhere in the Chaga country, on Kilimanjaro mountain, had a number of sons born to him, but lost them all, one after another. He sat down in his desolate house, brooding over his troubles, and at last burst out in wild wrath: "Who has been putting it into Iruwa's head to kill all my boys?"—a fairly literal rendering, which suggests that he thought an enemy had done this. (Iruwa would never have thought of it on his own account.) But if this is correct his conclusion is scarcely logical; yet how many, in the bitterness of their hearts, would have felt much the same, even if they had expressed it differently! "I will go and shoot an arrow at Iruwa." So he rose up and went to the smith's forge, and got him to make some iron arrow-heads. When they were ready he put them into his quiver, took up his bow, and said, "Now I am going to the farthest edge of the world, to the place where the sun comes up. The very moment I see it I will loose this arrow against it—*tichi!*" imitating the sound of the arrow. So he set out and walked, on and on, till he came to a wide meadow, where he saw a gateway and many paths, some leading up towards the sky, some downward to the earth. And he stood still, waiting till the sun should rise, and keeping very quiet. After a while he heard a great noise, and the earth seemed to shake with the trampling of many feet, as if a great procession were approaching. And he heard people shouting one to another: "Quick! Quick! Open the gate

[1] *Volksbuch*, p. 144.

for the King to pass through!" Presently he saw many men coming towards him, all goodly to look on and shining like fire. Then he was afraid, and hid himself in the bushes. Again he heard these men crying: "Clear the way where the King is going to pass!" They came on, a mighty host, and all at once, in the midst of them, he was aware of the Shining One, bright as flaming fire, and after him followed another long procession. But suddenly those in front stopped and began asking each other, "What is this horrible smell here, as if an earth-man had passed?" They hunted all about till they found the man, and seized him and brought him before the King, who asked, "Where do you come from, and what brings you to us?" And the man answered, "Nay, my lord, it was nothing—only sorrow—which drove me from home, so that I said to myself, let me go and die in the bush." Then said the King, "But how about your saying you wanted to shoot me? Go on! Shoot away!" The man said, "O my lord, I dare not—not now!" "What do you want of me?" "You know that without my telling you, O chief!" "So you want me to give you your children back?" The King pointed behind him, saying, "There they are. Take them home with you!" The man looked up and saw all his sons gathered in front of him; but they were so beautiful and radiant that he scarcely knew them, and he said, "No, O chief, I cannot take them now. They are yours, and you must keep them." So Iruwa told him to go home and look out carefully on the way, for he should find something that would greatly please him. And he should have other sons in place of those he had lost.

And so it came to pass, for in due time other sons were born to him, who all lived to grow up. And what he found on the road was a great store of elephants' tusks, so that when his neighbours had helped him to carry them home he was made rich for life.

One must not too hastily conclude that the man's desire for sons was only selfish, and that, so long as he had enough to work for him and keep up his position in the tribe, he did not care whether they were the same ones he had lost or not. But it is easy to understand that he did not feel comfortable with these strange, bright beings, who, one must remember, had died as small children, perhaps as babies. It is a remarkable point that they should have been found in the company of the sun-god; for as a rule the Bantu think of their dead as living underground. These same Chaga people point out their mountain tarns as entrances to the ghost world, and have many legends which assume it to be below rather than above. As they have been a good deal in touch with the Masai, and, indeed, to some extent mixed with them, this idea may perhaps be derived from an outside, probably a Hamitic, source. Though the Masai, apparently, concern themselves very little with the spirit world.

Another Bantu-speaking tribe subjected to strong Hamitic influence is that of the Banyaruanda, by Lake Kivu, on the confines of British and Belgian territory. Their royal family and the clans composing the aristocracy are taller and lighter-complexioned than the cultivators who form the bulk of the population, and also markedly different in feature, though they have adopted the speech of the Bahutu, as they call the indigenous peasants. The name of their High God, Imana, is one I have been unable to trace beyond Ruanda. As we saw in the last chapter, he certainly seems to be regarded definitely as a person, and a beneficent as well as a just one, if we are to allow any weight to the legends.

Here is one recorded by Père Hurel.[1]

The Girls who wanted New Teeth

A number of young girls agreed together to " go and get teeth created for them." [2] But one of their companions was unable to join the party. This girl's mother was dead, and

---

[1] *La Poésie chez les primitifs*, p. 27.

[2] This, as it stands, is obscure, and no explanation is given. It may mean that, having lost their first teeth, they thought a special act of creation was needed to procure the second set ; but they would seem to have been beyond the usual age for that process. Or they may only have wanted their teeth to be made white and even.

she had a stepmother who kept her hard at work and otherwise made her life a burden, so that she had become a poor, stunted drudge, ill-clothed and usually dirty. As for going to ask for new teeth, this was quite out of the question. So when her friends came back and showed her their beautiful teeth she said nothing, but felt the more, and went on with her work. When the cows came home in the evening she lit the fire in the kraal, so that the smoke might drive away the mosquitoes, and then helped with the milking,[1] and when that was done served the evening meal. After supper she slipped away, took a bath, oiled herself, and started out without anyone seeing her. Before she had gone very far in the dark she met a hyena, who said to her, "You, maiden, where are you going?" She answered, "I'm going where all the other girls went. Father's wife would not let me go with them, so I'm going by myself." The hyena said, "Go on, then, child of Imana!" and let her go in peace. She walked on, and after a while met a lion, who asked her the same question. She answered him as she had done the hyena, and he too said, "Go on, child of Imana!" She walked on through the night, and just as dawn was breaking she met Imana himself, looking like a great, old chief with a kind face. He said to her, "Little maid, where are you going?" She answered, "I have been living with my stepmother, and she always gives me so much to do that I could not get away when the other girls came to ask you for new teeth, and so I came by myself." And Imana said, "You shall have them," and gave her not only new teeth, but a new skin, and made her beautiful all over. And he gave her new clothes and brass armlets and anklets and bead ornaments, so that she looked quite a different girl, and then, like a careful father, he saw her on her way home, till they had come so near that she could point out her village. Then he said, "When you get home whatever you do you must not laugh or smile at anyone, your father or your stepmother or anyone else." And so he left her.

---

[1] This is exceptional, as in most cattle-keeping Bantu tribes the girls are strictly forbidden to go near the cattle. The Hereros are another exception.

When her stepmother saw her coming she did not at first recognize her, but as soon as she realized who the girl was she cried out, " She's been stealing things at the chief's place ! Where did she get those beads and those bangles ? She must have been driving off her father's cows to sell them. Look at that cloth ! Where did you get it ? " The girl did not answer. Her father asked her, " Where did you pick up these things ? "—and still she did not answer. After a while they let her alone. The step-mother's spiteful speeches did not impress the neighbours, who soon got to know of the girl's good fortune, and before three days had passed a respectable man called on her father to ask her in marriage for his son. The wedding took place in the usual way, and she followed her young husband to his home. There everything went well, but they all—his mother and sisters and he himself—thought it strange that they never saw her laugh.

After the usual time a little boy was born, to the great joy of his parents and grandparents. Again all went well, till the child was four or five years old, when, according to custom, he began to go out and herd the calves near the hut. One day his grandmother, who had never been able to satisfy her curiosity, said to him, " Next time your mother gives you milk say you will not take it unless she smiles at you. Tell her, if she does not smile you will cry, and if she does not do so then you will die ! " He did as she told him, but his mother would not smile ; he began to cry, and she paid no attention ; he went on screaming, and presently died. They came and wrapped his body in a mat, and carried it out into the bush—for the Banyaruanda do not bury their dead—and left it there. The poor mother mourned, but felt she could not help herself. She must not disobey Imana's commandment. After a time another boy was born. When he was old enough to talk and run about his grandmother made the same suggestion to him as she had done to his brother, and with the same result. The boy died, and was carried out to the bush. Again a baby was born—this time a bonny little girl.

55

When she was about three years old her mother one evening took her on her back and went out to the bush where the two little bodies had been laid long ago. There, in her great trouble, she cried to Imana, "*Yee, baba wee!* O my father! O Imana, lord of Ruanda, I have never once disobeyed you; will you not save this little one?" She looked up, and, behold! there was Imana standing before her, looking as kind as when she had first seen him, and he said, "Come here and see your children. I have brought them back to life. You may smile at them now." And so she did, and they ran to her, crying, "Mother! Mother!" Then Imana touched her poor, worn face and eyes dimmed with crying and her bowed shoulders, and she was young again, tall and straight and more beautiful than ever; the story says: "He gave her a new body and new teeth." He gave her a beautiful cloth and beads to wear, and he sent his servants to fetch some cows, so many for each of the boys. Then he went with them to their home. The husband saw them coming, and could not believe his eyes—he was too much astonished to speak. He brought out the one stool which every hut contains, and offered it to the guest, but Imana would not sit down yet. He said, "Send out for four more stools." So the man sent and borrowed them from the neighbours, and they all sat down, he and his wife and the two boys, and Imana in the place of honour. Then Imana said, "Now look at your wife and your children. You have got to make them happy and live comfortably with them. You will soon enough see her smiling at you and at them. It was I who forbade her to laugh, and then some wicked people went and set the children on to try to make her do so, and they died. Now I have brought them back to life. Here they are with their mother. Now see that you live happily together. And as for your mother, I am going to burn her in her house, because she did a wicked thing. I leave you to enjoy all her belongings, because you have done no wrong." Then he vanished from their sight, and while they were still gazing in astonishment a great black cloud gathered over the grandmother's hut; there was a dazzling flash, followed by a terrible clap of thunder, and the hut, with every one and everything in it, was burned to ashes. Before they had quite recovered from the shock Imana once more appeared to them, in blinding light, and said to the husband, " Remember my words, and all shall be well with you! " A moment later he was gone.

The Thunder's Bride

In this story we find Imana associated with thunder and lightning, as the Zulu lord of Heaven and the Thonga Tilo are, so that we may suppose him to be a sky-god, or, at any rate, to have been such in the beginning. In the Ruanda story which follows,[1] the Thunder is treated as a distinct personage (as he is by the Nandi), but he is nowhere said to be identical with Imana.

There was a certain woman of Ruanda, the wife of Kwisaba. Her husband went away to the wars, and was absent for many months. One day while she was all alone in the hut she was taken ill, and found herself too weak and wretched to get up and make a fire, which would have been done for her at once had anyone been present. She cried out, talking wildly in her despair: " Oh, what shall I do? If only I had some one to split the kindling wood and build the fire! I shall die of cold if no one comes! Oh, if some one would but come—if it were the very Thunder of heaven himself! "

So the woman spoke, scarcely knowing what she said, and presently a little cloud appeared in the sky. She could not see it, but very soon it spread, other clouds collected, till the sky was quite overcast; it grew dark as night inside the hut, and she heard thunder rumbling in the distance. Then there came a flash of lightning close by, and she saw the Thunder standing before her, in the likeness of a man, with a little bright axe in his hand. He fell to, and had split all the wood in a twinkling; then he built it up and lit

---

[1] Père Hurel, *La Poésie chez les primitifs*, p. 21.

it, just with a touch of his hand, as if his fingers had been torches. When the blaze leapt up he turned to the woman and said, " Now, O wife of Kwisaba, what will you give me? " She was quite paralysed with fright, and could not utter a word. He gave her a little time to recover, and then went on: " When your baby is born, if it is a girl, will you give her to me for a wife? " Trembling all over, the poor woman could only stammer out, " Yes! " and the Thunder vanished.

Not long after this a baby girl was born, who grew into a fine, healthy child, and was given the name of Miseke. When Kwisaba came home from the wars the women met him with the news that he had a little daughter, and he was delighted, partly, perhaps, with the thought of the cattle he would get as her bride-price when she was old enough to be married. But when his wife told him about the Thunder he looked very serious, and said, " When she grows older you must never on any account let her go outside the house, or we shall have the Thunder carrying her off."

So as long as Miseke was quite little she was allowed to play out of doors with the other children, but the time came all too soon when she had to be shut up inside the hut. One day some of the other girls came running to Miseke's mother in great excitement. " Miseke is dropping beads out of her mouth! We thought she had put them in on purpose, but they come dropping out every time she laughs." Sure enough the mother found that it was so, and not only did Miseke produce beads of the kinds most valued, but beautiful brass and copper bangles. Miseke's father was greatly troubled when they told him of this. He said it must be the Thunder, who sent the beads in this extraordinary way as the presents which a man always has to send to his betrothed while she is growing up.[1] So Miseke had always to stay indoors and amuse herself as best she could—when she was not helping in the house-

---

[1] It is not uncommon in some African tribes for a grown man to bespeak a girl, for himself or for his son, while she is still a baby.

work—by plaiting mats and making baskets. Sometimes her old playfellows came to see her, but they too did not care to be shut up for long in a dark, stuffy hut.

One day, when Miseke was about fifteen, a number of the girls made up a party to go and dig *inkwa*,[1] and they thought it would be good fun to take Miseke along with them. They went to her mother's hut and called her, but of course her parents would not hear of her going, and she had to stay at home. They tried again another day, but with no better success. Some time after this, however, Kwisaba and his wife both went to see to their garden, which was situated a long way off, so that they had to start at daybreak, leaving Miseke alone in the hut. Somehow the girls got to hear of this, and as they had already planned to go for *inkwa* that day they went to fetch her. The temptation was too great, and she slipped out very quietly, and went with them to the watercourse where the white clay was to be found. So many people had gone there at different times for the same purpose that quite a large pit had been dug out. The girls got into it and fell to work, laughing and chattering, when, suddenly, they became aware that it was growing dark, and, looking up, saw a great black cloud gathering overhead. And then, suddenly, they saw the figure of a man standing before them, and he called out in a great voice, " Where is Miseke, daughter of Kwisaba? " One girl came out of the hole, and said, " I am not Miseke, daughter of Kwisaba. When Miseke laughs beads and bangles drop from her lips." The Thunder said, " Well, then, laugh, and let me see." She laughed, and nothing happened. " No, I see you are not she." So one after another was questioned and sent on her way. Miseke herself came last, and tried to pass, repeating the same words that the others had said; but the Thunder insisted on her laughing, and a shower of beads fell on the ground. The Thunder caught her up and carried her off to the sky and married her.

Of course she was terribly frightened, but the Thunder

[1] White clay, used for painting pots, which is found in dry stream-beds.

proved a kind husband, and she settled down quite happily and, in due time, had three children, two boys and a girl. When the baby girl was a few weeks old Miseke told her husband that she would like to go home and see her parents. He not only consented, but provided her with cattle and beer (as provision for the journey and presents on arrival) and carriers for her hammock, and sent her down to earth with this parting advice: "Keep to the high road; do not turn aside into any unfrequented bypath." But, being unacquainted with the country, her carriers soon strayed from the main track. After they had gone for some distance along the wrong road they found the path barred by a strange monster called an *igikoko*, a sort of ogre, who demanded something to eat. Miseke told the servants to give him the beer they were carrying: he drank all the pots dry in no time. Then he seized one of the carriers and ate him, then a second—in short, he devoured them all, as well as the cattle, till no one was left but Miseke and her children. The ogre then demanded a child. Seeing no help for it, Miseke gave him the younger boy, and then, driven to extremity, the baby she was nursing, but while he was thus engaged she contrived to send off the elder boy, whispering to him to run till he came to a house.[1] "If you see an old man sitting on the ash-heap in the front yard that will be your grandfather; if you see some young men shooting arrows at a mark they will be your uncles; the boys herding the cows are your cousins; and you will find your grandmother inside the hut. Tell them to come and help us." The boy set off, while his mother kept off the ogre as best she could. He arrived at his grandfather's homestead, and told them what had happened, and they started at once, having first tied the bells on their hunting-dogs. The boy showed them the way as well as he could,

[1] This might seem like a contradiction if the turning aside had really meant going far astray. But Miseke was in familiar country; the bypath into which her men had turned was not so very far from the right road, though shunned on account of the monster which haunted it. Being screened from the sun in her hammock, or, rather, carrying-basket, she would not have seen them take the wrong turning in time to direct them.

but they nearly missed Miseke just at last; only she heard the dogs' bells and called out. Then the young men rushed in and killed the ogre with their spears. Before he died he said, "If you cut off my big toe you will get back everything belonging to you." They did so, and, behold! out came the carriers and the cattle, the servants and the children, none of them any the worse. Then, first making sure that the ogre was really dead, they set off for Miseke's old home. Her parents were overjoyed to see her and the children, and the time passed all too quickly. At the end of a month she began to think she ought to return, and the old people sent out for cattle and all sorts of presents, as is the custom when a guest is going to leave. Everything was got together outside the village, and her brothers were ready to escort her, when they saw the clouds gathering, and, behold! all of a sudden Miseke, her children, her servants, her cattle, and her porters, with their loads, were all caught up into the air and disappeared. The family were struck dumb with amazement, and they never saw Miseke on earth again. It is to be presumed that she lived happily ever after.

Climbing into Heaven

All primitive peoples, quite naturally, think of the sky as a solid vault, which joins the earth at the horizon—the place where, as the Thonga people say, the women can hit it with their pestles. Only no one now living has ever been able to reach that place. And even the tales about people who have got into the Heaven country do not represent them as having reached it in that way. Either they climb a tree, or they ascend by means of a rope,[1] or the spider obligingly spins a thread for them. The Zulus had an old saying: "Who can plait a rope for ascending, that he may go to heaven?"[2] implying that such a thing is utterly impossible. Yet in the "Praises"

---

[1] I have never seen it explained how the rope gets into position.
[2] *Ubani ongapot' igoda lokukupuka aye ezulwini?*

(*Izibongo*) of King Senzangakona, the father of Tshaka, he is said to have accomplished this feat.

> The son of Jama the king, he twisted a cord;
> Fearless he scaled the mansion of Heaven's lord,
> Who over this earth of ours the blue vault hollowed.
> And the ghosts of the house of Mageba fain would have followed,
> But never will they attain,
> Though they strive again and again
> For the pass that cannot be won by spear or by sword—
> No hold for the wounded feet that bleed in vain.[1]

No one appears to know anything more about this adventure of Senzangakona's. It is not said that he returned from his expedition, and, as tradition states that he died a natural death, it would not seem to refer to his departure from this world.

The Road to Heaven

The Baronga (in the neighbourhood of Delagoa Bay) have a very old song, which runs something like this:

> Oh, how hard it is to find a cord!
> How I would love to plait a cord and go up to the sky!
> I would find rest!

The Ronga story of a mortal who found the way there is as follows. There was once a girl who was sent by her mother to fetch water from the river. On the way, talking and laughing with her companions, she dropped her earthen jar and broke it. " Oh, what shall I do now? " she cried, in great distress, for these large jars are not so easily replaced, and she knew there would be trouble awaiting her on her return. She exclaimed, "*Bukali bwa ngoti!* Oh, that I had a rope! " and, looking up, sure enough she saw a rope uncoiling itself from a cloud. She seized it and climbed, and

---

[1] A very free paraphrase of

> Mnta ka' Jama, owapot' igoda laya lafika ezukwini
> Lapa izituta za Magweba zingayikufika,
> Zoba 'kukwela zapuke amazwanyana.

The literal rendering of the last two words is " that they may break their little toes."

VENDA GIRL PUTTING MAIZE-COBS INTO THE GRAIN-STORE
Photo A. M. Duggan-Cronin. By permission of the McGregor Museum, Kimberley

soon found herself in the country above the sky, which appeared to be not unlike the one she had left. There was what looked like a ruined village not far off, and an old woman sitting among the ruins called to her, " Come here, child ! Where are you going ? " Being well brought up and accustomed to treat her elders with politeness, she answered at once, and told her story. The old woman told her to go on, and if she found an ant creeping into her ear to let it alone. " It will not hurt you, and will tell you what you have to do in this strange country, and how to answer the chiefs when they question you."

The girl walked on, and in a little while found a black ant crawling up her leg, which went on till it reached her ear. She checked the instinctive impulse to take it out, and went on till she saw the pointed roofs of a village, surrounded by the usual thorn hedge. As she drew near she heard a tiny whisper: " Do not go in ; sit down here." She sat down near the gateway. Presently some grave old men, dressed in white, shining bark-cloth, came out and asked her where she had come from and what she wanted. She answered modestly and respectfully, and told them she had come to look for a baby.[1] The elders said, "Very good ; come this way." They took her to a hut where some women were at work. One of them gave her a *shirondo* [2] basket, and told her to go to the garden and get some of the new season's mealies. She showed no surprise at this unexpected request, but obeyed at once, and (following the directions of the ant

[1] This seems to need explanation. Nothing, so far, has been said about a baby. I was tempted to think that the narrator might have forgotten the real beginning of the story, which was that the girl had been carrying her baby brother on her back and dropped him into the water when stooping to fill her jar. But M. Junod (from whose book *Chants et contes des Baronga*, p. 237, this story is taken) would not hear of this suggestion when I asked him. I cannot help thinking that this version is a confusion of two different stories, one of a girl breaking a jar (or, as in a Chaga tale, letting the monkeys get into the bean-patch), and another of a married woman who was tricked into drowning her baby and, in the end, got it back from the lord of Heaven. This is given in Duff Macdonald's *Africana*, vol. i, p. 298.

[2] A round basket with sloping sides, used chiefly for carrying mealies. There is quite an art in filling these baskets so as to make them hold the largest possible quantity ; great nicety of arrangement is required.

in her ear) pulled up only one stalk at a time, and arranged the cobs carefully in the basket, so as not to waste any space. When she returned the women praised her for performing her task so quickly and well, and then told her first to grind the corn and then to make porridge. Again instructed by the ant, she put aside a few grains before grinding, and, when she was stirring the porridge, threw these grains in whole, which, it seems, is a peculiar fashion in the cooking of the Heaven-dwellers. They were quite satisfied with the way in which the girl had done her work, and gave her a place to sleep in. Next morning the elders came to fetch her, and conducted her to a handsome house, within which a number of infants were laid out on the ground, those on one side wrapped in red cloth, on the other in white. Being told to choose, she was about to pick up one of the red bundles, when the ant whispered, " Take a white one," and she did so. The old men gave her a quantity of fine cloth and beads, as much as she could carry in addition to the baby, and sent her on her way home. She reached her village without difficulty, and found that every one was out, as her mother and the other women were at work in the gardens. She went into the hut, and hid herself and the baby in the inner enclosure. When the others returned from the fields, towards evening, the mother sent her younger daughter on ahead to put on the cooking-pots. The girl went in and stirred the fire ; as the flames leapt up she saw the treasures her sister had brought home, and, not knowing how they had come there, she was frightened, and ran back to tell her mother and aunts. They all hurried in, and found the girl they had thought lost, with a beautiful baby and a stock of cloth to last a lifetime. They listened to her story in great astonishment ; but the younger sister was seized with envy, and wanted to set off at once for that fortunate spot. She was a rude, wilful creature, and her sister, knowing her character, tried to dissuade her, or, at any rate, to give her some guidance for the road. But she refused to listen. " You went off without being told anything by anybody, and I shall go without listening to anyone's advice."

Accordingly when called by the old woman she refused to stop, and even spoke insultingly; whereupon the crone said, "Go on, then! When you return this way you will be dead!" "Who will kill me, then?" retorted the girl, and went on her way. When the ant tried to get into her ear she shook her head and screamed with impatience, refusing to listen when it tried to persuade her. So the ant took itself off in dudgeon.

In the same way she gave a rude answer to the village elders when they asked her why she had come, and when requested to gather mealies she pulled up the stalks right and left, and simply ravaged the garden. Having refused to profit by the ant's warnings, she did not know the right way to prepare the meal or make the porridge, and, in any case, did the work carelessly. When taken to the house where the babies were stored she at once stretched out her hand to seize a red-wrapped one; but immediately there was a tremendous explosion, and she was struck dead. "Heaven," we are told, gathered up her bones, made them into a bundle, and sent a man with them to her home. As he passed the place where she had met with the ant that insect called out, "Are you not coming back dead? You would be alive now if you had listened to advice!" Coming to the old woman's place among the ruins, the carrier heard her cry, "My daughter, haven't you died on account of your wicked heart?" So the man went on, and at last he dropped the bones just above her mother's hut. And her sister said, "She had a wicked heart, and that is why Heaven was angry with her."

There are points here which remind us of a familiar story in Grimm's fairy-tales, and we shall meet with others still more like it later on. There are other stories of people who ascended to the Heaven country, some of which will be given in the next chapter.

CHAPTER V: MORTALS WHO HAVE ASCENDED TO HEAVEN

IN the instances hitherto mentioned, where a rope has been spoken of as the means of reaching the Heaven country, no explanation is offered as to the origin of the rope, or the means by which it became available. There are some stories and legends, possibly older, where the communication is said to be established through the spider's web. When Mulungu was compelled to leave the earth, say the Yaos, " he said, 'I cannot climb a tree ' " (as though that were the obvious way of reaching the sky), and went to call the spider, who " went on high, and returned again and said, ' I have gone on high nicely. . . . You now, Mulungu, go on high.' " That is, we may suppose, he spun his web (the narrator probably did not see why the spider should not be able to do this upward as well as downward) till it reached the sky, and spun another thread coming down. The Subiya also say that Leza ascended to heaven by a spider's thread.

This notion occurs in a tale [1] of, in some respects, much later development. It comes, like those about Kalunga already given, from Angola, and relates to " the son of Kimanaweze." Kimanaweze seems to be a mythical personage, perhaps originally identical with the first man, as, according to Héli Chatelain, " much of what the natives say of him corresponds with what the Amazulu tell of their Unkulunkulu." He figures in more than one folk-tale. The one I am about to give is further remarkable, not merely for personifying the Sun (which, to a certain extent, is done by the Wachaga), but for giving him the Moon as a wife. The Bantu in general speak of the Moon as a man, and say that he has two wives, the Evening Star and the Morning Star, which they do not realize to be one and the same.

The Daughter of the Sun and Moon

Kimanaweze's son, when the time came for him to choose a wife, declared that he would not " marry a woman of the

[1] Chatelain, *Folk-tales of Angola*, p. 31.

earth," but must have the daughter of the Sun and Moon.
He wrote " a letter of marriage "—a modern touch, no
doubt added by the narrator [1]—and cast about for a messenger
to take it up to the sky. The little duiker (*mbambi*) refused,
so did the larger antelope, known as *soko*, the hawk, and the
vulture. At last a frog came and offered to carry the letter.
The son of Kimanaweze, doubtful of his ability to do this,
said, " Begone! Where people of life, who have wings, gave
it up dost thou say, ' I will go there '? " But the frog
persisted, and was at last sent off, with the threat of a thrash-
ing if he should be unsuccessful. It appears that the Sun
and Moon were in the habit of sending their handmaidens
down to the earth to draw water, descending and ascending
by means of a spider's web. The frog went and hid himself
in the well to which they came, and when the first one filled
her jar he got into it without being seen, having first placed
the letter in his mouth. The girls went up to heaven, carried
their water-jars into the room, and set them down. When
they had gone away he came out, produced the letter, laid
it on a table, and hid.

After a while " Lord Sun " (*Kumbi Mwene*) came in,
found the letter, and read it. Not knowing what to make
of it, he put it away, and said nothing about it. The frog
got into an empty water-jar, and was carried down again
when the girls went for a fresh supply. The son of Kimanaweze, getting no answer, refused at first to believe that the
frog had executed his commission; but, after waiting for
some days, he wrote another letter and sent him again. The
frog carried it in the same way as before, and the Sun, after
reading it, wrote that he would consent, if the suitor came
himself, bringing his ' first-present '—the usual gift for
opening marriage negotiations. On receiving this the young
man wrote another letter, saying that he must wait till told
the amount of the ' wooing-present,' or bride-price (*kilembu*).

He gave this to the frog, along with a sum of money, and it
was conveyed as before. This time the Sun consulted his wife,
who was quite ready to welcome the mysterious son-in-law.

---

[1] We often find stories brought up to date in this way.

She solved the question of providing refreshments for the invisible messenger by saying, " We will cook a meal anyhow, and put it on the table where he leaves the letters." This was done, and the frog, when left alone, came out and ate. The letter, which was left along with the food, stated the amount of the bride-price to be " a sack of money." He carried the letter back to the son of Kimanaweze, who spent six days in collecting the necessary amount, and then sent it by the frog with this message : " Soon I shall find a day to bring home my wife." This, however, was more easily said than done, for when his messenger had once more returned he waited twelve days, and then told the frog that he could not find people to fetch the bride. But the frog was equal to the occasion. Again he had himself carried up to the Sun's palace, and, getting out of the water-jar, hid in a corner of the room till after dark, when he came out and went through the house till he found the princess's bed-chamber. Seeing that she was fast asleep, he took out one of her eyes without waking her, and then the other.[1] He tied up the eyes in a handkerchief, and went back to his corner in the room where the water-jars were kept. In the morning, when the girl did not appear, her parents came to inquire the reason, and found that she was blind. In their distress they sent two men to consult the diviner, who, after casting lots, said (not having heard from them the reason of their coming), " Disease has brought you ; the one who is sick is a woman ; the sickness that ails her the eyes. You have come, being sent ; you have not come of your own will. I have spoken." The Sun's messengers replied, " Truth. Look now what caused the ailment." He told them that a certain suitor had cast a spell over her, and she would die unless she were sent to him. Therefore they had best hasten on the marriage. The men brought back word to the Sun, who said, " All right. Let us sleep. To-morrow they shall take her down to the earth." Next day, accordingly, he gave orders for the spider to "weave a large cobweb" for sending his daughter down. Meanwhile the frog had gone

[1] The frog's magic powers are implied, if not explicitly stated.

ZULU DIVINERS IN CONSULTATION

Photo Natal Museum, Pietermaritzburg

down as usual in the water-jar and hidden himself in the bottom of the well. When the water-carriers had gone up again he came out and went to the village of the bridegroom and told him that his bride would arrive that day. The young man would not believe him, but he solemnly promised to bring her in the evening, and returned to the well.

After sunset the attendants brought the princess down by way of the stronger cobweb and left her by the well. The frog came out, and told her that he would take her to her husband's house; at the same time he handed back her eyes. They started, and came to the son of Kimanaweze, and the marriage took place. And they lived happy ever after—on earth, for, as the narrator said, "They had all given up going to heaven; who could do it was Mainu the frog."

In its present form, as will have been noticed, this story is strongly coloured by Portuguese influence. The water-carriers, the Sun's house, with its rooms and furniture, the bag of money, all belong to present-day Loanda. But, for all that, the groundwork is essentially African. The frog and the diviner would, by themselves, be sufficient to prove this. (The frog, by the way, is usually a helpful creature in African folklore.) The glaring improbabilities in the story must not be regarded too critically; it is constantly taken for granted, as we shall find when considering the animal stories proper, that any animal may speak and act like a human being—though the frog, in this instance, seems to possess more than ordinary human powers. The specially strong cobweb prepared for the daughter's descent, while the water-carriers had been going up and down every day without difficulty, may have been necessitated by the number of the bride's attendants; but we are not told why they should have returned and left her alone at the foot of the heavenly ladder.[1]

---

[1] The people of the Lower Congo have a story about the spider fetching fire from heaven at the request of Nzambi, who is here regarded as the Earth-mother and the daughter (according to R. E. Dennett) of Nzambi Mpungu, the "first father," or the personified sky. (Other authorities insist that everywhere in Africa the relation of sky and earth is that of husband and wife.) He was helped by the tortoise, the woodpecker, the rat, and the sandfly, whom he conveyed up by means of his thread. The story may be found in Dennett, Folk-lore of the Fjort [Fiote], p. 74.

In other cases we find people reaching the Heaven country by climbing a tree, as is done by the mother in the Yao tale of " The Three Women." In the Zulu story [1] of " The Girl and the Cannibals " a brother and sister, escaping from these ogres, climb a tree and reach the Heaven country.

The Heaven-tree

And there is a curious tradition among the Wachaga [2] about a mysterious tree. A girl named Kichalundu went out one day to cut grass. Finding it growing very luxuriantly in a certain place, she stepped on the spot and sank into a quagmire. Her companions took hold of her hands and tried to pull her out, but in vain ; she vanished from their sight. They heard her singing, " The ghosts have taken me. Go and tell my father and mother," and they ran to call the parents. The whole countryside gathered about the place, and a diviner advised the father to sacrifice a cow and a sheep. This was done, and they heard the girl's voice again, but growing fainter and fainter, till at last it was silent, and they gave her up for lost. But after a time a tree grew up on the spot where she had disappeared. It went on growing, until at last it reached the sky. The herd-boys, during the heat of the day, used to drive their cattle into its shade, and themselves climbed up into the spreading branches. One day two of them ventured higher than the rest, and called out, " Can you see us still ? " The others answered, " No ! Do come down again ! " but the two daring fellows refused. "We are going on into the sky— to *Wuhu*, the World Above ! " Those were their last words, for they were never seen again. And the tree was called *Mdi Msumu*, "the Story-tree."

The Tale of Murile

From the same region of Kilimanjaro comes the story of Murile, who also reached the Upper World, though neither by a rope nor a tree, and also came back.[3]

[1] Callaway, *Nursery Tales*, pp. 145 and 147.   [2] Gutmann, *Volksbuch*, p. 152.
[3] Raum, *Versuch*, p. 307.

MORTALS ASCENDED TO HEAVEN

A man and his wife living in the Chaga country had three sons, of whom Murile was the eldest. One day he went out with his mother to dig up *maduma*,[1] and, noticing a particularly fine tuber among those which were to be put by for seed, he said, "Why, this one is as beautiful as my little brother!" His mother laughed at the notion of comparing a *taro* tuber with a baby; but he hid the root, and, later, when no one was looking, put it away in a hollow tree and sang a magic song over it. Next day he went to look, and found that the root had turned into a child. After that at every meal he secretly kept back some food, and, when he could do so without being seen, carried it to the tree and fed the baby, which grew and flourished from day to day. But Murile's mother became very anxious when she saw how thin the boy was growing, and she questioned him, but could get no satisfaction. Then one day his younger brothers noticed that when his portion of food was handed to him, instead of eating it at once, he put it aside. They told their mother, and she bade them follow him when he went away after dinner, and see what he did with it. They did so, and saw him feeding the baby in the hollow tree, and came back and told her. She went at once to the spot and strangled the child which was "starving her son."

When Murile came back next day and found the child dead he was overcome with grief. He went home and sat down in the hut, crying bitterly. His mother asked him why he was crying, and he said it was because the smoke hurt his eyes. So she told him to go and sit on the other side of the fireplace. But, as he still wept and complained of the smoke when questioned, they said he had better take his father's stool and sit outside. He picked up the stool, went out into the courtyard, and sat down. Then he said, "Stool, go up on high, as my father's rope does when he hangs up his beehive in the forest!"[2] And the stool rose

---

[1] A kind of arum (*Colocasia*), the roots of which are used as food by the Wachaga; the *taro* of Polynesia.

[2] He would throw one end of a rope up so as to pass over a branch, and then fasten it to the beehive, which would then be hauled up into place. These hives (made from the hollowed section of a log) are placed in trees by many East African

up with him into the air and stuck fast in the branches of a tree. He repeated the words a second time, and again the stool moved upward. Just then his brothers happened to come out of the hut, and when they saw him they ran back and said to their mother, "Murile is going up into the sky!" She would not believe them. "Why do you tell me your eldest brother has gone up into the sky? Is there any road for him to go up by?" They told her to come and look, and when she saw him in the air she sang:

> "*Mrile, wuya na kunu!*
> *Wuya na kunu, mwanako!*
> *Wuya na kunu!*"
>
> ["Murile, come back hither!
> Come back hither, my child!
> Come back hither!"]

But Murile answered, "I shall never come back, Mother! I shall never come back!"

Then his brothers called him, and received the same answer; his father called him—then his boy-friends, and, last of all, his uncle (*washidu*, his mother's brother, the nearest relation of all). They could just hear his answer, "I am not coming back, Uncle! I am never coming back!" Then he passed up out of sight.

The stool carried him up till he felt solid ground beneath his feet, and then he looked round and found himself in the Heaven country. He walked on till he came to some people gathering wood. He asked them the way to the Moon-chief's kraal, and they said, "Just pick up some sticks for us, and then we will tell you." He collected a bundle of sticks, and they directed him to go on till he should come to some people cutting grass. He did so, and greeted the grass-cutters when he came to them. They answered his greeting, and when he asked them the way said they would show him if he would help them for a while with their work.

tribes and left till full of honey, when the bees are smoked out, escaping through a hole made for the purpose in the back of the hive. The Zulus and other South African Bantu appear to content themselves with taking the honey found in hollow trees or holes in the rock, where the wild bees make their nests.

So he cut some grass, and they pointed out the road, telling him to go on till he came to some women hoeing. These, again, asked him to help them before they would show him the way, and, in succession, he met with some herd-boys, some women gathering beans, some people reaping millet, others gathering banana-leaves, and girls fetching water—all of them sending him forward with almost the same words. The water-carriers said, " Just go on in this direction till you come to a house where the people are eating." He found the house, and said, " Greeting, house-owners ! Please show me the way to the Moon's kraal." They promised to do so if he would sit down and eat with them, which he did. At last by following their instructions he reached his destination, and found the people there eating their food raw. He asked them why they did not use fire to cook with, and found that they did not know what fire was. So he said, " If I prepare nice food for you by means of fire what will you give me ? " The Moon-chief said, " We will give you cattle and goats and sheep." Murile told them to bring plenty of wood, and when they came with it he and the chief went behind the house, where the other people could not see them. Murile took his knife and cut two pieces of wood, one flat and the other pointed, and twirled the pointed stick till he got some sparks, with which he lit a bunch of dry grass and so kindled a fire. When it burned up he got the chief to send for some green plantains, which he roasted and offered to him. Then he cooked some meat and various other foods. The Moon-chief was delighted when he tasted them, and at once called all the people together, and said to them, " Here is a wonderful doctor come from a far country ! We shall have to repay him for his fire." The people asked, "What must be paid to him ? " He answered, " Let one man bring a cow, another a goat, another whatever he may have in his storehouse." So they went to fetch all these things. And Murile became a rich man. For he stayed some years at the Moon's great kraal and married wives and had children born to him, and his flocks and herds increased greatly. But in the end a longing for his home came over him.

And he thought within himself: "How shall I go home again, unless I send a messenger before me? For I told them I was never coming back, and they must think that I am dead."

He called all the birds together and asked them one by one, "If I send you to my home what will you say?" The raven answered, "I shall say, *Kuruu! kuruu!*" and was rejected. So, in turn, were the hornbill, the hawk, the buzzard, and all the rest, till he came to Njorovi, the mocking-bird, who sang:

> *Mrile etsha kilalawu*
> *Tira ngama.*
> *Mrile etsha kilalawu*
> *Mdeye mafuda na kiliko!*

> ["Murile is coming the day after to-morrow,
> Missing out to-morrow.
> Murile is coming the day after to-morrow.
> Keep some fat in the ladle for him!"]

Murile was pleased with this, and told her to go. So she flew down to earth and perched on the gate-post of his father's courtyard and sang her song. His father came out and said, "What thing is crying out there, saying that Murile is coming the day after to-morrow? Why, Murile was lost long ago, and will never come back!" And he drove the bird away. She flew back and told Murile where she had been. But he would not believe her; he told her to go again and bring back his father's stick as a token that she had really gone to his home. So she flew down again, came to the house, and picked up the stick, which was leaning in the doorway. The children in the house saw her, and tried to snatch it from her, but she was too quick for them, and took it back to Murile. Then he said, "Now I will start for home." He took leave of his friends and of his wives, who were to stay with their own people, but his cattle and his boys came with him. It was a long march to the place of descent,[1] and Murile began to grow very tired. There

[1] We are not told how the cattle were to be got down, but probably they had to go down the slope where the sky joins the earth at the horizon, which would account for the journey being longer than Murile's when he came up by means of the magic stool!

was a very fine bull in the herd, who walked beside Murile
all the way. Suddenly he spoke and said, " As you are so
weary, what will you do for me if I let you ride me? If
I take you on my back will you eat my flesh when they kill
me?" Murile answered, " No! I will never eat you!"
So the bull let him get on his back and carried him home.
And Murile sang, as he rode along :

> " Not a hoof nor a horn is wanting !
>   Mine are the cattle—hey !
> Nought of the goods is wanting ;
>   Mine are the bairns to-day.
> Not a kid of the goats is wanting ;
>   My flocks are on the way.
> Nothing of mine is wanting ;
>   Murile comes to-day
> With his bairns and his cattle—hey ! "

So he came home. And his father and mother ran out
to meet him and anointed him with mutton-fat, as is the
custom when a loved one comes home from distant parts.
And his brothers and every one rejoiced and wondered
greatly when they saw the cattle. But he showed his father
the great bull that had carried him, and said, " This bull
must be fed and cared for till he is old. And even if you
kill him when he is old I will never eat of his flesh." So
they lived quite happily for a time.

But when the bull had become very old Murile's father
slaughtered him. The mother foolishly thought it such a
pity that her son, who had always taken so much trouble
over the beast, should have none of the beef when every one
else was eating it. So she took a piece of fat and hid it in
a pot. When she knew that all the meat was finished she
ground some grain and cooked the fat with the meal and
gave it to her son. As soon as he had tasted it the fat spoke
and said to him, " Do you dare to eat me, who carried you
on my back? You shall be eaten, as you are eating me ! "

Then Murile sang : " O my mother, I said to you, ' Do
not give me to eat of the bull's flesh! ' " He took a second
taste, and his foot sank into the ground. He sang the same

words again, and then ate up the food his mother had given him. As soon as he had swallowed it he sank down and disappeared.

Other people who tell the story simply say, " He died." Be that as it may, that was the end of him.

The inhabitants of the Moon country, according to this legend, were very much like the earth-dwellers, except that they seem to have been less advanced in culture, having no knowledge of cooking or of fire. I have not come across any other reference to the Moon-chief, or his kraal, though, as already stated, the Bantu in general, when they think about the matter at all, describe the Moon as a man, like the Arabs and our Saxon forefathers.[1]   In Nyasaland they give names to the Moon's two wives : the Evening Star is Chekechani, a poor housekeeper, who, during the fortnight he spends with her, starves him till he pines away to nothing. Puikani, the Morning Star, brings him back to life,[2] and feeds him up till he becomes quite round at the end of the month. The Giryama, in Kenya, call the planet Venus " the Moon's wife," but no one seems to have recorded any story connected with this expression.

Tailed Heaven-folk

The Ronga notion, too, as we have seen, appears to be that the dwellers above the sky are not very different from those beneath it. But we find here and there (so far only in detached fragments) traces of belief in a race of Heaven-dwellers distinct from ordinary mortals. For instance, they are sometimes said to have tails. One clan of the Wachaga claims that its ancestor fell from the sky during a rainstorm. He belonged to a race called the Wakyambi, living in the sky, " far above the sun," and having tails. This ancestor, finding himself among tailless beings, and feeling ashamed of his peculiar appearance, secretly cut off his tail ; consequently his descendants have none. Another legend says

---

[1] The Wasu, in Pare (south-east of Kilimanjaro), are an exception : they say that the sun is the father and the moon the mother of mankind.

[2] At new moon they say, *mwezi wafa*, " the moon is dead."

that once upon a time a man and a woman came down from the sky on a cloud and lighted on the hill Molama, in Machame. In the morning the inhabitants of the place found them standing there, and saw that they had tails like cows. When asked where they came from they answered, " God has sent us down on a cloud. We are looking for a place to live in." The people replied, " If you want to live with us you must have your tails cut off." They consented, and settled in that place, whither their descendants still come to sacrifice. It is said that cattle were sent down to them from the sky; they found them standing in front of their hut on the second morning.

The Wasu, the neighbours of the Wachaga on the southeast, speak of certain tailed beings inhabiting the clouds. Their nature is not very clear, but they are said to be always at war with the " good old people "—the ghosts of the human dead. " Sometimes," says a missionary long resident in Pare,[1] " they are held to be kind spirits who give people cattle, sometimes evil beings who bring disaster." It would probably be nearer the mark to say that, like ordinary human ghosts, they are beneficent or the reverse, according to their state of mind and the behaviour of the living.

Some of the Congo tribes, also, believe in the existence of ' Cloud folk' having tails. It is probable that if we could get at the folklore of all the tribes intervening between these two widely separated localities we should find the same notion everywhere. Outside the Bantu area the Lang'o, in the region of the Upper Nile (who, like the Wachaga, say that the first human pair had tails), and the Ewe, in West Africa, have traditions to the same effect, and something not very different comes out in the folk-tales of the Masai.

Whether, as one writer has suggested, these myths imply some dim race-memory of an ape ancestry our knowledge is not sufficient to decide; the general trend of Bantu thought (as shown in stories about baboons, for instance) would seem to negative such a conclusion. One might also ask whether the custom among some primitive tribes of

[1] Dannholz, *Im Banne des Geisterglaubens*, p. 24.

wearing an artificial tail (as the principal, if not the sole, article of dress) could be the origin or the result of the tradition.

The Celestial Bellman

Murile—who reversed the action of Prometheus in bringing fire *to*, not *from*, heaven—is a somewhat mysterious figure, perhaps surviving from some forgotten mythology which, if recovered, would bridge some gaps in his story. There is a queer, fragmentary legend[1] about a person called Mrule, " the stranger from the sky," who may or may not have been originally the same as Murile. He had only one leg, and of the rest of his body only half was like a man ; the other side was covered with grass.[2] He first alighted among the Masai (probably in the steppe to the north-west of Kilimanjaro), and went on thence to " our hill-country," ascending the mountain at Shira, hopping on his one leg. He was unable to speak. If he met anyone he only made a sound like *mremrem*. So it is hardly surprising that the people fled before him and barricaded themselves in their huts. He wandered on from place to place, and could get food nowhere. When he came to a homestead the inmates would call to him through their barred doors to go away. Naturally displeased, he found his way to the chief's place, but was not more kindly received there.[3] Then at last he spoke:

> " I am Mrule!
> If ye reject me here below
> Back to heaven I must go ! "

It was high noon, with the sun just overhead. He sprang into the air, rose straight up towards the sun, and was never seen on earth again.

[1] Gutmann, *Volksbuch*, p. 150.

[2] We shall meet with these half-men everywhere ; they will be fully discussed in Chapter XIII. The grass growing out of one side is curious. I do not remember anything like it elsewhere, except in Zulu accounts of the *Inkosazana*, a strange being described as the Queen of Heaven, and in those of certain mysterious monsters. The half-men usually have nothing on their non-human side, or else it is made of wax.

[3] One is reminded of a story by Mr H. W. Nevinson—one hopes not true—of an unfortunate Negro sailor shipwrecked on the Norfolk coast.

But not long after this the chief fell into the fire, burning himself badly. His people consulted the diviners, who answered, " You have sinned against Mrule. You all said, ' He will bring ill-luck to the country if we take him in. Who ever saw a being with one leg? ' And the chief never asked him, ' What brings you here? ' Because no one asked him anything he went away. But he is surely a great healer." Thus spoke the diviners. But all this time tortoises had been collecting in the plain. They gathered themselves into a long procession and came marching up to the chief's homestead, where they arranged themselves in a circle round the spot from which Mrule had ascended. And their leader chanted:

" Propitiate, propitiate, and, when ye have done so, asperse! "

The diviners interpreted this saying to the chief, and he at once sent for a black cow which had lately calved, a sheep, and the " water of expiation." They sacrificed the cow and the sheep, made a cut in the neck of the tortoise-chief, and took a drop of blood from him. Then they mixed this with the blood of the sacrifices and the water, and sprinkled the chief with it—also the whole of the ground within the circle of tortoises. So the curse was lifted, the tortoises went their way into the plain, and the chief recovered from his injuries.

In quite recent times a legend has grown up out of one of those rumours which arise no one knows how. " It was after the first white men had come into our country." [1] One day at noon a man appeared, floating in the air. He was light-complexioned, and held a bell in either hand. And he cried, with a loud voice:

" Pay that thou owest to thy brother!
Hast thou a beast of his, give it back!
Hast thou a goat of his, give it back!
    Thus saith the King.
Let every stranger in the land return to his own home;
Every child held in pawn shall go free to his father's house.
Cease from violence; break the spear!
    Thus saith the King."

[1] The first European to reach Chaga was Rebmann, in 1848.

At sunset he was seen again. Sometimes he appeared in one place, sometimes in another; but he never touched the earth. The chief of Moshi (was this the famous Mandara, properly called Rindi?) ordered his men to keep a look-out for him. They sat and stared at the sky till the cool of the evening drove them indoors. But they never saw him more.

CHAPTER VI: THE GHOSTS AND THE GHOST COUNTRY

THE core of Bantu religion, we may say, is the cult of the dead.

The belief in a High God is more or less vague— by some tribes it is almost forgotten, or, at any rate, not much regarded—but everywhere among Bantu-speaking peoples the spirits of the departed are recognized, honoured, and propitiated. There is not the slightest doubt that these people believe in something which survives the death of the body. No African tribe can be said with certainty to think that death ends all, perhaps not even the Masai,[1] of whom this has been asserted in a somewhat haphazard fashion. The universal Bantu custom of offerings to the spirits of deceased relatives is surely a sufficient proof to the contrary.

One cannot expect to find a reasoned theory of spiritual existence among people as relatively primitive as these, nor complete agreement between the beliefs of different tribes, or even between individuals of the same tribe. But, generally speaking, it is everywhere held that something, which we will call the ghost, lives on when the body dies, and can, to some extent, influence the affairs of the living. The ghosts can communicate with the living through dreams, through signs and omens, and through the medium of diviners or prophets. They may bring disaster on the family or the tribe if offended by neglect or, sometimes, as a judgment on some undiscovered sin. They are not invariably malignant, as sometimes stated; in fact, they are quite often regarded with affectionate respect, and show themselves helpful to their kinsfolk in time of need.

Spirit not Immortal

Though the ghost survives the body for an indefinite period it is not necessarily thought of as living on for ever. Some people distinctly state (perhaps only after having been

---

[1] See Hollis, *The Masai*, p. 307.

forced by questioning to think the matter out) that after the lapse of several generations they simply go back to nothingness, except in the case of outstanding personalities, remembered beyond the circle of their immediate descendants, such as ancient chiefs and tribal benefactors. In other words, the ghosts last only as long as they are remembered by the living : the parents and grandparents are always commemorated and sacrificed to ; the three preceding generations maintain a precarious existence, fighting for a share in the offerings and occasionally forcing attention by terrifying apparitions ; any older than these are said to " go to pieces." Where reincarnation is definitely believed in, as seems to be the case to a great extent, life lasts as long as there is a child of the line to carry it on, and only comes to an end if the family dies out. Yet another view prevails among the Wazaramo,[1] a tribe of Tanganyika Territory, in the immediate neighbourhood of Dar-es-Salaam. With them family ghosts (those of father, grandfather, and maternal uncle) are called *makungu*, and are honoured and propitiated in the usual way. With the passing of generations they lose their individuality, and are merged in the host of spirits known collectively as *vinyamkela* or *majini*. The difference between these two classes is variously stated, but every one seems to be agreed that the latter are the more powerful of the two, while both have more power than ordinary *kungu* ghosts. Some say that the *vinyamkela* (singular *kinyamkela*) are the ghosts of children, the *majini* those of adults, while others hold that the former were in their lifetime kindly, inoffensive people, the *majini* men of violence. This last name is of comparatively recent introduction, being borrowed from the Arabic *jinn* ; the earlier name for such a ghost was *dzedzeta*, or, according to some, *mwene mbago*, which means " lord (or lady) of the forest." This being is invisible, except to the ' doctors,' whose business is to exorcize him, and has his abode in hollow trees. The *kinyamkela* is also, as a rule, invisible, but when he (or she) appears it is as half a human body, " with one leg, one hand, one eye, and one

[1] Klamroth, in *Zeitschrift für Kolonialsprachen*, pp. 46–70 and 118–124.

ear." I shall have something more to say about these half-human beings later on.

Abode of the Ghosts

Different accounts are given as to the whereabouts of the ghosts, but the most general notion seems to be that they remain for some time in or about the grave, or perhaps at a certain place in the hut they inhabited during life, and afterwards depart to the country of the dead, which is imagined to be underground. Here they live very much as they did on earth, as one gathers from the numerous legends of persons who have reached this country and come back to tell the tale.

The Yao chief Matope, who died near Blantyre in 1893, was buried, according to local custom, in his hut, which was then shut up and left to fall into ruin. A year after his death the headman brought out his stool and sprinkled snuff round it as an offering to his spirit. I was told that this would be done again in the following year ; after that he would cease to haunt the spot. It was not said on this occasion where he was expected to go.

The Wazaramo believe ghosts as a rule to be mischievous: thus persons passing near a recent grave after dark may be pelted with stones by the *kungu*—a trick which is also sometimes played by the *kinyamkela*. But this characteristic is by no means universal.

The Dead return in Animal Form

Another very general belief is that the dead are apt to reappear in animal forms, most usually those of snakes or lizards, though, apparently, almost any animal may be chosen. The Atonga of Lake Nyasa say that by taking certain medicines a person can ensure his changing after death into whichever animal he may fancy. Some say that their great chiefs come back as lions. Wizards of a specially noisome kind can turn themselves at will, while living, into hyenas or leopards—it is not so clear whether they assume the forms of these animals after death. The precautions taken by way of annihilating, if that were possible, the dead bodies of such people would seem to have the object of preventing this.

The Country of the Dead

The ghost country can be reached through caves or holes in the ground; a favourite incident in folk-tales is the adventure of a man who followed a porcupine or other such creature into its burrow, and by and by found himself in the village of the dead. Mr Melland [1] says that by the Wakuluwe (a tribe near the south end of Lake Tanganyika) the *fisinzwa* (ghosts) " are supposed to remain in a village in the centre of the earth." Casalis,[2] an early observer of the Basuto (about 1840), says: " All natives place the spirit world in the bowels of the earth. They call this mysterious region *mosima*, the abyss." This word in recent dictionaries is said to mean only: " a hole in the ground, den, hole of a wild animal," so that the other signification, whether primary or derived, has probably been forgotten. The spirit country is very generally known by a name related to the Swahili *kuzimu*. The stem *-zimu*, or a similar form, occurs in many languages, meaning either a spirit or the kind of monstrous ogre who will be discussed later.

The Bapedi of the Transvaal used to say that the gateway to Mosima was in their country, and could be entered by anyone who had the courage. It seems to have been necessary for two or more persons to go together; they held each other's hands before entering the pass, and shouted: " Ghosts, get out of the way! We are going to throw stones! " After which they passed in without difficulty.

As already stated, the ghosts are believed to lead much the same life in their village as they did on the upper earth; but details vary from place to place. Some of Casalis' informants described valleys always green (no droughts such as South African farmers dread) grazed over by immense herds of beautiful hornless cattle. Others seemed to think that the life was but a dull one, " without joy or sorrow."

---

[1] *Through the Heart of Africa*, p. 24.   [2] *Les Bassoutos*, p. 261.

The Wakuluwe shades are described as weary and home-sick, which is the reason why from time to time they come up and fetch a relative to keep them company. In their country it is always night—the absence of daylight is not as a rule mentioned in these accounts—but "the village . . . is said to be lighted by a mightier light than [any on] earth, and the spirits wear shining clothes, and the huts are thatched with shining grass."

On Kilimanjaro the spirit land may be reached by plunging into pools, but there are also certain gateways—perhaps some of the caves which abound in the sides of that mountain. The gates are all closed nowadays—more's the pity!

The Haunted Groves

But sometimes the ghosts have their dwelling above ground, in the "sacred groves" where the dead are buried. This custom of burial in the forest is very general in East Africa; the trees of the burying-ground are never cut down, and care is taken to protect them, as far as possible, against the bush-fires which rage at the end of the dry season. Hence in Nyasaland you will find here and there, towering over the level scrub, a clump of tall trees, and in their shade some pots, a broken hoe or two, or the fragments of a bow will mark the place of graves.

In these groves the spirits sometimes hold their revels: people in distant villages have heard their drums. There are places deep in the woods where the earth has been swept clean, as if for a dancing-floor, and here they assemble. Passers-by may hear faint music, but see no one; the sounds seem to be in front, but when they have gone on a little way they are heard behind them.

In Nyasaland there are ghosts which haunt particular hills, probably those where old chiefs have been buried, and there are strange accounts given of "the spirits' hill"[1]— *piri la mizimu*—where women passing by carrying pots on their heads have had the pots taken from them by baboons. One is left to infer that the baboons are shapes assumed by

[1] Scott, *Dictionary*, p. 416.

the ghosts, though this is not expressly stated, and elsewhere one finds baboons mentioned only as wizards' familiars, not as reincarnated ancestors. There are bananas grown on the spirits' hill—you can cut a bunch and eat some; but if you carry any away they will have disappeared before you reach your village.

Ghost Stories : the Kinyamkela's Bananas

Near Mkongole, in the Zaramo country, there was once a hollow tree haunted by a *kinyamkela*. Two boys from Mkongole, Mahimbwa and Kibwana, strolling through the woods, happened to come upon this tree, and saw that the ground had been swept clean all round it and that there was a bunch of bananas hanging from a branch. They took the bananas down, ate them, and went home quite happy. But that night, when they were both asleep in the ' boys' house ' of their village, they were awakened by a queer noise, and saw the one-legged, one-armed *kinyamkela* standing in the doorway. He called out to them : " You have eaten my bananas ! You must die ! " And with that they were suddenly hit by stones flying out of the darkness. There was a regular rain of stones, lumps of earth, and even human bones. The boys jumped up, ran out, and took refuge in another hut, but the stones followed them there. This went on for four nights—apparently without anyone getting seriously hurt—and then a doctor named Kikwilo decided to take the matter in hand. He said to the boys, " You have eaten the *kinyamkela's* bananas ; that is why he comes after you." He took a gourd, twice seven small loaves of bread, a fowl, some rice, and some bananas, and went to the *kinyamkela's* tree, where he laid the things down, saying, " The boys are sorry for what they did. Can you not leave them alone now ? " That night the *kinyamkela* appeared again to Mahimbwa and Kibwana, and said, " It's all right now ; the matter is settled ; but don't let it happen again."

So there was peace in the village, and all would have been well if the business had stopped there. But there was a certain man named Mataula, a wood-carver, addicted to hemp-smoking (this is perhaps mentioned to show that he was not quite responsible), who was, unluckily, absent at the time. When he came back and heard the story he declared that some one must have been playing a trick on the boys, and announced that he would sit up that night and see what happened. So he loaded his gun and waited. The *kinyamkela* must have heard his words, for as soon as it was dark he began to be pelted with bones and all sorts of dirt, and at last an invisible hand began to beat him with a leg-bone. He could not fire, as he could see no one, and was quite helpless to defend himself against the missiles. The neighbours had no cause to bless him, for they began to be persecuted similarly, and at last the whole population had to emigrate, as life in the village had become unendurable.[1]

Some well-authenticated reports from clergy of the Universities' Mission who have seen and felt lumps of mud thrown about without visible agency make one wonder whether stories like this ought not to be taken seriously. Similar occurrences nearer home have sometimes been satisfactorily explained, but not always.

Kwege and Bahati

Another story from Uzaramo[2] shows the dead coming back in the form of birds. This is less usual than for them to come as snakes or lions, except in the special case of a murdered man or woman, as will be illustrated by the story of Nyengebule to be told presently.

There was once upon a time a man who married a woman of the Uwingu clan (*uwingu* means 'sky') who was named Mulamuwingu, and whose brother, Muwingu, lived in her old home, a day or two's journey from her husband's.

The couple had a son called Kwege, and lived happily enough till, in course of time, the husband died, leaving his wife with her son and a slave, Bahati, who had belonged to an old friend of theirs and had come to them on that friend's death.

[1] Klamroth, in *Zeitschrift für Kolonialsprachen*, p. 118.
[2] *Ibid.*, p. 128.

Now the *tabu* of the Sky clan was *rain*—that is, rain must never be allowed to fall on anyone belonging to it; if this were to happen he or she would die.

One day when the weather looked threatening Mula-muwingu said, " My son Kwege, just go over to the garden and pick some gourds, so that I can cook them for our dinner." Kwege very rudely refused, and his mother rejoined, " I am afraid of my *mwidzilo* (*tabu*). If I go to the garden I shall die." Then Bahati, the slave, said, " I will go," and he went and gathered the gourds and brought them back.

Next day Kwege's mother again asked him to go to the garden, and again he refused. So she said, " Very well; I will go; but if I die it will be your fault." She set out, and when she reached the garden, which was a long way from any shelter, a great cloud gathered, and it began to rain. When the first drops touched her she fell down dead.

Kwege had no dinner that evening, and when he found his mother did not come home either that day or the next (it does not seem to have entered into his head that he might go in search of her) he began to cry, saying, " Mother is dead! Mother is dead!" Then he called Bahati, and they set out to go to his uncle's village.

Now Kwege was a handsome lad, but Bahati was very ugly; and Kwege was well dressed, with plenty of cloth, while Bahati had only a bit of rag round his waist.

As they walked along Kwege said to Bahati, " When we come to a log lying across the path you must carry me over. If I step over it I shall die." For Kwege's *mwidzilo* was stepping over a log.

Bahati agreed, but when they came to a fallen tree he refused to lift Kwege over till he had given him a cloth. This went on every time they came to a log, till he had acquired everything Kwege was wearing, down to his leglets and his bead ornaments. And when they arrived at Muwingu's village and were welcomed by the people Bahati sat down on one of the mats brought out for them and told Kwege to sit on the bare ground. He introduced himself

GHOSTS AND THE GHOST COUNTRY

to Muwingu as his sister's son, and treated Kwege as his slave, suggesting, after a day or two, that he should be sent out to the rice-fields to scare the birds. Kwege, in the ragged kilt which was the only thing Bahati had left him, went out to the fields, looked at the flocks of birds hovering over the rice, and then, sitting down under a tree, wept bitterly. Presently he began to sing:

> " I, Kwege, weep, I weep!
> And my crying is what the birds say.
> Oh, you log, my *tabu*!
> I cry in the speech of the birds.
> They have taken my clothes,
> They have taken my leglets,
> They have taken my beads,
> I am turned into Bahati.
> Bahati is turned into Kwege.
> I weep in the speech of the birds."

Now his dead parents had both been turned into birds. They came and perched on the tree above him, listening to his song, and said, "*Looo!* Muwingu has taken Bahati into his house and is treating him like a free man and Kwege, his nephew, as a slave! How can that be?"

Kwege heard what they said, and told his story. Then his father flapped one wing, and out fell a bundle of cloth; he flapped the other wing and brought out beads, leglets, and a little gourd full of oil. His mother, in the same way, produced a ready-cooked meal of rice and meat. When he had eaten they fetched water (by this time they had been turned back into human beings), washed him and oiled him, and then said, " Never mind the birds—let them eat Muwingu's rice, since he has sent you to scare them while he is treating Bahati as his son! " So they sat down, all three together, and talked till the sun went down.

On the way back Kwege hid all the cloth and beads that his parents had given him in the long grass, and put on his old rag again. But when he reached the house the family were surprised to see him looking so clean and glossy, as if he had just come from a bath, and cried out, " Where did

89

you get this oil you have been rubbing yourself with? Did you run off and leave your work to go after it?" He did not want to say, "Mother gave it me," so he simply denied that he had been anointing himself.

Next day he went back to the rice-field and sang his song again. The birds flew down at once, and, seeing him in the same miserable state as before, asked him what he had done with their gifts. He said they had been taken from him, thinking that, while he was about it, he might as well get all he could. They did not question his good faith, but supplied him afresh with everything, and, resuming their own forms, they sat by him while he ate.

Meanwhile Muwingu's son had taken it into his head to go and see how the supposed Bahati was getting on with his job—it is possible that he had begun to be suspicious of the man who called himself Kwege. What was his astonishment to see a good-looking youth, dressed in a clean cloth, with bead necklaces and all the usual ornaments, sitting between two people, whom he recognized as his father's dead sister and her husband. He was terrified, and ran back to tell his father that Kwege was Bahati and Bahati Kwege, and related what he had seen. Muwingu at once went with him to the rice-field, and found that it was quite true. They hid and waited for Kwege to come home. Then, as he drew near the place where he had hidden his cloth, his uncle sprang out and seized him. He struggled to get away, but Muwingu pacified him, saying, "So you are my nephew Kwege after all, and that fellow is Bahati! Why did you not tell me before? Never mind; I shall kill him to-day." And kill him they did; and Kwege was installed in his rightful position. Muwingu made a great feast, inviting all his neighbours, to celebrate the occasion. "Here ends my story," says the narrator.

Kwege, it will be seen, is described as anything but a model son, who does not deserve the kindness of his very forbearing parents; but it is evidently reckoned for righteousness to him that he submitted to any amount of inconvenience and indignity rather than break his *mwidzilo*.

90

Another point to notice is the curious limitation in the powers of the ghosts. They can assume any form they please and go anywhere they wish; they can produce magical stores out of nowhere; but they never seem to suspect that Kwege is deceiving them when he says he has been robbed of their gifts. Why Kwege should not have exposed Bahati when he reached his uncle's house is not clear, unless, with African fatalism,[1] he felt sure that he would not be believed.

"False Bride" Stories

This story reminds one of Grimm's "Goose Girl," as far as Bahati's imposture is concerned; but the theme is a world-wide one. In Angola the story of Fenda Madia has probably come from Portugal, and has nothing to do with the ghosts, but the Zulu "Untombiyapansi" (more shortly told by McCall Theal as "The Girl and the Mbulu") is genuine African. Here a girl on her way to her sister's kraal (her parents being dead) is overtaken by an imbulu, "a fabulous creature which can assume the human form, but can never part with its tail." It tricks her out of her clothes, rides on her ox, and personates her on arriving at the village, where it is received as the chief's daughter, while Untombiyapansi is sent to scare the birds. She summons her dead parents from underground by striking the earth with a brass rod, and they appear in their own proper form and succour her. The imbulu is detected and killed, and the chief, already married to her sister, takes Untombiyapansi as his second wife.[2]

The Makonde people,[3] in Tanganyika Territory, have a story of an orphan, who deserves more sympathy than Kwege. He was bullied by the other boys, who robbed him of the animals he had caught when he was more successful than they. So one day he proposed that they should go to hunt

[1] It is scarcely fair to use this expression as if it applied to all Africans; but the characteristic is noticeable among tribes who have suffered from slave-raids or the oppression of more powerful neighbours.

[2] Callaway, Nursery Tales, p. 303.

[3] The Makonde Plateau is near the East Coast, south of Lindi and to the north of the river Ruvuma. This story was collected by Mr Frederick Johnson.

91

in a certain wood, where his father and mother were buried. When they came to the grave he told the others to sit down, saying, " If you see anything coming out don't run." Then he began to sing (his companions joining in the chorus):

> " Father! Father! come out of your grave!
> CHORUS : *Ngondo liyaya!* The raiders come!
> They treat your child like the meanest slave.
> *Ngondo liyaya!* The raiders come!
> I trapped my rats with weariful toil;
> *Ngondo liyaya!* The raiders come!
> They've robbed me of all my hard-won spoil.
> *Ngondo liyaya!* The raiders come!
> ' You've no father or mother! ' they said.
> *Ngondo liyaya!* The raiders come!
> ' Your parents have gone to the Place of the Dead! '
> *Ngondo liyaya!* The raiders come! "

There is a certain attractive simplicity about the literal translation of what follows:

> Now came a snake from the grave there and lay down and coiled itself, and the boys wanted to run, and he said, " Do not run." And they sat there, clapping their hands. That snake came from the grave of his father. And he arose and sang at the grave of his mother, and a snake also came from that place and coiled itself there. And he sang again—

nearly the same song as before:

> " Father! Mother! from Dead Men's Town,
> CHORUS : *Ngondo liyaya!* The raiders come! [1]
> Come forth, come forth, and swallow them down,
> Who scorned and wronged me day by day,
> And robbed me of all my lawful prey.
> ' You've no father or mother! ' they said.
> ' Your parents have gone to the Place of the Dead! ' "

The snakes then rose up and swallowed all the boy's companions. Their son sang again, and they retired into their holes, while he went back to the village. The parents of the other boys asked him about them, but he only answered, " I do not know; they left me in the forest."

---

[1] Repeated after each line, as before.

As the boys did not come home their parents consulted a diviner, who told them that " the orphan had hidden his companions." So they questioned the orphan lad, and he told every one who had lost a boy to bring him a slave— a touch which cannot be very recent. They did so, and he set off for the grave with his newly acquired retinue, all singing together. He called once more on his parents, and the boys all came out, safe and sound, and marched back to the village. The orphan lad went with his slaves to an un- occupied piece of land in the bush, where they built a new village and he became a chief and lived there with his people.[1]

An African 'Holle' Story

How a girl reached the land of the ghosts and came back is told by the Wachaga.[2] Marwe and her brother were ordered by their parents to watch the bean-field and drive away the monkeys. They kept at their post for the greater part of the day, but as their mother had not given them any food to take with them they grew very hungry. They dug up the burrows of the field-rats, caught some, made a fire, roasted their game, and ate it. Then, being thirsty, they went to a pool and drank. It was some distance off, and when they came back they found that the monkeys had descended on the bean-patch and stripped it bare. They were terribly frightened, and Marwe said, " Let's go and jump into the pool." But her brother thought it would be better to go home without being seen and listen to what their parents were saying. So they stole up to the hut and listened through a gap in the banana-leaves of the thatch. Father and mother were both very angry. " What are we to do with such good-for-nothing creatures? Shall we beat them? Or shall we strangle them?" The children did not wait to hear any more, but rushed off to the pool. Marwe threw herself in, but her brother's courage failed him, and he ran back home and told the parents: " Marwe has gone into the pool." They went down at once, quite

---

[1] Johnson, " Notes on Kimakonde."
[2] Gutmann, *Volksbuch*, p. 117.

forgetting the hasty words provoked by the sudden discovery of their loss, and called again and again, " Marwe, come home! Never mind about the beans; we can plant the patch again!" But there was no answer. Day after day the father went down to the pool and called her—always in vain. Marwe had gone into the country of the ghosts.

You entered it at the bottom of the pool. Before she had gone very far she came to a hut, where an old woman lived, with a number of children. This old woman called her in and told her she might stay with her. Next day she sent her out with the others to gather firewood, but said, " You need not do anything. Let the others do the work." Marwe, however, did her part with the rest, and the same when they were sent out to cut grass or perform any other tasks. She was offered food from time to time, but always made some excuse for refusing it. (The living who reach the land of the dead can never leave it again if they eat while there—a belief met with elsewhere than in Africa.) So time went on, till one day she began to weary, and said to the other girls, "I should like to go home." The girls advised her to go and tell the old woman, which she did, and the old body had no objection, but asked her, " Shall I hit you with the cold or with the hot? " It is not easy to see what is meant by this question, but in all stories of this kind, which are numerous, the departing visitor to the ghost land is given a choice of some kind—sometimes between two gifts, sometimes between two ways of going home. Perhaps the meaning of the alternative here proposed has been lost in transmission or in translation. The good girl always chooses the less attractive article or road, and Marwe asked to be " hit with the cold." The woman told her to dip her arms into a pot she had standing beside her. She did so, and drew them out covered with shining bangles. She was then told to dip her feet, and found her ankles adorned with fine brass and copper chains. Then the woman gave her a skin petticoat worked with beads, and said, " Your future husband is called Sawoye. It is he who will carry you home."

She went with her to the pool, rose to the surface, and left her sitting on the bank. It happened that there was a famine in the land just then. Some one saw Marwe, and ran to the village saying that there was a girl seated by the pool richly dressed and wearing the most beautiful ornaments, which no one else in the countryside could afford, the people having parted with all their valuables to the coast-traders in the time of scarcity. So the whole population turned out, with the chief at their head. They were filled with admiration of her beauty. (It seems that her looks had not suffered in the ghost country, in spite of her not eating.) They all greeted her most respectfully, and the chief wanted to carry her home; but she refused. Others offered, but she would listen to none till a certain man came along, who was known as Sawoye. Now Sawoye was disfigured by a disease from which he had suffered called *woye*, whence his name. As soon as she saw him Marwe said, " That is my husband." So he picked her up and carried her home and married her.

This is a somewhat unusual kind of wedding, from the Bantu point of view: nothing is said about the parents. But the whole circumstances were unusual : it is not every day that a girl comes back from the country of the dead, having had her destined husband pointed out by the chieftainess of the ghosts.

We are not told, but I think we must be meant to understand, that Sawoye soon lost his disfiguring skin disease and appeared as the handsomest man in the clan. With the old lady's bangles they bought a fine herd of cattle and built themselves the best house in the village. And they would have lived happy ever after if some of his neighbours had not envied him and plotted to kill him. They succeeded, but his faithful wife found means to revive him, and hid him in the inner compartment of the hut. Then, when the enemies came to divide the spoil and carry Marwe off to be given to the chief as his wife, Sawoye came out, fully armed, and killed them all. After which he and Marwe were left in peace.

95

Other 'Holle' Stories

Two interesting variants come from the Ngonde country. One is described by a learned German writer as " psychologically incomprehensible"; but if he had a complete version before him he would seem curiously to have missed the point. A woman is " persuaded by another "—evidently a jealous co-wife—to throw away her baby, because it is weakly: other versions show that he ought to have added " in the hope of getting it back improved in health and looks." The rest of the story is much the same as that of " La Route du ciel," and follows much more naturally from its opening than does that tale, except that the jealous woman, instead of being struck dead, gets only half a baby, with one arm, one leg, and so on.[1]

In the other story the opening is more mysterious: the mother, coming to a river too deep to ford, heard a voice telling her to throw her baby into the water, and she would be able to walk over dryshod. She did so, and the water parted to let her cross; but when she had reached the other side she could not find the child again. She had to go home without it, and was told by her husband to go away and never come back till she had found it. Wandering through the forest, she met, one after another, a lion, a leopard, a crocodile, and other animals, all, apparently, suffering from ophthalmia, who asked her where she was going, requested of her a most unpleasant service, and after she had rendered it allowed her to pass on. She then met a very old man, who told her that she would shortly come to a place where the path divided, and would hear a voice on one side saying *mbo*, and one on the other side saying *ndi*. She was to follow the first, which she did, and arrived at a hut, where a woman showed her a number of beautiful children and told her to choose one. There is the usual sequel: the envious neighbour disregards all advice and meets in the end with her deserts—in this case by having to carry home a wretched, diseased, and crippled infant.[2]

---

[1] Unpublished; quoted by Dr Fülleborn, in *Das deutsche Njassa- und Ruwumagebiet*, p. 335.

[2] Nauhaus, "Was sich die Konde in Deutsch-Ostafrika erzählen."

A SWAZI MOTHER AND BABY

Photo A. M. Duggan-Cronin. By permission of the McGregor Museum, Kimberley

The incident of the stream stands alone, so far as I know, in stories of this type. The dividing of a river occurs more than once in a very different connexion—in traditions of tribal migrations, as when one of the Ngoni chiefs was said to have struck the Zambezi with his stick, to let the people cross.[1] The voices—from the river and from the two paths—may belong to some bit of forgotten mythology. In one of the hare stories which form the subject of Chapter XVII the hyena tells the hare that when crossing the river he may hear a voice ordering him to throw away his bread. This, of course, is a trick on the hyena's part, but seems to be accepted as a possible occurrence, and may be an echo of some belief in river-spirits.

Do the Dead return to Life ?

The possibility of the dead returning to life is frequently assumed in folk-tales,[2] but I do not know that it is seriously believed in at the present day, as seems to be the case for the visits of living men and women to the Underworld. The Rev. Donald Fraser relates an extraordinary incident[3] : a man was thought to have died, but came to, and said that he had reached the ghosts' country, where he saw and spoke to people, but none would answer him ; in fact, they showed him decidedly that they did not want him, and he had to come back.

The Wazaramo appear to have a divinity called Kolelo, who lives in a cave in the form of a huge serpent. Remembering the very common belief that the spirits of the dead come back in the form of snakes, it may be considered probable that this Kolelo was originally an ancestral ghost. He played a great part in the troubles of 1905 (known as the "Majimaji Rebellion") in what was then German East Africa ; but his legend will come in more fittingly in Chapter XVI.

[1] The Rev. T. Cullen Young thinks this may have arisen from the fact that the Ngoni had never seen a log canoe, which might be described as a stick ('log,' 'tree,' and 'stick' might sometimes be expressed by the same word), and misunderstood as the tradition was passed on.

[2] As in the story of "Tangalimlibo," Theal, *Kaffir Folklore*, p. 54.

[3] *Winning a Primitive People*, p. 126.

CHAPTER VII: THE AVENGER OF BLOOD

THE usual unwritten law of primitive peoples is, in theory at least, " a life for a life," the clan of the murdered man being entitled to kill the murderer, if they can get hold of him ; if not, one of his family, or, at any rate, a member of the same clan. No difference was originally made between intentional and accidental killing, though this distinction came to be recognized later. In time the principle of ransom came into force—the *weregild* of our Saxon ancestors. The Yaos would express it thus in a case where the relations had failed to kill the murderer out of hand and had captured a relative of his : " You have slain our brother ; we have caught yours ; and we will send him after our brother—or keep him as a slave—unless you pay a ransom." This last alternative has tended more and more to become the usual practice in Africa.

Murder of a Relative

But a difficulty arose when a man killed one of his own relations. In that case who could demand compensation? for the slayer and the slain were of the same clan. And the general belief about this shows that such a thing is regarded with horror and as almost unthinkable. Such a man would be seized by a kind of madness—the Anyanja call it *chirope*,[1] and say, " The blood of his companion enters his heart ; it makes him just like a drunk man." Or, as the Yaos say,[2] " He will become emaciated, lose his eyesight, and ultimately die a miserable death." Though the owner of a slave in theory had the power of life and death, he was afraid of *chirope* if he killed him. He could escape only by being ' doctored ' with a certain charm, which, one may suppose, would not be too easily procured.

The Warrior's Purification

A man who had killed another in battle also had to be ' doctored,' for fear that he should be haunted by the ghost

[1] Scott, *Dictionary*, p. 96.   [2] Duff Macdonald, *Africana*, vol. i, p. 168.

of the slain—no doubt because, from the nature of the case, the dead man's kin could not follow the usual procedure. With the Zulus [1] the 'doctoring' (*ukuqunga*) was a long and complicated process, involving various *tabus*: an essential point was that the warrior must cut open the corpse of his foe before it began to swell. This precaution (the neglect of which rendered him liable to be possessed by the avenging ghost—a form of insanity known as *iqungo*) has, not unnaturally, been misunderstood and given rise to reports of "atrocities," "mutilation of the dead," and so on, as happened in the Zulu War of 1879.

The Two Brothers

There is a well-known story, current, probably, among all the South African Bantu, in which the secret murder of a brother is brought to light and avenged. It is usually called "Masilo and Masilonyane," though the Zulu variant has a different name. In some versions the guilty brother is killed when detected, but in what would appear to be the oldest and most authentic he is driven from the clan and becomes an outcast. Perhaps we find the beginning of a change from the older view in one case, where he is said to have been killed, not by a member of the family, but by a servant (*mohlanka*) of Masilonyane's—presumably not a member of the clan.

In the most usual form of the story [2] the two brothers, Masilo and Masilonyane, went hunting together and happened upon a ruined village. The younger, Masilonyane, went straight on through the ruins with his dogs, while his brother turned aside and skirted round them. In the middle of the ruins Masilonyane found a number of large earthen pots turned upside down. He tried to turn up one of the largest, but it resisted all his efforts. After he had tried in vain several times he called to his brother for help, but

---

[1] Colenso, *Zulu-English Dictionary*, p. 513.

[2] I have here, more or less, combined two versions : one by S. H. Edwards, in the South African *Folk-Lore Journal*, vol. i, p. 139, and the other by Jacottet, in his *Treasury of Ba-Suto Lore*, p. 56.

Masilo refused, saying, " Pass on. Why do you trouble
about pots?" Masilonyane persevered, however, and at
length succeeded in heaving up the pot, and in doing so
uncovered a little old woman who was grinding red ochre
between two stones. Masilonyane, startled at this appari-
tion, was about to turn the pot over her again, but she
remonstrated: " My grandchild, do you turn me up and
then turn me upside down again?" She then requested
him to carry her on his back. Before he had time to refuse
she jumped up and clung to him, so that he could not get
rid of her. He called Masilo, but Masilo only jeered and
refused to help him. He had to walk on with his burden,
till, at last, seeing a herd of springbok, he thought he had
found a way of escape, and said, " Grandmother, get down,
that I may go and kill one of these long-legged animals, so
that I may carry you easily in its skin." She consented, and
sat down on the ground, while Masilonyane called his dogs
and made off at full speed after the game. But as soon as
he was out of her sight he turned aside and hid in the hole
of an ant-bear. The old woman, however, was not to be
defeated. After waiting for a time and finding that he did
not come back she got up and tracked him by his footprints,
till she came to his hiding-place. He had to come out and
take her up again, and so he plodded on for another weary
mile or two, till the sight of some hartebeests gave him
another excuse for putting her down. Once more he hid,
and once more she tracked him ; but this time he set his
dogs on her, and they killed her. He told the dogs to eat
her, all but her great toe, which they did. He then took an
axe and chopped at the toe, when out came many cattle, and,
last of all, a beautiful cow, spotted like a guinea-fowl.

This incident, monstrous as it appears to us—especially
as there has been no hint that the old woman was of unusual
size ; indeed, she was not too big to be carried on Masilonyane's back—is not uncommon in Bantu folklore, and in
some cases seems to link on to the legend of the Swallowing
Monster. Now Masilo, who had shirked all the unpleasant
part of the day's adventures, came running up and demanded

a share of the cattle. Masilonyane, not unnaturally, refused, and they went on together.

After a while Masilonyane said he was very thirsty, and his brother said he knew of a water-hole not far off. They went there, and found that it was covered with a large, flat stone. They levered up the stone with their spears, and Masilonyane held it while Masilo stooped to drink. When he, in his turn, stooped to reach the water Masilo dropped the stone on him and crushed him to death. Then he collected the cattle and started to drive them home. Suddenly he saw a small bird perching on the horn of the speckled cow; it sang:

> "*Chwidi! Chwidi!* Masilo has killed Masilonyane, because of his speckled cow!"

(People say it was Masilonyane's heart which was changed into a bird.) Masilo threw a stone at the bird, and seemed to have killed it, but it came to life again, and before he had gone very far he saw it sitting on the cow's horn, and killed it once more, as he thought.

When he reached his home all the people crowded together and greeted him. "*Dumela!* Chief's son! *Dumela!* Chief's son! Where is Masilonyane?" He answered, "I don't know; we parted at the water-hole, and I have not seen him since." They went to look at the cattle, and exclaimed in admiration, "What a beautiful cow! Just look at her markings!"

While they were standing there the little bird flew up with a great whirring of wings and perched on the horn of the speckled cow and sang:

> "*Chwidi! Chwidi!* Masilo has killed Masilonyane, all for his speckled cow!"

Masilo threw a stone at the bird, but missed it, and the men said, "Just leave that bird alone and let us hear." The bird sang the same words over and over again, and the people heard them clearly. They said, "So that is what you have done! You have killed your younger brother." And

Masilo had nothing to say. So they drove him out of the village.

A different version from North Transvaal [1] makes the cattle come out of a hollow tree, and says nothing about the old woman. It also prefixes to the story some incidents not found elsewhere, which show Masilonyane in a less favourable light than that in which we have so far regarded him. At any rate, he does something, by his arrogance, to provoke his elder brother's enmity. Their father had entrusted them with the means of buying a beast or two to start a herd—the recognized manner of providing for sons. Masilonyane (here called Mashilwane), by clever trading and repeated strokes of good luck, soon became richer than his brother, and so provoked Masilo's envy. Mashilwane did nothing to conciliate him; on the contrary, he kept on boasting of his prosperity, and even, when his wife died, said, "I am Mashilwane, whom death cannot touch!"

Another point of difference in this version is that it is one of Mashilwane's dogs who reveals the murder and leads the clansmen to the place where the body is hidden. In the other there is no question of the body; indeed, in one form of the story the murdered man comes to life again, the bird suddenly taking his shape. On the whole the North Transvaal version seems later and more consciously elaborated— perhaps in response to questions from European auditors.

A hunter's dogs figure in a story from Angola,[2] where an elder brother kills a younger, being envious of his success. He gives part of the body to the two dogs, but they refuse to eat it; instead they lift up their voices and denounce him. He kills and buries them; they come to life, follow him home, and report the whole affair in the village. The story ends: "They wailed the mourning"; nothing is said about the fate of the murderer. A brother killing a brother is something quite outside the common course of law.

It is not entirely the same with a wife, who, by the nature of the case, must belong to a different clan; the duty of

[1] Hoffmann, *Zeitschrift für Kolonialsprachen*, vol. vi, No. 5.
[2] Chatelain, *Folk-tales of Angola*, p. 127.

exacting retribution naturally falls on her relations once the crime is made known.

The Xosa Tale of Nyengebule

So it was with Nyengebule.[1] He had two wives, who, one day, went out together to collect firewood in the forest. The younger found a bees' nest in a hollow tree, and called her companion to help her take out the honeycomb. When they had done so they sat down and ate it, the younger thoughtlessly finishing her share, while the elder kept putting some aside, which she wrapped up in leaves to take home for her husband. Arriving at the kraal, each went to her own hut. The elder, on entering, found her husband seated there, and gave him the honeycomb. Nyengebule thanked her for the attention, and ate the honey, thinking all the time that Nqandamate, the younger wife, who was his favourite, would also have brought him some, especially as he was just then staying in her hut. When he had finished eating he hastened thither and sat down, expecting that she would presently produce the titbit. But he waited in vain, and at last, becoming impatient, he asked, " Where is the honey? " She said, " I have not brought any." Thereupon he lost his temper and struck her with his stick, again and again. The little bunch of feathers which she was wearing on her head (as a sign that she was training for initiation as a doctor) fell to the ground; he struck once more in his rage; she fell, and he found that she was dead. He made haste to bury her, and then—he is shown as thoroughly selfish and callous throughout—he gathered up his sticks and set out for her parents' kraal, to report the death (which he would represent as an accident) and demand his *lobolo*-cattle [2] back. But the little plume which had fallen from her head when he struck her turned into a bird and flew after him.

When he had gone some distance he noticed a bird sitting on a bush by the wayside, and heard it singing these words :

[1] South African *Folk-Lore Journal*, July 1879.

[2] A man who loses his wife before she has had any children is entitled to get back the cattle he paid on his marriage—unless her parents can give him another daughter instead of her.

A Zulu Woman Diviner

Photo Mariannhill Mission

" I am the little plume of the diligent wood-gatherer,
   The wife of Nyengebule.
   I am the one who was killed by the house-owner, wantonly !
   He asking me for morsels of honeycomb."

It kept up with him, flying alongside the path, till at last
he threw a stick at it. It paid no attention, but kept on as
before, so he hit it with his knobkerrie, killed it, threw it
away, and walked on.

But after a while it came back again and repeated its song.
Blind with rage, he again threw a stick at it, killed it, stopped
to bury it, and went on his way.

As he was still going on it came up again and sang :

" I am the little plume of the diligent wood-gatherer . . ."

At that he became quite desperate, and said, " What shall
I do with this bird, which keeps on tormenting me about a
matter I don't want to hear about? I will kill it now, once
for all, and put it into my bag to take with me." Once more
he threw his stick at the little bird and killed it, picked it up,
and put it into his *inxowa*—the bag, made from the skin of
some small animal, which natives carry about with them to
supply the place of a pocket. He tied the bag up tightly
with a thong of hide, and thought he had now completely
disposed of his enemy.

So he went on till he came to the kraal of his wife's relations, where he found a dance going on. He became so
excited that he forgot the business about which he had come,
and hurried in to join in the fun. He had just greeted his
sisters-in-law when one of them asked him for snuff. He
told her—being in a hurry to begin dancing and entirely
forgetful of what the bag contained—to untie the *inxowa*,
which he had laid aside. She did so, and out flew the bird—
dri-i-i! It flew up to the gate-post, and, perching there,
began to sing:

" *Ndi 'salana sika' Tezateza
   'Mfazi Unyengebule ;
   Ndingobulewe 'Mninindhlu ngamabom,
   Ebendibuza amanqatanqata obusi.*"

He heard it, and, seeing that every one else had also

heard it, started to run away. Some of the men jumped up and seized hold of him, saying, " What are you running away for? " He answered—his guilty conscience giving him away against his will—" Me! I was only coming to the dance. I don't know what that bird is talking about."

It began again, and its song rang out clearly over the heads of the men who were holding him :

" Ndi 'salana sika' Tezateza . . ."

They listened, the meaning of the song began to dawn on them, and they grew suspicious. They asked him, " What is this bird saying? " He said, " I don't know."

They killed him.

With this brief statement the story closes, leaving to the imagination the clamour that arose, the cries of the mother and sisters, the brothers rushing for their kerries, the doomed man's frantic struggles. . . . *Bambulala*, "They killed him."

Father Torrend says :

> Tales of this kind, showing that every crime finds an unexpected revealer, appointed by a superior power, are very common in the whole of the Zambezi region. In this particular tale [which will be given presently] the revealer is a child . . . in others it is a little dog, but in tales far more numerous it is a little bird which no killing can prevent from rising from the dead and singing of the criminal deed until punishment is meted out to the guilty person.[1]

One such story was collected by Mrs Dewar [2] among the Winamwanga, to the north of Lake Nyasa, on the farthest edge of the " Zambezi region," since their country is near the sources of the Chambezi.[3] As set down by her it is very short, but it may be worth while to reproduce it here, as it gives the notes of the bird's song.

> Once upon a time there was a man and his younger brother. The younger brother was chief. [It is not explained how this happened, but no doubt he was the son of the ' Great Wife,' and as such his father's heir.] One day when he climbed a *mpangwa*

---

[1] *Bantu Folklore*, p. 17.   [2] *Chinamwanga Stories*, p. 29.

[3] But the story is not confined to that region, its underlying motive being practically universal.

tree [which bears an edible fruit, much liked] his elder brother killed him. Afterwards he came to life again as a little bird and sang:

Nzye!　Nzye! Nzye! Nzye!　Wa- nko-me-la　pa chi-mpa-ngwa

["*Nzye!* [a mere exclamation] He has killed me because of the *mpangwa* fruit,
The *mpangwa* by the roadside.
Doesn't it help us in time of need?"]

That is all, but the rest is not difficult to guess. The bird's song seems somewhat obscure, but probably means that the young man was gathering the fruit to eat in a time of scarcity. This is a detail stressed in the next story,[1] though the other incidents are quite different.

Out of the Mouths of Babes

Once upon a time there was a married couple who had two children. Not long after the birth of the second the wife said she wanted to go and see her mother. The husband agreed, and they set out. It happened to be a time of famine, and they had little or nothing to eat, so when they came to a wild fig-tree by the wayside the man climbed it and began to shake down the fruit.[2] The wife and the elder child picked up the figs and ate them as fast as they fell. Presently there fell, among the rest, a particularly large and fine one. The husband called out: "My wife, do not eat that fig! If you do I will kill you."[3] The wife, not without spirit, answered, "Hunger has no law. And, really, would you kill me, your wife, for a fig? I am eating it; let us see whether you dare kill me!"

She ate the fig, and her husband came down from the tree and picked up his spear.

[1] Torrend, *Bantu Folklore*, p. 9.
[2] It is edible, but somewhat insipid, and not considered worth eating when anything better is to be had.
[3] The selfish and greedy husband and father is frequently held up to reprobation in folk-tales. Refusal to share food with others is looked on as something worse than mere lack of manners—it is "simply not done."

"My fig! Where has it gone?" he said, pointing the weapon at her.

She answered, "I have eaten it."

He said not another word, but stabbed her. As she fell forward on her knees the baby she was carrying on her back stared at him over her shoulder. He took no notice, only saying, "My children, let us go now, as I have killed your mother."

The elder boy picked up his little brother and put him on his back. The baby, Katubi, looked behind him at the dead woman and began to cry. His brother sang:

> "How can I silence Katubi?
> Oh, my dear Katubi!
> How can I silence Katubi?" [1]

The father asked him what he was saying, but he said, "I am not speaking; it is only baby crying." The father said, "Let us go on. You shall eat when you get there." They went on and on, and at last the baby himself began to sing:

> "Silence Katubi!
> My brother has become my mother!"

That is, he is carrying him on his back, as his mother had been doing.

The father heard it, and, thinking it was the elder boy who sang, said, "What are you talking about, you little wretch? I am going to kill you. What, are you going to tell tales when we get to your grandmother's?" The child, terrified, said, "No! I won't say anything!"

Still they went on, and the baby kept looking behind him, and after a while began again:

---

[1] The baby's name is significant; it means: "Expose the truth"—literally, "Make the thing white." These songs, of which each line is usually repeated at least twice, are an essential feature in the story. The words are always known to some, at any rate, of the audience, who sing them in chorus every time they occur. Bishop Steere says (*Swahili Tales*, p. vii): "It is a constant characteristic of popular native tales to have a sort of burden, which all join in singing. Frequently the skeleton of the story seems to be contained in these snatches of singing, which the story-teller connects by an extemporized account of the intervening history."

"What a lot of vultures
Over the fig-tree at Moya's!
What a lot of vultures!"

And he cried again. The father asked, "What are you crying for?" and the boy said that he was not crying; he was only trying to quiet the baby. The man, looking back, saw a number of vultures hovering over the place he had left, and as he did so he heard the song again:

"What a lot of vultures!"

The boy, when asked once more why the baby was crying, answered, "He is crying for Mother!" And the father said, "Nonsense! Let us get on. You're going to see your grandmother!"

The same incident was repeated, till the father, in a rage, turned back and began beating both the children. The boy asked, "Are you going to kill me, as you killed Mother?" The furious man shouted, "I do mean to kill you!" However, he held his hand for the moment, and the boy slipped past him and went on in front, and presently the baby's voice was heard again:

"What a lot of vultures!"

They reached the village at last, and the man exchanged greetings with his mother-in-law. He seems to have failed to satisfy her when she inquired after his wife, for, on the first opportunity, she questioned the little boy: "Now where has your mother been left?" The child shook his head, and did not speak for a while. Then he said, "Do you expect to see Mother? She has been killed by Father— all for the sake of a wild fruit!"

At the same moment the baby began to sing:

"What a lot of vultures!"

The grandmother must have been convinced by this portent, for she questioned the boy no further, but only said, "Stop, Baby! We are just going to kill your father also!" She set some men to dig a deep, narrow hole inside the hut, while she prepared the porridge. When the hole was ready she had a mat spread over it, and then brought in the porridge and sent the boy to call his father to supper. The guilty man came in, saw the mat spread in what appeared to be the best place, and immediately sat down on it. The grandmother had large pots of boiling water ready, and as soon as he had fallen into the hole they poured it over him and killed him.[1]

The significance of this story is emphasized by the fact that " the revealer is a little being which might have been thought to have no notion of right or wrong." This is still more strongly brought out—in a somewhat crude fashion—in Father Torrend's alternative version, where it is actually the unborn child which makes its way into the world to proclaim the father's guilt.

The same people, the Bwine-Mukuni, have another tale, which we need not reproduce in full, where a young chief, killed by his covetous companions, "was changed into a little bird with pretty colours," which, though not merely killed but burnt to ashes, revives and flies to the house of the dead man's sister. Its song has a certain beauty.

A i-ri-re nti-ngi-ni! A i-ri-re nti-ngi-ni! Ka-ra-te-re-nte-nta ko-ni ka-ka-swa kwi-ro-nga kwi-ro-nga rya-bo A i-ri-re nti-ngi-ni!

---

[1] This mode of execution seems in the folk-tales to be considered appropriate for aggravated cases of murder, like the above, or as an effectual means of putting an end to extra-human pests, like the *imbulu* of the Zulu story referred to in a previous chapter. In another version, also given by Father Torrend, the man is speared by his wife's brothers.

[Let the big drum roll! (CHORUS : Let the big drum roll!)
It flaps the wings, the little bird that has come out from the deep river,
From the great river of God. Let the big drum roll!]

There are six stanzas. In the fourth Nemba, the chief's sister, is called on to begin threading beads for the mourners to wear. The last verse is as follows :

Let the big drum roll! Let the big drum roll!
The land Where-I-wash-the-wrongs,
It is far from this place to which you have brought me,
Me who have no feet.[1] Let the big drum roll!

This is explained by Torrend as referring to Bantu notions of a future life, and his note may fitly close this chapter.

The souls, though " having no feet," are supposed to go to a deep river of God, far away, not a simple *mulonga* " river," but a *rironga*, " big, deep river," where God washes the wrongs clean and where birds with beaks all white—that is, innocent souls—cry vengeance against the spilling of blood.[2]

[1] I have nowhere else seen any reference to this notion. In whatever form the dead are supposed to appear they are normally assumed to have their full complement of limbs. Is there a belief that some kinds of birds are without feet, as was formerly said about the bird of Paradise ? The " birds with white beaks " are mentioned in the third verse of the song.

[2] *Bantu Folklore*, p. 25.

CHAPTER VIII: HEROES AND DEMI-GODS

GREAT chiefs, or men otherwise distinguished, whose memory lives on after many generations, are not only honoured beyond the worship paid to ordinary ghosts, but become the subjects of many a legend. Some of these heroes are plainly mythical, others are known to have actually existed, and some historical persons have become legendary without receiving divine honours. One knows that the genesis of myths is not confined to remote ages; they may spring up any day, even in civilized countries: there have been at least three well-known examples within the last twenty years. I remember being present at a conversation during which, as I believe, a legend was nipped in the bud. Some Zulus, after consulting together in undertones, asked Miss Colenso, very respectfully, whether it was true that her father had prophesied before his death that his house (Bishopstowe, near Pietermaritzburg) would be burned down. She answered that very likely he might have said, some time or other, that if due precautions were not taken a fire might reach the house during the grass-burning season—which, in fact, actually happened, owing, however, to a sudden change of wind rather than to any lack of care. I fear the questioners were disappointed; but one can imagine how the story would have grown if not discouraged.

The Ox-eater

In the countries to the west of Lake Victoria there is a cult of a being known as Ryang'ombe, or Lyang'ombe, concerning whom curious legends are current. His name means " Eater of an ox "; in full it is, in the language of the Baziba, Kashaija Karyang'ombe, " the little man who eats an [whole] ox." The name is distinctly Bantu, and is connected with his story. In Ruanda and Urundi, where his worship is fully developed, it does not seem to be entirely understood; and another indication of his Bantu origin is to be found in the fact that the mysteries of Ryang'ombe are supposed specially to belong to the Bahutu, the Bantu agricultural community; and, though the Batusi aristocracy frequently take part in them, there is a very strict rule that the reigning chief must never have been initiated into this particular rite. This seems strange, as Rehse, writing of the Baziba, says that Ryang'ombe is "the spirit of the cattle, *only* venerated by the Bahima." [1] But there is much in the whole subject which still awaits investigation. The Baziba tell a story which differs considerably from the Ruanda legend as given by P. Arnoux [2] and by Johanssen; [3] but, for all one knows, both may circulate side by side—in one of the countries at any rate. Some feats of his remind one strongly of the Zulu Hlakanyana, but the latter is merely a trickster, and never, so far as I know, attained the status of a national hero, or became an object of worship. Ryang'ombe, according to this story, [4] spoke before he was born, and ate a whole ox immediately after his entrance into the world. His father told him of a terrible ogre, Ntubugezi, notorious for killing people; Ryang'ombe at once made for the giant's abode, insulted and defied him, and made him give up eleven head of cattle, which he (Ryang'ombe) swallowed at once. He then attacked another ogre, Ntangaire, and swallowed him whole, but did not long enjoy his triumph, for Ntangaire cut his way out and killed him. In the Ruanda legend, likewise, Ryang'ombe's mortal career ends disastrously, though after a different fashion.

Ryang'ombe in Ruanda

The Banyaruanda give Ryang'ombe's family affairs in great detail. His father was Babinga, described as the "king of the *imandwa*"; [5] his mother, originally called Kalimulore, [6] was an uncomfortable sort of person, who had

[1] The Bahima are the Hamitic invaders who form the pastoral aristocracy in Buganda, Bunyoro, and elsewhere. In Ruanda they are called Batusi.

[2] *Anthropos* (1913), vol. viii. [3] *Ruanda*, pp. 109–111. [4] H. Rehse, *Kiziba*, p. 371.

[5] The *imandwa* are a superior order of spirits, distinct from the common herd of ghosts, who are called *bazimu*, and mostly thought of as malevolent. All the *imandwa* are known by name; many of them are in one way or another related to Ryang'ombe, and each has his or her own special ritual.

[6] After the birth of her son she was known as Nyiraryang'ombe ('Mother of Ryang'ombe').

H

the power of turning herself into a lioness, and took to killing her father's cattle, till he forbade her to herd them, and sent some one else in her place. She so frightened her first husband that he took her home to her parents and would have no more to do with her. After her second marriage, to Babinga, there seems to have been no further trouble. It is not clear how Babinga could have been " king of the ghosts " while still living, but when he died his son, Ryang'ombe, announced that he was going to take his father's place. This was disputed by one of Babinga's followers named Mpumutimuchuni, and the two agreed to decide the question by a game of *kisoro*,[1] which Ryang'ombe lost. Perhaps we are to understand by the long story which follows that he passed some time in exile; for he went out hunting, and heard a prophecy from some herd-lads which led to his marriage. After some difficulties with his parents-in-law he settled down with his wife, and had a son, Binego, but soon left them and returned to his own home.

As soon as Binego was old enough his mother's brother set him to herd the cattle; he speared a heifer the first day, a cow and her calf the next, and when his uncle objected he speared him too. He then called his mother, and they set out for Ryang'ombe's place, which they reached in due course, Binego having, on the way, killed two men who refused to leave their work and guide him, and a baby, for no particular reason. When he arrived he found his father playing the final game with Mpumutimuchuni. The decision had been allowed to stand over during the interval, and Ryang'ombe, if he lost this game, was not only to hand over the kingdom, but to let his opponent shave his head—that is, deprive him of the crest of hair which marked his royal rank. Binego went and stood behind his father to watch the game, suggested a move which enabled him to win, and when Mpumutimuchuni protested stabbed him. Thus he secured his father in the kingship, which, apparently, was so far counted to him for righteousness as to outweigh all the

---

[1] A game variously known as *mankala, mweso, bao, msuo*, etc., and played all over Africa, either on a board or with four rows of holes scooped in the ground.

murders he had committed. Ryang'ombe named him, first as his second-in-command and afterwards as his successor, and Binego, as will be seen, avenged his death. Like all the *imandwa*, with the exception of Ryang'ombe himself, who is uniformly kind and beneficent, he is thought of as mischievous and cruel, and propitiated from fear, especially when the diviner has declared, in a case of illness, that Binego is responsible. During these ceremonies, and also in the mysteries celebrated from time to time, certain persons are not only recognized as mediums of Ryang'ombe, Binego, or other *imandwa*, but actually assume their characters and are addressed by their names for the time being.

Ryang'ombe's Death

The story of his death is as follows.

Ryang'ombe one day went hunting, accompanied by his sons, Kagoro and Ruhanga, two of his sisters, and several other *imandwa*. His mother tried to dissuade him from going, as during the previous night she had had four strange dreams, which seemed to her prophetic of evil. She had seen, first, a small beast without a tail; then an animal all of one colour; thirdly, a stream running two ways at once; and, fourthly, an immature girl carrying a baby without a *ngobe*.[1] She was very uneasy about these dreams, and begged her son to stay at home, but, unlike most Africans, who attach great importance to such things, he paid no attention to her words, and set out. Before he had gone very far he killed a hare, which, when examined, was found to have no tail. His personal attendant at once exclaimed that this was the fulfilment of Nyiraryang'ombe's dream, but Ryang'ombe only said, "Don't repeat a woman's words while we are after game." Soon after this they encountered the second and third portents (the "animal all of one colour" was a black hyena), but Ryang'ombe still refused to be impressed. Then they met a young girl carrying a baby, without the usual skin in which it is supported. She stopped Ryang'ombe

[1] The skin in which an African woman carries a baby on her back. The Zulus call it *imbeleko*.

and asked him to give her a *ngobe*. He offered her the skin of one animal after another; but she refused them all, till he produced a buffalo hide. Then she said she must have it properly dressed, which he did, and also gave her the thongs to tie it with. Thereupon she said, "Take up the child." He objected, but gave in when she repeated her demand, and even, at her request, gave the infant a name. Finally, weary of her importunity, he said, "Leave me alone!" and the girl rushed away, was lost to sight among the bushes, and became a buffalo. Ryang'ombe's dogs, scenting the beast, gave chase, one after the other, and when they did not return he sent his man, Nyarwambali, to see what had become of them. Nyarwambali came back and reported: "There is a beast here which has killed the dogs." Ryang'ombe followed him, found the buffalo, speared it, and thought he had killed it, but just as he was shouting his song of triumph it sprang up, charged, and gored him. He staggered back and leaned against a tree; the buffalo changed into a woman, picked up the child, and went away.

At the very moment when he fell a bloodstained leaf dropped out of the air on his mother's breast. She knew then that her dream had in fact been a warning of disaster; but it was not till a night and a day had passed that she heard what had happened. Ryang'ombe, as soon as he knew he had got his death-wound, called all the *imandwa* together, and told first one and, on his refusal, another to go and call his mother and Binego. One after another all refused, except the maidservant, Nkonzo, who set off at once, travelling night and day, till she came to Nyiraryang'ombe's house and gave her the news. She came at once with Binego, and found her son still living. Binego, when he had heard the whole story, asked his father in which direction the buffalo had gone; having had it pointed out, he rushed off, overtook the woman, brought her back, and killed her, with the child, cutting both in pieces. So he avenged his father.

Ryang'ombe then gave directions for the honours to be paid him after his death; these are, so to speak, the charter of the Kubandwa society which practises the cult of

IMANDWA INITIATION CEREMONY

From "Anthropos," by permission of the Rev. Father Schmidt

MOUNT SABINYO

Photo J. E. Tracy Philipps

the *imandwa*. He specially insisted that Nkonzo, as a reward for her services, should have a place in these rites, and, accordingly, we find her represented by one of the performers in the initiation ceremony, as photographed by P. Schumacher. Then " at the moment when his throat tightened " he named Binego as his successor, and so died.

Here Ryang'ombe appears as a headstrong adventurer, whose principal virtue is courage, and it is a little difficult to gather from his story, as here related, why he should have been credited with so many good qualities. He shows some affection for his mother (though not sufficient to make him consider her wishes) and for his son, and gratitude to the poor dependent who fulfilled his last request—but that is all one can say.

Spirits inhabiting Volcanoes

The definition of a myth, as laid down by the Folk-Lore Society, is : " A story told to account for something " ; of a legend : "A story told as true, but consisting either of fact or fiction, or both indifferently." The story of Ryang'ombe would seem to come under both definitions, for it is certainly (at least in Ruanda—in Kiziba it is more like an ordinary fairy-tale) told as true, and it is held to account not only for the *kubandwa* mysteries (of which P. Arnoux has given a very full account in the seventh and eighth volumes of *Anthropos*), but for certain volcanic phenomena.

The Virunga volcanoes, north of Lake Kivu, are a striking feature of the Ruanda country. They are among the few still active in Africa, and there have been several remarkable eruptions in quite recent times. It appears that after his death Ryang'ombe took up his abode in the Muhavura volcano, the most easterly of the group, where he still lives, though occasionally migrating to Karisimbi, about midway between Lake Kivu and the smaller lake, Bolere. The memory of former eruptions is preserved in accounts of battles between Ryang'ombe and his enemy, Nyiragongo, who then lived in Mount Mikeno. Ryang'ombe, with his fiery sword, cleft this mountain from top to bottom, and drove Nyiragongo westward to the mountain which still bears his name. He then cut off the top of this peak with his sword, threw Nyiragongo into it, and piled hot stones on him to keep him down. One is reminded of Enceladus, buried under Etna by Zeus.

The other *imandwa*, Ryang'ombe's relatives and dependents, are supposed to be living with him in Muhavura. As already mentioned, they are, in the main, spiteful and mischievous, and a great part of his energy is devoted to keeping them within bounds. The inferior ghosts, the *bazimu*, are by some said to haunt their former dwelling-places; others say that the good ones—*i.e.*, those who during their lifetime were initiated into the *kubandwa* mysteries—go to join Ryang'ombe in Muhavura, while the 'profane' (*nzigo*) are sent to Nyiragongo.[1] This notion may be due to the Hamitic invaders, as the idea of a future state of rewards and punishments is, in general, foreign to Bantu thought. The absence of any really moral distinction ('good' being simply synonymous with 'initiated'), coupled with the recent date of the earliest missions to Ruanda, would negative the supposition of Christian influence.

Names Common to Ruanda and Buganda

Before quitting the subject of Ryang'ombe I should like to call attention to an interesting point. Dr Roscoe, writing of Buganda, speaks of "the fetish Lyang'ombe,"[2] but gives no details about him. In the absence of any further information it is impossible to determine whether the name alone was carried from Ruanda into Kiziba, and thence into Buganda, whether it was accompanied by any elements of the original story, or whether a fresh one grew up in its new

[1] *Anthropos* (1912), vol. vii.

[2] *The Northern Bantu*, p. 134. This word—of which anthropologists are now somewhat shy—is used by Dr Roscoe as the equivalent of *ejembe*, literally, 'a horn,' because the objects in question are usually horns, filled with charms of all sorts and believed to be the abode, for the time being, of some particular spirit. The Baganda speak of "the horn of Lyang'ombe," "the horn of Nambaga," and so on. It seems hardly correct to speak of "the fetish Lyang'ombe," as it is the horn, and not the spirit, which is the 'fetish'—if that word must be used.

home. It is evident that some, at any rate, of the Ruanda myths, if they were ever heard, would be speedily forgotten in a country with no active volcanoes.

Then there is Mukasa. In Buganda he is the most important of the 'gods'—*i.e.*, heroes or demi-gods, originally ghosts, and quite distinct from Katonda, the creator, probably also from Gulu, the sky-god. He has much the same character as Ryang'ombe in Ruanda, being " a benign god, who never asked for human life," and, perhaps, a man of old time, deified on account of his benevolence. But the Banyaruanda make Mukasa the son-in-law of Ryang'ombe, and so far from being of a kindly disposition that his wife died of his cruel treatment. He was, curiously enough, the ferryman on the Rusizi, the river which runs out of Lake Kivu into Tanganyika. The story of his marriage seems to be connected with some traditional hostility between two sections of the Ruanda people.

Another point to notice is that the 'mediums'—people possessed by the 'gods' (*balubale*), through whom they give their oracles—are called in Luganda *emandwa*, which, as mentioned above, is the name for the superior class of spirits in Ruanda.

Culture-heroes

Dr Haddon says : " The term hero is usually applied to one who stands out from among ordinary mortals by his . . . conspicuous bravery or sustained power of endurance . . . but [also by] inventiveness, moral or intellectual qualities, or the introduction of new cults." [1] This might apply to Ryang'ombe. 'Culture-heroes' are those who have done anything " to improve the conditions of human existence." I suppose we might reckon among these the Thonga chief who taught his people to peg out hides on the ground in order to dress them. The earlier process was for a number of men to stand round, hold the edges of the hide in their teeth, and lean back till it was sufficiently stretched. It is not clear how far this is to be taken seriously, but we have

[1] *Encyclopædia of Religion and Ethics*, vol. vi, p. 633.

a distinct culture-hero in Kintu, who brought goats, sheep, fowls, millet, and the banana into Buganda. Several tribes have a legend of a mighty hunter who came into the country with trained dogs and, like Theseus, cleared out dangerous wild beasts or fought with monsters. Such was Mbega of the Wakilindi, whom we shall meet in the next chapter.

Such also was Kibwebanduka, the tribal hero of the Wazaramo, who led them from Khutu to their present home (probably about 1700), and drove out the cannibal Akamba, who were then occupying it.[1] It is said that his footprints and those of his dog are still to be seen on a rock somewhere in Khutu, to the north-west of the Zaramo country. The Baziba have a similar hero, Kibi, who came from Bunyoro.

Sometimes animals figure as culture-heroes; one of the hare's many adventures turns on this notion, though sometimes the same story is told of an unnamed man or boy, who combines his benefits with flagrant cheating. One example of this, though not the best or most typical, occurs in the story of Hlakanyana (told in Chapter XI, below). Meanwhile the tale of Sudika-Mbambi will serve to illustrate what has just been said. It comes, like that of " The Son of Kimanaweze," given in Chapter V, from Angola.[2]

Sudika-Mbambi the Invincible

Sudika-Mbambi was the son of Nzua dia Kimanaweze, who married the daughter of the Sun and Moon. The young couple were living with Nzua's parents, when one day Kimanaweze sent his son away to Loanda to trade. The son demurred, but the father insisted, so he went. While he was gone certain cannibal monsters, called *makishi*, descended on the village and sacked it—all the people who were not killed fled. Nzua, when he returned, found no houses and no people; searching over the cultivated ground, he at last came across his wife, but she was so changed that

---

[1] I do not know whether there is any warrant for this accusation against the Akamba. Cannibalism is regarded with horror by the East African tribes in general, though some of them are very sure that their neighbours practise it. For Kibwebanduka see Klamroth, in *Zeitschrift für Kolonialsprachen*, p. 44.

[2] Chatelain, *Folk-tales of Angola*, p. 85.

he did not recognize her at first. "The *makishi* have destroyed us," was her explanation of what had happened.

They seem to have camped and cultivated as best they could; and in due course Sudika-Mbambi ('the Thunderbolt') was born. Like others who will be mentioned later, he was a wonder-child, who spoke before his entrance into the world, and came forth equipped with knife, stick, and "his *kilembe*"—a 'mythic plant,' explained as "life-tree," which he requested his mother to plant at the back of the house. Scarcely had he made his appearance when another voice was heard, and his twin brother Kabundungulu was born. The first thing they did was to cut down poles and build a house for their parents. Ryang'ombe and (as we shall see) Hlakanyana were similarly precocious, but their activities were of a very different character. Soon after this Sudika-Mbambi announced that he was going to fight the *makishi*. He told Kabundungulu to stay at home and to keep an eye on the *kilembe*: if it withered he would know that his brother was dead; he then set out. On his way he was joined by four beings who called themselves *kipalendes* and boasted various accomplishments—building a house on the bare rock (a sheer impossibility under local conditions), carving ten clubs a day, and other more recondite operations, none of which, however, as the event proved, they could accomplish successfully. When they had gone a certain distance through the bush Sudika-Mbambi directed them to halt and build a house, "in order to fight the *makishi*." As soon as he had cut one pole all the others needed cut themselves. He ordered the *kipalende* who had said he could erect a house on a rock to begin building, but as fast as a pole was set up it fell down again. The leader then took the work in hand, and it was speedily finished.

Next day he set out to fight the *makishi*, with three *kipalendes*, leaving the fourth in the house. To him soon after appeared an old woman, who told him that he might marry her granddaughter if he would fight her (the grandmother) and overcome her. They wrestled, but the old woman soon threw the *kipalende*, placed a large stone on top

121

of him as he lay on the ground, and left him there, unable to move.

Sudika-Mbambi, who had the gift of second-sight, at once knew what had happened, returned with the other three, and released the *kipalende*. He told his story, and the others derided him for being beaten by a woman. Next day he accompanied the rest, the second *kipalende* remaining in the house. No details are given of the fighting with the *makishi*, beyond the statement that " they are firing." [1] The second *kipalende* met with the same fate as his brother, and again Sudika-Mbambi was immediately aware of it. The incident was repeated on the third and on the fourth day. On the fifth Sudika-Mbambi sent the *kipalendes* to the war, and stayed behind himself. The old woman challenged him; he fought her and killed her—she seems to have been a peculiarly malignant kind of witch, who had kept her grand-daughter shut up in a stone house, presumably as a lure for unwary strangers. It is not stated what she intended to do with the captives whom she secured under heavy stones, but, judging from what takes place in other stories of this kind, one may conclude that they were kept to be eaten in due course.

Sudika-Mbambi married the old witch's granddaughter, and they settled down in the stone house. The *kipalendes* returned with the news that the *makishi* were completely defeated, and all went well for a time.

Treachery of the Kipalendes

The *kipalendes*, however, became envious of their leader's good fortune, and plotted to kill him. They dug a hole in the place where he usually rested and covered it with mats; when he came in tired they pressed him to sit down, which he did, and immediately fell into the hole. They covered it up, and thought they had made an end of him. His younger brother, at home, went to look at the ' life-tree,' and found that it had withered. Thinking that, perhaps,

---

[1] Through the Portuguese occupation (dating from the sixteenth century) guns would be familiar objects to the Angola natives.

there was still some hope, he poured water on it, and it grew green again.

Sudika-Mbambi was not killed by the fall; when he reached the bottom of the pit he looked round and saw an opening. Entering this, he found himself in a road—the road, in fact, which leads to the country of the dead. When he had gone some distance he came upon an old woman, or, rather, the upper half of one,[1] hoeing her garden by the way-side. He greeted her, and she returned his greeting. He then asked her to show him the way, and she said she would do so if he would hoe a little for her, which he did. She set him on the road, and told him to take the narrow path, not the broad one, and before arriving at Kalunga-ngombe's house he must "carry a jug of red pepper and a jug of wisdom."[2] It is not explained how he was to procure these, though it is evident from the sequel that he did so, nor how they were to be used, except that Kalunga-ngombe makes it a condition that anyone who wants to marry his daughter must bring them with him. We have not previously been told that this was Sudika-Mbambi's intention. On arriving at the house a fierce dog barked at him; he scolded it, and it let him pass. He entered, and was courteously welcomed by people who showed him into the guest-house and spread a mat for him. He then announced that he had come to marry the daughter of Kalunga-ngombe. Kalunga answered that he consented if Sudika-Mbambi had fulfilled the conditions. He then retired for the night, and a meal was sent in to him—a live cock and a bowl of the local porridge (funji). He ate the porridge, with some meat which he had brought with him; instead of killing the cock he kept him under his bed. Evidently it was thought he would assume that the fowl was meant for him to eat (perhaps we have here

[1] Half-beings are very common in African folklore, but they are usually split lengthways, having one eye, one arm, one leg, and so on. This case I thought to be quite unique, but have since come across something of the same sort in a manuscript from Nyasaland.

[2] What is meant by "a jug of wisdom" is not clear, but very likely it is merely a nonsense expression, used for the sake of the pun: ndungu is 'red pepper,' and ndunge 'wisdom.'

a remnant of the belief, not known to or not understood by the narrator of the story, that the living must not eat of the food of the dead), and a trick was intended, to prevent his return to the upper world. In the middle of the night he heard people inquiring who had killed Kalunga's cock; but the cock crowed from under the bed, and Sudika-Mbambi was not trapped.

Next morning, when he reminded Kalunga of his promise, he was told that the daughter had been carried off by the huge serpent called Kinyoka kya Tumba, and that if he wanted to marry her he must rescue her.

Sudika-Mbambi started for Kinyoka's abode, and asked for him. Kinyoka's wife said, "He has gone shooting." [1] Sudika-Mbambi waited awhile, and presently saw driver-ants approaching—the dreaded ants which would consume any living thing left helpless in their path. He stood his ground and beat them off; they were followed by red ants, these by a swarm of bees, and these by wasps, but none of them harmed him. Then Kinyoka's five heads appeared, one after the other. Sudika-Mbambi cut off each as it came, and when the fifth fell the snake was dead. He went into the house, found Kalunga's daughter there, and took her home to her father.

But Kalunga was not yet satisfied. There was a giant fish, Kimbiji, which kept catching his goats and pigs. Sudika-Mbambi baited a large hook with a sucking-pig and caught Kimbiji, but even he was not strong enough to pull the monster to land. He fell into the water, and Kimbiji swallowed him.

Kabundungulu, far away at their home, saw that his brother's life-tree had withered once more, and set out to find him. He reached the house where the *kipalendes* were keeping Sudika-Mbambi's wife captive, and asked where he was. They denied all knowledge of him, but he felt certain there had been foul play. "You have killed him.

---

[1] This need not mean that we must suppose Kinyoka to have been other than a real serpent. Readers of "Uncle Remus" will not need to be reminded that animals in folk-tales perform all sorts of actions which would be quite impossible if their real character were strictly kept in view.

Uncover the grave." They opened up the pit, and Kabundungulu descended into it. He met with the old woman, and was directed to Kalunga-ngombe's dwelling. On inquiring for his brother he was told, " Kimbiji has swallowed him." Kabundungulu asked for a pig, baited his hook, and called the people to his help. Between them they landed the fish, and Kabundungulu cut it open. He found his brother's bones inside it, and took them out. Then he said, " My elder, arise ! " and the bones came to life. Sudika-Mbambi married Kalunga-ngombe's daughter, and set out for home with her and his brother. They reached the pit, which, it would seem, had been filled in, for we are told that " the ground cracked," and they got out. They drove away the four *kipalendes*—one is surprised to learn that they did not kill them out of hand—and, having got rid of them, settled down to a happy life.

But the end of the story is decidedly disappointing. Kabundungulu felt that he was being unfairly treated, since his brother had two wives, while he had none, and asked for one of them to be handed over to him. Sudika-Mbambi pointed out that this was impossible, as he was already married to both of them, and no more was said for the time being. But some time later, when Sudika-Mbambi returned from hunting, his wife complained to him that Kabundungulu was persecuting them both with his attentions. This led to a desperate quarrel between the brothers, and they fought with swords, but could not kill each other. Both were endowed with some magical power, so that the swords would not cut, and neither could be wounded. At last they got tired of fighting and separated, the elder going east and the younger west. The narrator adds a curious sentence to the effect that Sudika-Mbambi is the thunder in the eastern sky and Kabundungulu the echo which answers it from the west.

Nature-myths of this sort, so far as I am aware, occur very rarely, if at all, among the Bantu, and I am inclined to doubt whether this conclusion really belongs to the story.

125

The Wonder-child

Many Bantu tribes have a tale which may well come under this heading. It has points of contact with those of Sudika-Mbambi (though the main theme is quite different) and Ryang'ombe on the one hand and, on the other, with the tricksters Huveane and Hlakanyana. The hero—always a wonder-child, like Ryang'ombe and Hlakanyana—is called by the Yaos Kalikalanje, by the Anyanja Kachirambe, by the Hehe Galinkalanganye,[1] by the Baronga Mutipi (in another story Mutikatika), and by the Lambas Kantanga. They all have the following points in common:

A woman gets into difficulties—usually when alone in the bush—and is helped by an ogre, a demon, or an animal (in one case a hyena; in another a lion), on promising to hand over to this being the next child to which she gives birth.

The birth takes place with unusual circumstances, and the child shows marvellous precocity.

The mother, about to hand him over to the devourer, finds him too sharp for her, and devises one stratagem after another, which he always defeats.

Finally the ogre (or other enemy) is killed.

The opening incident varies considerably in the different stories. In one the woman cannot lift her load of firewood by herself; in another it is her water-jar, with which her companions unkindly refuse to help her (in both these cases the birth is expected very shortly); others introduce the episode (which also occurs in several quite different stories) of the woman sent out by her husband to look for water in which there are no frogs. In the Angola story of Na Nzua the mother has a craving for fish, which can only be satisfied by her promising the child, when born, to the river-spirit Lukala. Except in the above particular, this story differs

---

[1] This, from various indications, would seem to be the form whence the preceding two are derived. It means " the one who was held over the fire " (from *kalanga*, ' roast,' ' scorch '), because as soon as he was born he told his mother to put him on a potsherd and hold him over the fire. This may be connected with a custom of passing new-born babies through the smoke. The Yao name has the same meaning, but is differently explained. *Kachirambe,* in Nyanja, has no meaning applicable to the story.

markedly from the rest. That of Kachirambe,[1] again, has an entirely different opening, and is altogether so curious that it may well be related here.

Kachirambe of the Anyanja

Some little girls had gone out into the bush to gather herbs. While they were thus busied one of them found a hyena's egg [2] and put it into her basket. Apparently none of the others saw it; she told them, somewhat to their surprise, that she had now picked enough, and hastened home. After she was gone the hyena came and asked them, "Who has taken my egg?" They said they did not know, but perhaps their companion who had gone home had carried it off. Meanwhile the girl's mother, on finding the egg in her basket, had put it on the fire. The hyena arrived and demanded the egg; the woman said it was burnt, but offered to give him the next child she had to eat. Apparently this callous suggestion was quite spontaneous on her part; but as there was no child in prospect just then she probably thought that the promise was quite a safe one, and that by the time its fulfilment became possible some way out could be found. The hyena, however, left her no peace, waylaid her every day when she went to the stream for water, and kept asking her when the child was to be produced. At last he said, "If you do not have that child quickly I will eat you yourself." She went home in great trouble, and soon after noticed a boil on her shin-bone, which swelled and swelled, till it burst, and out came a child.[3] He was fully armed, with bow, arrows, and quiver, had his little gourd of charms slung round his neck, and was followed by his

---

[1] Rattray, *Some Folk-lore Stories and Songs in Chinyanja*, p. 133.

[2] There is no attempt at explaining this, and I have seen no other mention of a hyena's egg. But this animal is, in popular belief, so abnormal that anything may be expected of it.

[3] This strange incident has several parallels, though none, so far as I am aware, in connexion with this particular story. The Wakuluwe (Tanganyika Territory) say that the first woman brought forth a child in this way, and the (non-Bantu) Nandi have a tradition that their first ancestor was an old man who produced a boy and a girl from the calf of his leg.

dogs! He announced himself in these words: "I, Kachirambe, have come forth, the child of the shin-bone!" The mother was struck with astonishment, but it does not seem to have occurred to her to go back on her promise. When next she went to draw water and the hyena met her with the usual question she replied, "Yes, I have borne a child, but he is very clever; you will never be able to catch him, but I myself will beguile him for you. I will tie you up in a bundle of grass, and tell Kachirambe to go and fetch it." So she tied up the hyena in a bundle of the long grass used for thatching, and left it lying beside the path. Kachirambe, when sent to fetch it, stood still a little way off, and said, "You, bundle, get up, that I may lift you the better!" And the bundle of grass rose up of itself. Kachirambe said, "What sort of bundle is this that gets up by itself? I have never seen the like, and I am not going to lift it, not I!" So he went home.

The hyena, after releasing himself from the grass, came back and said to the woman, "Yes, truly, that youngster of yours is a sharp one!" She told him to go in the evening and wait in a certain place; then she called Kachirambe and said, "I want you to set a trap in such and such a place for the rats; they have been destroying all my baskets." Kachirambe went and chose out a large, flat stone; then he cut a forked stick, and whittled the cross-piece and the little stick for the catch, and twisted some bark-string, and made a falling trap, of the kind called *diwa*, and set and baited it. In the evening his mother said to him, "The trap has fallen. Go and see what it has caught!" He said, "You, trap, fall again, so that I may know whether you have caught a rat!" The hyena, waiting beside the trap, heard him, lifted up the stone, and let it fall with a bang. Kachirambe said, "What sort of trap is it that falls twice? I have never seen such a one."

Next the mother told the hyena that she would send Kachirambe to pick beans. The boy took the basket and went to the field, but then he turned himself into a fly, and the hyena waited in vain. Kachirambe returned home with

128

a full basket, to his mother's astonishment. She was nearly at her wits' end, but thought of one last expedient; she sent him into the bush to cut wood. The night before he had a dream, which warned him that he was in great danger, so he took with him his bow, and his quiver full of arrows, and his 'medicine-gourd,' as well as a large knife. He climbed up into a tree which had dead branches, and began to cut. Presently he saw the hyena below, who said, "You are dead to-day; you shall not escape. Come down quickly, and I will eat you!" He answered, "I am coming down, but just open your mouth wide!" The hyena, with his usual stupidity, did as he was told, and Kachirambe threw down a sharp stick which he had just cut—it entered the hyena's mouth and killed him. Kachirambe then came down and went home; when drawing near the house he shot an arrow towards it, to frighten his mother, and said, "What have I done to you, that you should send wild beasts after me to eat me?" She, thoroughly scared, begged his pardon, and we are to suppose that he granted it, for the story ends here.

Galinkalanganye was not so forgiving; he contrived to change places with his mother after she was asleep, and it was she who was carried off by the hyena. Similarly, Mutipi's mother was eaten by the lion to whom she had promised her son, and Kalikalanje himself killed his mother, after he and his companions had shot Namzimu (the demon who had come to claim him). The tricks devised for handing over these lads to the enemy, and the stratagems by which they are defeated, vary in the different stories, but the bundle of grass appears in every one, and also in that of Huveane.

CHAPTER IX : THE WAKILINDI SAGA

A SAGA is defined by one authority as " a series of legends which follows in detail the lives and adventures of characters who are probably historical." We are therefore quite right in applying this name to the stories related about the high chiefs of Usambara, who are certainly historical characters, though perhaps not all of the adventures attributed to them ever really took place.

Usambara is one of the most beautiful countries to be found in Africa—a land of rocky hills and clear streams, of woods and fertile valleys. The upland pastures feed herds of cattle and countless flocks of sheep and goats ; the bottom lands and even the hill-slopes are carefully cultivated and bear abundant crops of plantains and sugar-cane, rice and maize and millet. The first European to visit this country was Krapf, the missionary, who walked overland from Rabai in 1848, and was overjoyed at the thought of planting a mission in such a little paradise. The paramount chief, Kimweri, received him hospitably, and consented to give him a piece of ground to build on, though circumstances prevented this plan from being carried out till the arrival of the Universities' Mission, some twenty years later. Krapf was greatly impressed, not only by the scenery and the abundant resources of the country, but by the evidences of order and good government which met him on every side.

This Kimweri, who died at a great age in 1869, seems to have been the fifth of his line. Its founder is described as an Arab who came from Pemba to the Zigula country and built his house on the hill Kilindi, in the district of Nguu, or Nguru. Here he settled down, married more than one wife, and had a numerous family. One of his wives, seemingly the youngest, or, at any rate, the latest married, had two sons, of whom the younger is the Shambala national hero, Mbega.[1]

---

[1] The main source of this narrative is a Swahili account, written by the late Abdallah bin Hemedi, and printed at the Universities' Mission, Magila.

130

THE GRAVE OF A LAMBA CHIEF
Photo Dr Clement M. Doke

SKULLS OF RELATIVES IN A ROCK-SHELTER
Photo H. R. Tate, formerly Provincial Commissioner in Kenya

Mbega, a Child of Ill-omen

Mbega would, in ordinary circumstances, have had short shrift, for he cut his upper teeth first, and such infants are, by most of the Bantu, considered extremely unlucky. Indeed, so strong is the belief that if allowed to grow up they would become dangerous criminals that in former times they were invariably put to death. At Rabai, on the now forsaken site of the old fortified village on the hill-top, a steep declivity is pointed out where such ill-omened babies were thrown down. It must have been the rarity of this occurrence that caused it to be regarded as unnatural, and so produced the belief. Mbega's parents, however, no doubt because his father despised such pagan superstitions (he must have been a Moslem, though his sons did not follow his faith), paid no attention to this custom, but on the contrary took every care of him, and he grew up strong and handsome and beloved by every one, except his half-brothers, the sons of the other wives. Their hostility could not injure him as long as his father lived, but both parents died while he was still a youth. He had a protector, however, in his elder brother, " his brother of the same father and the same mother "—a tie always thus carefully specified in a polygamous society. But this brother died, and the rest took on themselves the disposal of his property, which—along with the guardianship of the widow and children—should naturally have passed to Mbega. They did not even summon him to the funeral.

When all the proper ceremonies had been performed and the time came for "taking away the mourning," which means slaughtering cattle and making a feast for the whole clan, at, or after, which the heir is placed in possession, all the relatives were assembled, but not the slightest notice was taken of the rightful heir. Mbega, naturally, was deeply wounded—the record represents him as saying, " Oh, that my brother were alive ! I have no one to advise me, not one ; my father is dead, and my mother is dead! " So he went his way home, and wept upon his bed (*akalia kitandani pake*), and was ready to despair.

Mbega shut out from his Inheritance

The brothers chose the son of a more distant kinsman to succeed to the property and marry the widow, and handed over to him the dead man's house and a share of his cattle, dividing the rest among themselves. Mbega, hearing of this, as he could not fail to do, consulted with the old men of the village, and sent them to his brothers and the whole clan, with the following message: " Why do they not give me my inheritance? Never once when one of the family died have they called me to the funeral. What wrong have I done?"

When the messengers had finished speaking " those brothers looked each other in the eyes, and every man said to his fellow, ' Do you answer.' " At last one of them spoke up and said, " Listen, ye who have come, and we will tell you. That Mbega of yours is mad. Why should he send you to us instead of coming himself? Tell him that there is no man in our clan named Mbega. We do not want to see him or to have anything to do with him."

The old men asked what Mbega had done, that they should hate him so, and the spokesman replied that he was a sorcerer (*mchawi*) who had caused all the deaths that had taken place in the clan. Anyone might know that he was not a normal human creature, since he was a *kigego* who had cut his upper teeth first ; but his parents had been weak enough to conceal the fact and bring him up like any other child. He went on to say that when Mbega's mother died he and the others had consulted a diviner, who told them that Mbega was responsible (a cruel slander on a most affectionate son), and they had represented to their father that he ought to be killed, " but he would not agree through his great love for him." Now that Mbega's parents and his own brother were no more they would take things into their own hands, since, if let alone, he would exterminate the whole clan. They did not wish to have his blood on their hands, but let him depart out of the country on peril of his life, and, as for the messengers: " Do not you come here again with any word from Mbega." They replied, with the quiet dignity of aged councillors, " We shall not come again to you." So they returned to Mbega, who received them with the usual courtesies and would not inquire about their errand till they had rested and been fed and had a smoke. Then they told him all, and he said, " I have heard your words and theirs, and in truth I have no need to send men to them again. I, too, want no dealings with them."

Mbega, a Mighty Hunter

Now Mbega, though hated by his near kinsmen, was beloved by the rest of the tribe, more especially the young men, whom he took with him on hunting expeditions and taught the use of trained dogs, then a novelty in the country. His father, no doubt, had brought some with him from Pemba. The name of Mbega's own favourite dog, Chamfumu, has been preserved. The chronicler adds : " This one was his heart." It does not seem clear whether this phrase merely expresses the degree of his affection for this particular dog, or whether there is some hint that Mbega's life was bound up with him. This idea of the totem animal as 'external soul' was probably not strange to the old-time Washambala, but Abdallah bin Hemedi might well fail to understand it, and nothing of the sort appears anywhere else in the story.

The land was sorely plagued with wild beasts, which ravaged the flocks and destroyed the crops. We hear most of the wild swine, which still, in many parts of East Africa, make the cultivator's life a burden to him. Mbega and his band of devoted followers scoured the woods with the dogs, put a stop to the depredations of the animals, and supplied the villagers with meat.

When Mbega's messengers had reported the answer returned by his brothers he called his friends together, told them the whole story, and informed them that he would have to leave the country. They asked where he was going, and he replied that he did not know yet, but would find out by divination, and would then call them together and take leave of them.

We are given to understand that Mbega was highly skilled in magic—white magic, of course—and this may have lent some colour to his brothers' accusations. If the expression he used on this occasion (" I am going to use the sand-board ") is to be taken literally it seems to refer to the Arab method of divining by means of sand spread on a board, the knowledge of which Mbega's father may have brought with him from Pemba.

The young men protested against the notion of his leaving them, and declared that they would follow him wherever he went. He was determined not to allow this, knowing it would cause trouble with their parents, but said no more till he had decided on his course. He then consulted the oracle, and determined to direct his steps towards Kilindi, where he was well known. Next day, his friends being assembled, he told them he must leave them. He would not tell them where he was going, in case they should be asked by his brothers. They were very unwilling to agree to this, insisting that they would go with him, but were persuaded at last to give way. He sent for all his dogs and distributed them among the young men, keeping for himself seven couples, among them the great Chamfumu, " who was his heart." He also gave them his recipes for hunting-magic, in which, to this day, most natives put more faith than in the skill of the hunter or the excellence of his weapons.

Mbega goes to Kilindi

So Mbega went forth, carrying his spears, large and small, and his dog-bells, and his wallet of charms, and, followed by his pack, came on the evening of the second day to the gate of Kilindi town. It was already shut for the night, and, though those within answered his call, they hesitated to admit him till he had convinced them that he was indeed Mbega of Nguu, the hunter of the wild boar. Then the gate was thrown open, and the whole town rushed to welcome him, crying, " It is he! It is he! " They escorted him to the presence of the chief, who greeted him warmly, assigned him a dwelling, and gave orders that everything

A Zulu Doctor and Patient
Photo Natal Museum, Pietermaritzburg

possible should be done to honour him. " So they gave him a house, with bedsteads and Zigula mats "—about all that was usual in the way of furniture—and when all the people summoned for the occasion had gone their several ways rejoicing Mbega rested for two or three days.

He remained at Kilindi for many months, and not only cleared the countryside of noxious beasts, but secured the town by his magic against human and other enemies. He possessed the secret of raising such a thick mist as to render it invisible to any attacking force, and could supply charms to protect men and cattle from lions and leopards. He seems also to have had some skill as a herbalist, for we are told that he healed the sick. In these ways, and still more " because he was he," he made himself universally beloved. The chief's son, in particular, who insisted on making blood-brotherhood with him, worshipped him with all a youth's enthusiasm.

Death of the Chief's Son

As time went on all the wild pigs in the immediate neighbourhood of Kilindi were killed or driven away, and the cultivators had peace ; but one day it was reported that there was a number of peculiarly large and fierce ones in a wood two or three days' journey distant. Mbega at once prepared to set out, and the chief's son wished to go with him. Mbega was unwilling to take the risk, and his companions all tried to dissuade the young man, but he insisted, and they finally gave way, on condition of his getting his father's leave. The father consented, and he joined the party.

The pigs, when found, were indeed fierce : it is said they " roared like lions." The dogs, excited beyond their wont by a stimulant Mbega administered to them, were equally fierce, and when the hunters rushed in with their spears some of them were overthrown in the struggle and others compelled to take refuge in trees. A number of pigs were killed, but five men were hurt, and when the ground was cleared it was found that the chief's son was dead.

135

There could be no question of returning to Kilindi: Mbega knew he would be held responsible for the lad's death, and for once was quite at a loss. When the others said, "What shall we do?" he answered, "I have nothing to say; it is for you to decide." They said they must fly the country, and as he, being a stranger, did not know where to go they offered to guide him. So they set out together, fifteen men in all (the names of ten among them have been preserved by tradition), with eleven dogs—it would seem that three had perished in the late or some other encounter with the wild boars. Their wanderings, recorded in detail, ended in Zirai, on the borders of Usambara, where they settled for some time, and Mbega's fame spread throughout the country. The elders of Bumburi (in Usambara) sent and invited him to become their chief, " and he ruled over the whole country and was renowned for his skill in magic, and his kindness, and the comeliness of his face, and his knowledge of the law; and if any man was pressed for a debt Mbega would pay it for him." He married a young maiden of Bumburi, and no doubt looked forward to spending the rest of his life there. But he had reckoned without the men of Vuga.

Mbega called to be Chief of Vuga

Vuga, the most important community of Usambara, had for some time been at war with the hillmen of Pare. The headman, Turi, having heard reports of Mbega's great powers, especially as regards war-magic, first sent messengers to inquire into the truth of these reports, and then came himself in state to invite him to be their chief. He encamped with his party at Karange, a short distance from Bumburi, with beating of drums and blowing of war-horns. Mbega, hearing that they had arrived, prepared to go to meet them, and also to give some proof of his power. Having put on his robe of tanned bullock's hide and armed himself with sword, spear, and club, he sent off a runner, bidding him say, " Let our guest excuse me for a little, while I talk with the clouds, that the sun may be covered,

since it is so hot that we cannot greet each other comfortably."
For it was the season of the *kaskazi*, the north-east monsoon,
when the sun is at its fiercest.

The Vuga men were astonished at receiving this message,
but very soon they saw a mist rising, which spread till it
became a great cloud and quite obscured the sun. Mbega
had filled his magic gourd with water and shaken it up;
then taken a fire-brand, beaten it on the ground till the
glowing embers were scattered, and then quenched them
with the water from the gourd. The rising steam formed
the cloud, and the Vuga elders were duly impressed.

When, at last, they saw him face to face they felt that all
they had been told of him was true, so comely was his face
and so noble his bearing. Turi explained why he had
come, and after the usual steps had been taken for enter-
taining the guests Mbega agreed to accept the invitation on
certain conditions. These chiefly concerned the building
of his house and the fetching of the charms which he had
left in charge of his Kilindi friends at their camp in the
bush. These were to be taken to Vuga by a trusty messenger and hidden at a spot on the road outside the town,
which he would have to pass.

Everything being agreed upon, Mbega went to inform his
father-in-law, and ask his leave to take away his wife—an
interesting point, as indicating that the tribal organization
was matrilineal. It should also be noted that the father-in-
law, while consenting for his own part, said that his wife
must also be consulted. She, however, made no difficulty,
" but I must certainly go and take leave of my daughter."

Mbega than bade farewell to the elders of Bumburi,
insisting that he did not wish to lose touch with them and
enjoining on them to send word to him at Vuga of any
important matter. He wanted his wife's brother to accompany him, so that she might not feel cut off from all her
relatives; also four of the old men.

The party set out, travelling by night and resting by
day, when Mbega sacrificed a sheep and performed various
'secret rites,' which he explained to his brother-in-law.

137

On the following morning they reached the place where the charms had been deposited, and the man who had hidden them produced them and handed them over to Mbega, who gave them to his wife to keep. They camped in this place for the day, and when night came on a lion made his appearance. The men scattered and fled; Mbega followed the lion up and killed him with one thrust of his spear. When his men came back he gave most careful directions about taking off and curing the skin, for reasons which will appear later. They then set out once more, and reached Vuga by easy stages early in the morning. The war-drum was beaten, and was answered by drums from the nearest hills, and those again by others from more distant ones, proclaiming to the whole countryside that the chief had come. And from every village, far and near, the people thronged to greet him. His house was built, thatched, and plastered according to his instructions, and when it was finished he had cattle killed and made a feast for the workers, both men and women. He then sent for the lion-skin, which meanwhile had been carefully prepared, and had it made into a bed for his wife, who was shortly expecting her first child.

Soon after she had taken her place on this couch Turi's wife was sent for, and, she having called the other skilled women to attend on the queen, before long the cry of rejoicing, usual on such occasions, was raised. All the people came, bringing gifts and greetings, and Mbega had a bullock killed, and sent in some meat for the nurses. His first question to them was whether the birth had taken place on the lion-skin; when informed that it had he asked whether the child was a boy or a girl. They told him that it was a boy, and he asked, " Have you given him his ' praise-name ' yet ? " [1] They answered that they had not done so, where-

[1] The term used is *jina la mzaha*, translated by Madan, in his Swahili dictionary, as " nickname," but the meaning is really the same as the Zulu *isibongo*, an honorific title. Its use caused some heart-burnings in a later generation, when two branches of the family quarrelled. Stanley, in 1871, had some trouble with a kind of brigand called Simba Mwene, who had a fortified stronghold on the road to Unyanyembe, but this man, I believe, was in no way connected with the Wakilindi, and had assumed the title with no right to it.

upon he said that the boy's name was to be Simba, the Lion, and by this name he was to be greeted. Mbega's original name—the one first given him in his childhood—was Mwene, hence his son was to be greeted as Simba (son) of Mwene, which became a title handed down in the male line of the dynasty. But the name officially bestowed on the boy, at the usual time, was Buge.

As soon as the child was old enough his mother's kinsmen claimed him, and he was brought up by his uncles at Bumburi—another indication of mother-right in Usambara. Mbega afterwards married at least one other wife, and had several sons, but Buge's mother was the 'Great Wife,' and her son the heir. When he had arrived at manhood his kinsmen at Bumburi asked Mbega's permission to install him as their chief, which was readily granted. The lad ruled wisely, and bade fair to tread in his father's footsteps. His younger brothers, as they grew up, were also put in charge of districts, ruling as Mbega's deputies; this continued to be the custom with the Wakilindi chiefs, who also assigned districts to their daughters.

Mbega's Death and Burial

Now it came to pass that Mbega fell sick, but no one knew it except five old men who were in close attendance on him. His failing to appear in public created no surprise, for he had been in the habit, occasionally, of shutting himself up for ten days at a time and seeing no one, when it was given out that he was engaged in magic, as was, indeed, the case. His illness, which was not known even to his sons, lasted only three days, and the old men kept his death secret for some time. They sent messengers to Bumburi by night to tell Buge that his father was very ill and had sent for him. He set off at once, and, on arriving, was met by the news that Mbega was dead. The funeral was carried out secretly—no doubt in order to secure the succession by having Buge on the spot before his father's death was known. First a black bull was killed and skinned and the grave lined with its hide; then a black cat was found and killed and a boy and a girl chosen who had to lie down in the grave, side by side, and stay there till the corpse was lowered into it. This, no doubt, was a symbolical act, representing what in former times would have been a human sacrifice. When the corpse was laid in the grave the two came out of it, and were thenceforth *tabu* to each other : they were forbidden to meet again as long as they lived. Then the cat was placed beside the dead man and the grave filled in.

All this was done without the knowledge of the people in the town. The elders agreed to install Buge as successor to his father, and his wife was sent for from Bumburi. She arrived in the early morning, and at break of day the drums were sounded, announcing the death of the chief, and Buge sacrificed two bullocks at his father's grave. Then he was solemnly proclaimed as chief, and his younger brother Kimweri took his place at Bumburi.

Mboza and Magembe

Buge's reign was a short one ; when he died Shebuge, the son of his principal wife, was still under age. He had, by another wife, a son, Magembe, and a daughter, Mboza, somewhat older than her brother. She was a woman of considerable ability and great force of character, as is apparent from the fact that the elders consulted her about the succession. She advised them to appoint Kimweri, keeping her own counsel as to further developments, for she was determined that her own full brother, Magembe, should succeed him.

Kimweri died after a reign of eight years, and was buried with the same rites as his father and brother, Mboza hurrying on the funeral without waiting for her brothers. Shebuge and Magembe, unable to arrive in time, sent cattle for the sacrificial feast. Mboza summoned a council of the elders, and gave her vote in favour of electing Magembe to the chieftainship, to which they agreed. She then said that in her opinion the mourning had lasted long enough, and they should now end it with the usual feast, after which she would go home to Mwasha and—when the proper number of days had passed—send the herald (*mlao*) with orders for the warriors to go and fetch the chief (*zumbe*).

Now word was brought to Shebuge at Balangai that Magembe was about to be proclaimed chief of Vuga by his sister Mboza. He made no protest, but contented himself with saying that he certainly intended to claim his share of his father's treasure, and to call himself, henceforward, not Shebuge, but Kinyasi. This he explained to mean: " I walk alone; I have no fellow."

When six months had passed Mboza sent word that the *kitara* (as the Zulus would say, " the King's kraal ") was to be made ready, and messengers sent to fetch Magembe from Mulungui, where he lived. When she heard the signal-drums announcing his arrival she would set out for Vuga with her people. So far all her plans had worked smoothly, as no one dared oppose her, "for she was a woman of a fierce spirit and feared throughout the country, because of her skill in magic." But now she met with a check: her messengers, on their way to Mulungui, were intercepted by Shebuge Kinyasi's maternal uncles, who induced them to delay while they themselves started for Balangai and conducted their nephew in triumph to Vuga. The messengers reached Mulungui, and set out on the return journey with Magembe, but always, without knowing it, a stage behind his rival. When, with the dawn, they reached Kihitu the royal drums crashed out in the town, and, marching on, they were further perplexed by hearing the shouts of *Mbogo! Mbogo!* ('Buffalo!'), with which the multitude were greeting the new chief. They were speedily enlightened by people coming from the town. Magembe, as soon as he knew that matters were finally settled, left Usambara in disgust, never to return; but this comes a little later in the story; for the moment the chronicler is more concerned with Mboza.

That princess left Mwasha as soon as the boom of the great drum was heard, and by midday had halted at the villages just outside Vuga, when she heard from some people returning from the town, who stopped to greet her, the name of the new chief. She at once sent for the elders and some of the principal men. " Let them come hither to the gate, that I may question them ! " The men delivered their message to the Mlugu,[1] who asked : " Why so ? Can she not enter the town and greet the chief ? " Whereto the reply was brief and sufficient : " She does not want to do so."

So they all went out and found her standing in the road, staff in hand, her sword girt about her and her kerrie slung over her shoulder, and they greeted her, but she answered not a word. At last she spoke and said, " Who is the chief who has entered the town ? "

And the Mlugu answered, " It is Shebuge Kinyasi of Balangai." Said Mboza : " Whose counsel was this ? When I called you, together with all the men of your country, and said to you, men of Vuga, ' Let us now all of us choose the chief,' we chose Magembe. Who, then, has dared to change the decision behind my back ? "

Mboza emigrates and founds another Kingdom

They explained what had happened, and, once it had been made clear to her that Shebuge had already entered the *kigiri*,[2] she knew the matter was past remedy, and shook the dust of Vuga from her feet, sending back to Shebuge's uncles a message which the bearers could not understand, but took to be a curse, and were filled with fear accordingly. Shebuge, however, paid no heed to it.

Mboza, with her husband, her three sons and two daughters, her servants, and her cattle, left at once for Mshihwi, the husband's home country. There she founded a new settlement, which she called Vuga, as a rival to her brother's town. The local inhabitants were very ready to welcome her, and to all who came to greet her she distributed cattle and goats and announced her intentions : " I set this my son Shebuge as chief in this my town, and he shall be

---

[1] A high official ; the title is sometimes rendered 'Prince.'

[2] *Kigiri* is, properly, the mausoleum of the chiefs, which is placed in a special hut within the royal kraal. When the new chief has been introduced into this, in the course of his installation, his appointment is confirmed beyond recall. When she heard that this had taken place Mboza knew that her case was hopeless.

CHARMS USED IN THE LAMBA COUNTRY FOR PREVENTING THEFT
FROM GARDENS

Photos Dr Clement M. Doke

142

greeted as ' Lion Lord,' like as his uncle at Vuga." She thus
founded a rival line, and when, in the course of years, she
felt her end approaching she straitly charged all her children
never to set foot in the original Vuga, or to be induced, on
any pretext, to enter into friendly relations with their kinsmen there. To her eldest son she left all her charms, and
imparted to him her secret knowledge, to be made use of
in case of war—such as the magic for raising a mist and the
charms for turning back the enemy from the town. Her
last words to him were an injunction to keep up the feud
for ever, "you and your brothers, your sons and your
grandsons."

Shebuge's Wars and Death

Shebuge Kinyasi, for his part, was little disposed towards
conciliation, and the two Vugas were soon at war, which
continued till his attention was claimed in other directions.
Unlike his grandfather, Mbega, who is not extolled as a
warrior, but as a great hunter and a general benefactor to
his people, Shebuge was ambitious to distinguish himself
as a conqueror. He was successful for a time, making
tributary, not only all the districts now included in Usambara, but the Wadigo and other tribes as far as the coast
at Pangani, Tanga, and Vanga. The Wazigula, however,
refused to submit to him, and in a fight with them he was
cut off with a few followers and overpowered by numbers.
" They let off arrows like drops of rain or waves in a storm.
And Shebuge was hit by an arrow, and he died."

Next morning, when the Wazigula came to pick up the
weapons of the slain, they found a man sitting beside
Shebuge's body. He drew his bow on the first man who
approached him and shot him dead, and so with the next
and the next, but at last the rest surrounded him and
seized him, and asked, " Who art thou? " And he said,
" I am Kivava, a man overcome with sorrow and compassion." They said, "Wherefore are thy compassion and thy
sorrow? " He answered, " In your battle yesterday my
chief was slain." They asked him, " What chief? "

143

He told them: " In yesterday's fight Shebuge died. My fellows fled, but, as for me, I had sworn a free man's oath: this Shebuge who is dead was my friend at home; I bade farewell to my comrades; but, as for me, I cannot leave Shebuge. If I were to go back to Vuga, how should I face Shebuge's children, and his wives? My life is finished to-day. I was called ' the Chief's Friend '— I can no longer bear that name. It is better that I too should die as Shebuge has died."

They declared that they did not want to kill him, and turned to leave, but he, to provoke them, shot an arrow after them and hit the Zigula chief's son. Then at last they seized him, and he said, " Slay me not elsewhere, only on this spot where Shebuge is lying." So they slew him and left him there. And when they reached their village they told to all men the tale of Shebuge's friend, who kept troth and loved him to the death.

The fugitives of Shebuge's host, who meanwhile had reached the Ruvu river, heard the news on the following day; they gathered together and returned to the battlefield, which was quite deserted by the enemy. They made a bier and took up Shebuge's body and laid him on it, and so brought him back to Vuga for burial. And his son Kimweri succeeded him.

From thenceforth it was fixed that the chiefs of Vuga should bear the names of Kimweri and Shebuge in alternate generations. This Kimweri is he who was mentioned at the beginning of the chapter and is usually known as " the Great." With him we have definitely passed into the light of history, as known to Europeans—and there we may leave the Wakilindi.

CHAPTER X : THE STORY OF LIONGO FUMO

BISHOP STEERE wrote, in 1869, that " the story of Liongo is the nearest approach to a bit of real history I was able to meet with. It is said that a sister of Liongo came to Zanzibar, and that her descendants are still living there."[1]

Since reading these words I have been informed that there is now at Mombasa a family of the Shaka clan and tribe claiming descent from Liongo Fumo. Even apart from this, there seems every reason to believe that he had a real existence, though some mythical elements have been incorporated into his legend.

Shaka, which gives its name to one of the thirteen tribes (*miji*, or, as they are more usually called, *mataifa*) of Mombasa, was a small principality at the mouth of the Ozi river, founded in very early times by colonists from Persia. The ruins of Shaka may still be seen not very far from the present town of Kipini, and another group of ruins, somewhat nearer it, goes by the name of *Wangwana wa Mashah*, " the noblemen of the Shahs." The rulers of Shaka, to whose family Liongo Fumo belonged, bore the Persian title of Shah.

Liongo Fumo, Poet and Bowman

Shaka was conquered by Sultan Omar of Pate, whose dates are variously given, but he seems to have been more or less contemporary with our Edward III, one authority even putting him as early as 1306. It is therefore safe to say that Liongo flourished during the twelfth century, if not earlier. It is true that one informant said to me, " Liongo warred with the Portuguese," which would put him not earlier than the sixteenth century, but this is not supported by the general weight of authority.

Liongo's grave was pointed out to me at Kipini in 1912, also the site of the well outside the city gate which plays a

[1] *Swahili Tales*, p. vi.

part in his story, and even the exact spot where he met his death. Most people, there and at Lamu, knew, at any rate, the song which is handed down as having been sung by him in prison, and almost anyone you met, Swahili or Pokomo, could tell you his story.

Many poems attributed to him circulate in manuscript among educated Swahili, and some are recited from memory even by the illiterate. It was two poor labourers, working on a cotton plantation, who showed me Liongo's grave and were evidently quite familiar with the story. One of the poems was printed by Steere at the end of his *Swahili Tales*, with an English translation and a rendering into modern Swahili supplied by a native scholar at Zanzibar. As a rule, the language in which they are written is to a Swahili much as Chaucer's English is to us.

Liongo, as we have seen, was of the house of the Shaka " Mashah," but, though the eldest son, could not succeed his father, his mother having been one of the inferior wives. He seems, however, to have been in every way more able than his brother, the lawful Shah Mringwari. His extraordinary stature and strength, his courage, his skill with the bow, and his poetical talents have been celebrated over and over again in song and story. The Pokomo fisherfolk tell how he conquered them and imposed on them the " tribute of heads "—that is to say, from every large village two boys and two girls, from every small village one of each. Also how he was " a tall man " (*muntu muyeya*) and very strong, and once, leaving Shaka in the morning, walked to Gana (at or near the present Chara)—about two days' journey each way—and returned the same day.

Liongo and his brother were not on good terms. By whose fault the quarrel began we are not told, but it is quite conceivable that the elder, kept by no fault of his own out of a position which he considered his due, and which he was more competent to fill than Mringwari, chafed under a sense of injustice, which embittered his already overbearing temper. It does not appear that, like Absalom, he stole the hearts of the people, for Mringwari had always been the more popular of the two, and Liongo's high-handed ways soon made him hated; yet he always had some to love him. Like Napoleon, he seems to have had a gift that way, which he exercised when he chose. Among the poems attributed to him is the tender *Pani kiti*:

> Give me a chair that I may sit down
> And soothe my Mananazi,
> That I may soothe my wife,
> Who takes away my grief and heaviness.[1] . . .

Anyhow, the enmity between the two went so far that Liongo attempted Mringwari's life.

The "Hadithi yar Liongo"

A poem of uncertain date (not supposed to be written by him, but telling his story) relates how certain Galla, coming to Pate to trade, heard of Liongo from the sultan, who dwelt so much on his prowess that their curiosity was aroused, and they expressed a wish to see him. So he sent a letter to Liongo at Shaka, desiring him to come. Liongo replied "with respect and courtesy" that he would come, and he set out on the following day, fully armed and carrying three trumpets.[2] The journey from Shaka to Pate was reckoned at four days, but Liongo arrived the day after he had started. At the city gate he blew such a blast that the trumpet was split, and the Galla asked, "What is it? Who has raised such a cry?" He answered, "It is Liongo who has come!"

Liongo sounded his second trumpet, and burst it; he then took the third, and the townsfolk all ran together, the Galla among them, to see what this portended. He then sent a messenger to say, "Our lord Liongo asks leave to enter." The gate was thrown open, and he was invited in, all the Galla being struck with astonishment and terror at the sight of him. "This is a lord of war," they said; "he can put a hundred armies to flight."

He sat down, at the same time laying on the ground the

---

[1] Steere's translation, in *Swahili Tales*, p. 473.
[2] *Panda*, probably of ivory, like the great *siwa* of Lamu, still in existence.

wallet which he had been carrying. After resting awhile he took out from it a mortar and pestle, a millstone, cooking-pots of no common size, and the three stones used for supporting them over the fire.[1] The Galla stood by, gaping with amazement, and when at last they found speech they said to the sultan, " We want him for a prince, to marry one of our daughters, that a son of his may bring glory to our tribe." The sultan undertook to open the matter to Liongo, who agreed, on certain conditions (what these were we are not told), and the wedding was celebrated with great rejoicing at the Galla kraals. In due course a son was born, who, as he grew up, bade fair to resemble his father in strength and beauty.

It would seem as if Liongo had been living for some time at Pate (for he did not take up his abode permanently with the Galla)—no doubt as a result of the quarrel with his brother. But now some one—whether an emissary of Mringwari's or some of the Galla whom he had offended—stirred up trouble; " enmity arose against him," and, finding that the sultan had determined on his death, he left Pate for the mainland. There he took refuge with the forest-folk, the Wasanye and Wadahalo. These soon received a message from Pate, offering them a hundred *reals* (silver dollars) [2] if they would bring in Liongo's head. They were not proof against the temptation, and, unable to face him in fight, planned a treacherous scheme for his destruction. They approached him one day with a suggestion for a *kikoa*,[3] since a regular feast—in their roving forest life—" is not to be done." They were to dine off *makoma* (the fruit of the *Hyphaene* palm), each man taking his turn at climbing a tree and gathering for the party, the intention being to shoot Liongo when they had him at a disadvantage. However, when it came to his

---

[1] This poet describes Liongo as a giant, on the scale of Goliath of Gath. The Galla—who as a rule are tall men—" only reached to his knees." But most accounts speak of him merely as an ordinary human being of unusual stature and strength.

[2] Of course a touch inserted by some comparatively recent writer or copyist.

[3] Defined by Madan as " a meal eaten in common provided by each of those who join in it by turns." The one in the story was repeated as many times as there were people taking part.

turn, having chosen the tallest palm, he defeated them by shooting down the nuts, one by one, where he stood. This, by the by, is the only instance recorded of his marksmanship, though his skill with the bow is one of his titles to fame.

Liongo escapes from Captivity

The Wasanye now gave up in despair, and sent word to the sultan that Liongo was not to be overcome either by force or guile. He, unwilling to trust them any further, left them and went to Shaka,[1] where he met his mother and his son. His Galla wife seems to have remained with her people, and we hear nothing from this authority of any other wives he may have had. Here, at last, he was captured by his brother's men, seized while asleep—one account says : " first having been given wine to drink " : it was probably drugged. He was then secured in the prison in the usual way, his feet chained together with a post between them, and fetters on his hands. He was guarded day and night by warriors. There was much debating as to what should be done with him. There was a general desire to get rid of him, but some of Mringwari's councillors were of opinion that he was too dangerous to be dealt with directly : it would be better to give him the command of the army and let him perish, like Uriah, in the forefront of the battle. Mringwari thought this would be too great a risk, and there could be none in killing him, fettered as he was.

Meanwhile Liongo's mother sent her slave-girl Saada every day to the prison with food for her son, which the guards invariably seized, only tossing him the scraps.

Mringwari, when at last he had come to a decision, sent a slave-lad to the captive, to tell him that he must die in three days' time, but if he had a last wish it should be granted, " that you may take your leave of the world." Liongo sent word that he wished to have a *gungu* dance performed where he could see and hear it, and this was granted.

[1] Pate, in the poem I have been quoting from, but this is inconsistent with the further development of the narrative.

He then fell to composing a song, which is known and sung to this day:

> O thou handmaid Saada, list my words to-day!
> Haste thee to my mother, tell her what I say.
> Bid her bake for me a cake of chaff and bran, I pray,
> And hide therein an iron file to cut my bonds away,
> File to free my fettered feet, swiftly as I may;
> Forth I'll glide like serpent's child, silently to slay.

When Saada came again he sang this over to her several times, till she knew it by heart—the guards either did not understand the words or were too much occupied with the dinner of which they had robbed him to pay any attention to his music. Saada went home and repeated the song to her mistress, who lost no time, but went out at once and bought some files. Next morning she prepared a better meal than usual, and also baked such a loaf as her son asked for, into which she inserted the files, wrapped in a rag.

When Saada arrived at the prison the guards took the food as usual, and, after a glance at the bran loaf, threw it contemptuously to Liongo, who appeared to take it with a look of sullen resignation to his fate.

When the dance was arranged he called the chief performers together and taught them a new song—perhaps one of the " Gungu Dance Songs " which have been handed down under his name. There was an unusually full orchestra: horns, trumpets, cymbals (*matoazi*), gongs (*tasa*), and the complete set of drums, while Liongo himself led the singing. When the band was playing its loudest he began filing at his fetters, the sound being quite inaudible amid the din; when the performers paused he stopped filing and lifted up his voice again. So he gradually cut through his foot-shackles and his handcuffs, and, rising up in his might, like Samson, burst the door, seized two of the guards, knocked their heads together, and threw them down dead. The musicians dropped their instruments and fled, the crowd scattered like a flock of sheep, and Liongo took to the woods, after going outside the town to take leave of his mother, none daring to stay him.

THE STORY OF LIONGO FUMO

Liongo undone by Treachery at last

Here he led an outlaw's life, raiding towns and plundering travellers, and Mringwari was at his wits' end to compass his destruction. At last Liongo's son—or, as some say, his sister's son [1]—was gained over and induced to ferret out the secret of Liongo's charmed life, since it had been discovered by this time that neither spear nor arrow could wound him. The lad sought out his father, and greeted him with a great show of affection; but Liongo was not deceived. He made no difficulty, however, about revealing the secret—perhaps he felt that his time had come and that it was useless to fight against destiny. When his son said to him, after some hesitation, " My father, it is the desire of my heart—since I fear danger for you—that I might know for certain what it is that can kill you," Liongo replied, " I think, since you ask me this, that you are seeking to kill me." The son, of course, protested : " I swear by the Bountiful One I am not one to do this thing ! Father, if you die, to whom shall I go ? I shall be utterly destitute."

Liongo answered, " My son, I know how you have been instructed and how you will be deceived in your turn. Those who are making use of you now will laugh you to scorn, and you will bitterly regret your doings ! Yet, though it be so, I will tell you ! That which can slay me is a copper nail driven into the navel. From any other weapon than this I can take no hurt." The son waited two days, and on the third made an excuse to hasten back to Pate,[2] saying that he was anxious about his mother's health. Mringwari, on receiving the information, at once sent for a craftsman and ordered him to make a copper spike of the kind required. The youth was feasted and made much of

[1] His nearest relation and rightful heir, in Bantu usage ; but this would not be the case in Moslem law, whether Arab or Persian, and most accounts call the traitor his son. This was the promising son of the Galla wife. We hear of no other children ; yet there must have been more if it is true that there are direct descendants of his now living.

[2] Liongo seems to have been living unmolested for some time at Shaka, where he may have rallied some followers to his cause, while Mringwari, apparently, had retreated to Pate.

for the space of ten days, and then dispatched on his errand, with the promise that a marriage should be arranged for him when he returned successful. On arriving at Shaka he was kindly welcomed by his father (who perhaps thought that, after all, he had been wrong in his suspicions), and remained with him for a month without carrying out his design—either from lack of opportunity or, as one would fain hope, visited by some compunction. As time went on Mringwari grew impatient and wrote, reproaching him in covert terms for the delay. " We, here, have everything ready "—*i.e.*, for the promised wedding festivities, which were to be of the utmost magnificence. It chanced that on the day when this letter arrived Liongo, wearied out with hunting, slept more soundly than usual during the midday heat. The son, seizing his opportunity, screwed his courage to the sticking-place, crept up, and stabbed him in the one vulnerable spot.

Liongo started up in the death-pang and, seizing his bow and arrows, walked out of the house and out of the town. When he had reached a spot half-way between the city gate and the well at which the folk were wont to draw water his strength failed him : he sank on one knee, fitted an arrow to the string, drew it to the head, and so died, with his face towards the well.

The townsfolk could see him kneeling there, and did not know that he was dead. Then for three days neither man nor woman durst venture near the well. They used the water stored for ablutions in the tank outside the mosque ; when that was exhausted there was great distress in the town. The elders of the people went to Liongo's mother and asked her to intercede with her son. " If she goes to him he will be sorry for her." She consented, and went out, accompanied by the principal men, chanting verses (perhaps some of his own poems) " with the purpose of soothing him." Gazing at him from a distance, she addressed him with piteous entreaties, but when they came nearer and saw that he was dead she would not believe it. " He cannot be killed ; he is angry, and therefore he does not speak ; he is brooding over his wrongs in his own mind and refuses to hear me!" So she wailed; but when he fell over they knew that he was dead indeed.

They came near and looked at the body, and drew out the copper needle which had killed him, and carried him into the town, and waked and buried him. And there he lies to this day, near Kipini by the sea.

The Traitor's Doom

The news reached Pate, and Mringwari, privately rejoicing at the removal of his enemy, sent for Mani Liongo, the son (who meanwhile had been sumptuously entertained in the palace), and told him what had happened, professing to be much surprised when he showed no signs of sorrow. When the son replied that, on the contrary, he was very glad Mringwari turned on him. "You are an utterly faithless one! Depart out of my house and from the town; take off the clothes I have given you and wear your own, you enemy of God!" Driven from Pate, he betook himself to his Galla kinsmen, but there he was received coldly, and even his mother cast him off. So, overcome with remorse and grief, he fell into a wasting sickness and died unlamented.

The Pokomo tradition has it that Liongo's enemies, having made use of the son for their own purposes, slew him, for they said, "If you kill a snake you must cut off its head. If you do not cut off its head it will bite again. Therefore it is better to kill this son also!" Hamisi wa Kayi, who told the story to Bishop Steere at Zanzibar, said, "And they seized that young man and killed him, and did not give him the kingdom." In any case he reaped the due reward of his treason.

The mourning for Liongo, in which the townsfolk of Shaka joined with his mother, shows that she was not alone in the more favourable view of him. "Liongo was our sword and spear and shield; there is none to defend us now he is gone!"

The grave, as I saw it in 1912, was a slight elevation in the ground, which might once have been a barrow. It was roughly marked at the head and foot with rows of white stones, evidently remnants of a complete rectangle. The native overseer in charge of the plantation in which it was situated told me that he and the European superintendent had measured the grave some time before, and found its length from east to west to be "fourteen paces"—some twelve or fourteen yards, suggesting that Liongo might, indeed, have been a giant whose knees were level with the head of a tall Galla. He and others said that the grave had formerly been marked with an inscribed stone " seven hundred years old "—but some European had dug it up and taken it away. As far as I know it has never been traced. So much for Liongo. With all his faults he had

> The genius to be loved, so let him have
> The justice to be honoured in his grave.

The idea of the charmed life, protected against every weapon but one, or vulnerable in one point only, is familiar from European mythology (Balder, Siegfried, Achilles), but it is still a matter of living belief in Africa. Chikumbu, a Yao chief living on Mlanje in 1893, could, I was assured, be killed by one thing only—a splinter of bamboo ; he had 'medicines' against everything else. A generation or two earlier Chibisa, a chief of the Mang'anja, was proof against everything but a 'sand-bullet,' which killed him as he stood on an ant-hill shouting his war-song.

Since writing this chapter I have found a curious parallel in a Rumanian ballad which is quoted in Panait Istrati's *Les Haidoucs*. The brigand Gheorghitza, who could be killed in one way only, was shot with a silver bullet, by a close friend turned traitor, " in the seat of the soul " (*un peu au-dessus du nombril, où cela fait mal aux vaillants*). He seized his gun, leaned against a rock, and took aim at his false friend, but death came upon him as he knelt. For three days none durst come near him; then one Beshg Elias went up to the body, cut off the head, and carried it to Bucharest. And all who met him wept when they saw the head of Gheorghitza, " so beautiful was he ! "

CHAPTER XI : THE TRICKSTERS
HLAKANYANA AND HUVEANE

WE find two curious figures in the mythology of the South-eastern Bantu. Huveane belongs to the Bapedi [1] and Bavenda, in the Eastern Transvaal. We have met with him before, as the First Man (though, incongruously enough, we also hear about his father) and, in some sense, the creator; but, as was stated at the time, he also appears in a very different character. Hlakanyana plays a conspicuous part in Zulu folklore; he no longer belongs to mythology proper, being more on the level of Jack the Giant-killer and Tom Thumb in our own fairy-tales. But there seems to be some uncertainty about his real nature. One of his names is Ucakijana, which means the Little Weasel, and though the people who told his story to Bishop Callaway explained this by saying he was like a weasel for his small size and his cunning, it may well be that he had actually been an animal to begin with. Some of his adventures are exactly the same as those which by other Bantu tribes are ascribed to the hare, the really epic figure in their folklore, and the authentic ancestor of Uncle Remus's Brer Rabbit. It is quite possible, though I do not know of any direct evidence for this, that he was originally a totem animal, and, as such, a mysterious power, like the Algonkin hare, in North America, who made the world.

As for Huveane, his name is a diminutive of Huve (or Hove)—a name given in some accounts to his father. Some of the Bushman tribes have a divinity Huwe (or Uwe) who created and preserves all wild things, and to whom they pray to give them food. In Angola Huwe (represented, of course, by a masked man) is said to appear to the young Bushmen when they are being initiated into manhood.

It might be thought that the Bantu had borrowed the idea of Huve, if not of Huveane, from the Bushmen; but Miss Bleek, who knows more about the Bushmen than anyone

---

[1] A branch of the great Suto-Chuana group of tribes, between Pretoria and Pietersburg. They are perhaps better known as Sekukuni's people.

else, is of opinion, for several reasons, that the reverse is
more likely to be true.

The name of Huveane's father varies a good deal; some
call him Hodi, others, again, Rivimbi or Levivi. The
Thonga [1] clans in the Spelonken district of the Transvaal
have heard of him in a very confused and fragmentary way,
probably from the Bavenda, but it is the latter, along with
the Bapedi, who really know the legend.

Huveane produces a Child

Of this legend there are various versions, none apparently
complete, but they can be used to supplement each other.
One, obtained from the Masemola section of the Bapedi, [2]
begins in a way which recalls the story of Murile. Only
whereas Murile cherished a *Colocasia* tuber, which magically
developed into an infant, Huveane is quite baldly stated to
have " had a baby." The narrator seems to see nothing
improbable in this (though Huveane's parents and their
neighbours did), and no explanation is given of this extraordinary proceeding; but the Basuto have a story resembling
this in which the result is produced by the boy having swallowed some medicine intended for his mother. Another
version has it that Huveane modelled a baby in clay and
breathed life into it. This may possibly have some vague
connexion with the idea of his having originated the human
race; it may, on the other hand, be due to some echo of
missionary teaching.

The creation idea had, no doubt, fallen more or less into
the background by the time the story had taken shape as
above; but in any case one must not be troubled by such
incongruities as the existence of Huveane's parents. The
impossibility of such a situation would never occur to the
primitive mind.

Huveane kept his child in a hollow tree, and stole out

---

[1] The tribe of which the Delagoa Bay Baronga are a branch. They extend from
St Lucia Bay, in the south, to the Sabi river, in the north. Some clans of the Bila
section of the tribe, now known as Magwamba, are isolated in the Eastern Transvaal.

[2] Hoffmann, in *Zeitschrift für Kolonialsprachen*, vol. vi, p. 238.

early every morning to feed it with milk before it was time for him to begin herding the sheep and goats. His parents noticed that he used to take the milk, and could not make out what he did with it; so one day his father followed him stealthily, saw him feeding the child, hid till Huveane had gone away, and carried the baby to his wife. They then placed it among the firewood and other things stacked up under the eaves of the hut. When Huveane brought the flock home he went straight to his tree and found no baby there. He went into the courtyard, sat down by the fire, where his parents were seated, and did not speak, only looking miserable. His mother asked him what was the matter, and he said the smoke was hurting his eyes. " Then you had better go out and sit somewhere else." He did so, but remained gloomy. At last his mother told him to go and fetch a piece of wood from the pile, which he did, and found the baby wrapped in a sheepskin and quite safe. His parents, relieved to find that he had recovered his spirits, let him have his way, and he went on caring for the child, whom he called Sememerwane sa Matedi a Telele, " One who causes much trouble."

Huveane plays Tricks with the Stock

His parents continued, however, to be uneasy; they could not understand how the child had been produced, and the neighbours, when the story leaked out, began to talk of witchcraft. Huveane did not trouble himself, but went on herding his father's stock and devising practical jokes to play upon him. When a ewe or goat had twins, which not infrequently happened, he took one of the lambs or kids and shut it up in a hollow ant-heap. In this way he gradually collected a whole flock. Some one, who had noticed that the ewes, when driven out in the morning, always collected round the ant-heaps, told Huveane's father, and the latter followed his son to the pasture, heard the bleating of the lambs and kids inside the ant-heaps, took away the stones which blocked the entrance, and seized the lambs to take them to their mothers. But as he did not know to which mother each belonged the result was confusion worse confounded. Huveane, exasperated beyond endurance, struck his father with the switch he had in his hand. No doubt this helped to bring matters to a crisis, but for the moment the old man was too much impressed with the sudden increase of the flock to be very angry. In the evening, when the villagers saw the full number being driven home, they were filled with envy, and asked him where he had got all those animals. He told the whole story, which gave rise to endless discussions.

Plans for Huveane's Destruction

It was certain that Huveane could be up to no good; he must have produced those sheep and goats by magic—and how came he to have a child and no mother for it? He certainly ought to be got rid of. They put it to his father that the boy would end by bewitching the whole village. They handed him some poison, and in the evening, when Huveane was squatting by the fire, his mother brought him a bowl of milk. He took it, but, instead of drinking, poured it out on the ground. The neighbours took counsel, and suggested to the father that he should dig a pit close to the fireplace, where Huveane was in the habit of sitting, and cover it over. But Huveane, instead of sitting down in his usual place, forced himself in between his brothers, who were seated by the fire, and in the struggle for a place one of them fell into the pit. Next they dug another pit in the gateway of his father's enclosure, where he would have to pass when he came home with the flocks in the evening. He jumped over the pitfall, and all his sheep and goats did likewise.

This having failed, some one suggested that a man with a spear should be tied up in a bundle of grass, a device adopted, as we have seen, by Kachirambe's mother. This was done, and Huveane's father sent him to fetch the bundle. He took his spear with him—to his father's surprise—and, when near enough, threw it with unerring aim. The man inside jumped up and ran away. Huveane returned to his father, saying, " Father, I went to do as you told me, but the grass has run away."

HLAKANYANA AND HUVEANE

Huveane's Practical Jokes

The villagers were driven to the conclusion that it was quite impossible to compass Huveane's destruction by any stratagem, however cunning, and they were fain to let him be. He knew that he was a match for them, and thenceforth set himself to fool them by pretended stupidity. Whatever tricks he played on them he knew that he was safe.

One day he found a dead zebra, and sat down on it while watching his flock. In the evening, when he returned and was asked where he had been herding that day, he said, " By the striped hill." Three or four days running he gave the same answer, and, his relatives' curiosity being roused, some of them followed him and found the zebra—by this time badly decomposed. They told him, " Why, this is game ; if you find an animal like this you should heap branches over it, to keep the hyenas away, and come and call the people from the village to fetch the meat." Next day Huveane found a very small bird lying dead ; he heaped branches over it and ran home with the news. Half the village turned out, carrying large baskets ; their feelings on beholding the ' game' may be imagined. One of the men informed him that this kind of game should be hung round one's neck ; he did this next day, and was set down as a hopeless idiot. Several other tricks of the same kind are told of him ; at last, one day, his father, thinking he should no longer be left to himself, went herding with him. When the sun was high he became very thirsty ; Huveane showed him a high rock, on the top of which was a pool of water, and knocked in a number of pegs, so that he could climb up. They both went up and drank ; then Huveane came down, took away the pegs, one by one, and ran home, where his mother had prepared the evening meal. Huveane ate all that was ready ; then he took the empty pots, filled them with cow dung, and ran off to drive in the pegs and let his father come down. The old man came home and sat down to the supper, which, as his graceless son now informed him, had been magically changed, so as to be entirely uneatable. After this the parents and neighbours alike seem to have felt that there was nothing to be done with Huveane, except to put up with him as best they could. We hear nothing more about the child in the hollow tree.

It almost seems as if the trick played by Huveane on his father were a kind of inverted echo of one tradition about the High God, whom some call Huveane. " His abode is in the sky. He created the sky and the earth. He came down from the sky to make the earth and men. When he had finished he returned to the sky. They say he climbed up by pegs,[1] and after he had gone up one step he took away the peg below him, and so on, till he had drawn them all out and disappeared into the sky." [2]

Some say that all the incidents detailed above belong, not to Huveane (whom the narrators call the Great God, Modimo o Moholo), but to his son Hutswane, who, it is believed, will one day come again, bringing happiness and prosperity to mankind—a somewhat unexpected conclusion after all that we have heard about him.

Hlakanyana's Precocious Development and Mischievous Pranks

" Uhlakanyana is a very cunning man; he is also very small, of the size of a weasel "—*icakide*; hence his other name. He is " like the weasel; it is as though he really was of that genus; he resembles it in all respects." As already stated, it is probable that he really was a weasel, though the fact had been so far forgotten by the time the story was written down as we have it that the narrators thought the name needed explanation. Why the weasel was chosen does not seem clear: his exploits are credited by most of the Bantu to the hare, by a few to the jackal.[3]

Hlakanyana was a chief's son. Like Ryang'ombe, he spoke before he was born; in fact, he repeatedly declared

---

[1] No doubt driven into the solid vault of the sky, where it was believed to join the earth at the horizon.

[2] Hoffmann, in *Zeitschrift für Eingeborenensprachen*, vol. xix, p. 270.

[3] Callaway, *Nursery Tales*, p. 3.

SOME OF THE BOYS WHO OBJECTED TO HLAKANYANA'S COMPANY

Photo Austin Hughes, Pietermaritzburg

his impatience to enter the world. No sooner had he made his appearance than he walked out to the cattle-kraal, where his father had just slaughtered some oxen, and the men were sitting round, ready for a feast of meat. Scared by this portent—for they had been waiting for the birth to be announced—they all ran away, and Hlakanyana sat down by the fire and began to eat a strip of meat which was roasting there. They came back, and asked the mother whether this was really the expected baby. She answered, " It is he"; whereupon they said, " Oh, we thank you, our queen. You have brought forth for us a child who is wise as soon as he is born. We never saw a child like this child. This child is fit to be the great one among all the king's children, for he has made us wonder by his wisdom." [1]

But Hlakanyana, thinking that his father did not take this view, but looked upon him as a mere infant, asked him to take a leg of beef and throw it downhill, over the kraal fence (the gateway being on the upper side). All the boys and men present were to race for it, and " he shall be the man who gets the leg." They all rushed to the higher opening, but Hlakanyana wormed his way between the stakes at the lower end of the kraal, picked up the leg, and carried it in triumph to meet the others, who were coming round from the farther side. He handed it over to his mother, and then returned to the kraal, where his father was distributing the rest of the meat. He offered to carry each man's share to his hut for him, which he did, smeared some blood on the mat (on which meat is laid to be cut up), and then carried the joint to his mother. He did this to each one in turn, so that by the evening no house had any meat except that of the chief's wife, which was overstocked. No wonder that the women cried out, " What is this that has been born to-day? He is a prodigy, a real prodigy !" His next feat was to take out all the birds which had been caught in the traps set by the boys, and bring them home, telling his mother to cook them and cover the pots, fastening down the lids. He then went off to sleep in the boys' house (*ilau*),

---

[1] Callaway, *Nursery Tales*, p. 8.

which he would not ordinarily have entered for several years to come, and overbore their objections, saying, " Since you say this I shall sleep here, just to show you ! " He rose early in the morning, went to his mother's house, got in without waking her, opened the pots, and ate all the birds, leaving only the heads, which he put back, after filling the lower half of the pots with cow dung, and fastened down the lids. Then he went away for a time, and came back to play Huveane's trick on his mother. He pretended to have come in for the first time, and told her that the sun had risen, and that she had slept too long—for if the birds were not taken out of the pot before the sun was up they would turn into dung. So he washed himself and sat down to his breakfast, and when he opened the pots it was even as he had said, and his mother believed him. He finished up the heads, saying that, as she had spoilt his food, she should not have even these, and then announced that he did not consider himself her child at all, and that his father was " a mere man, one of the people and nothing more." He would not stay with them, but would go on his travels. So he picked up his stick and walked out, still grumbling about the loss of his birds.

He goes on his Travels

When he had gone some distance and was beginning to get hungry he came upon some traps with birds in them and, beginning to take them out, found himself stuck fast. The owner of the traps was a 'cannibal'—or, rather, an ogre— who, finding that birds had more than once disappeared from his traps, had put sticks smeared with birdlime in front of them. Now he came along to look at them, and found Hlakanyana, who, quite undisturbed, addressed him thus: " Don't beat me, and I will tell you. Take me out and cleanse me from the birdlime and take me home with you. Have you a mother? " The ogre said he had. Hlaka-nyana, evidently assuming that he was to be eaten, said that if he were beaten and killed at once his flesh would be ruined for the pot. " I shall not be nice; I shall be bitter.

Cleanse me and take me home with you, that you may put me in your house, that I may be cooked by your mother. And do you go away and just leave me at your home. I cannot be cooked if you are there; I shall be bad; I cannot be nice." The hare, in some stories, uses the same stratagem to escape being eaten.

The ogre, a credulous person, like most of his kind, did as he was asked, and handed Hlakanyana over to his mother, to be cooked next morning.

When the ogre and his younger brother were safely out of the way Hlakanyana proposed to the old woman that they should "play at boiling each other." He got her to put on a large pot of water, made up the fire under it, and when it was beginning to get warm he said, "Let us begin with me." She put him in and covered the pot. Presently he asked to be taken out, and then, saying that the fire was not hot enough, made it up to a blaze and began, very rudely, to unfasten the old woman's skin petticoat. When she objected he said: "What does it matter if I have unfastened your dress, I who am mere game, which is about to be eaten by your sons and you?" He thrust her in and put on the lid. No sooner had he done so than she shrieked that she was being scalded; but he told her that could not be, or she would not be able to cry out. He kept the lid on till the poor creature's cries ceased, and then put on her clothes and lay down in her sleeping-place. When the sons came home he told them to take their 'game' and eat; he had already eaten, and did not mean to get up. While they were eating he slipped out at the door, threw off the clothes, and ran away as fast as he could. When he had reached a safe distance he called out to them, "You are eating your mother, you cannibals!" They pursued him hot-foot; he came to a swollen river and changed himself into a piece of wood. They came up, saw his footprints on the ground, and, as he was nowhere in sight, concluded he had crossed the river and flung the piece of wood after him. Safe on the other bank, he resumed his own shape and jeered at the ogres, who gave up the pursuit and turned back.

He kills a Hare, gets a Whistle, and is robbed of it

Hlakanyana went on his way, and before very long he
spied a hare. Being hungry, he tried to entice it within
reach by offering to tell a tale, but the hare would not be
beguiled. At last, however (this part of the story is not
very clear, and the hare must have been a different creature
from the usual Bantu hare!), he caught it, killed it, and
roasted it, and, after eating the flesh, made one of the
bones into a whistle. He went on, playing his whistle
and singing:

> " *Ngahlangana no Nohloya*
> *Sapekapekana*
> *Ngagwanya*
> *Wapekwa wada wavutwa.*"

> [" I met Hloya's mother,
> And we cooked each other.
> I did not burn;
> She was done to a turn."]

In time he came to a large tree on the bank of a river,
overhanging a deep pool. On a branch of the tree lay an
iguana,[1] who greeted him, and Hlakanyana responded
politely. The iguana said, " Lend me your whistle, so that
I can hear if it will sound." Hlakanyana refused, but the
iguana insisted, promising to give it back. Hlakanyana
said, " Come away from the pool, then, and come out here
on to the open ground; I am afraid near a pool. I say
you might run into the pool with my whistle, for you are a
person that lives in deep water." The iguana came down
from his tree, and when Hlakanyana thought that he was
at a safe distance from the river he handed him the whistle.
The iguana tried the whistle, approved the sound, and
wanted to take it away with him. Hlakanyana would not
hear of this, and laid hold of the iguana as he was trying to
make off, but received such a blow from the powerful tail
that he had to let go, and the iguana dived into the river,
carrying the whistle with him.

---

[1] This is the word used by Callaway (probably unaware that there are no
iguanas on the African continent) to translate *uxamu*, which is really the monitor
lizard (*Monitor niloticus*).

HLAKANYANA AND HUVEANE

In a Xosa version it is Hlakanyana who steals the whistle from the iguana.

One of the Ronga stories about the hare describes him as challenging a poor gazelle to the game of "cooking each other." Having killed her, he made her horns into a kind of trumpet, which he used to sound an alarm of war.

In fact, this trick, in one form or other, and attributed to different actors, is found throughout the Bantu area. Compare the case of Jack and the Cornish giant.

Hlakanyana again went on till he came to a place where a certain old man had hidden some bread.[1] He ran off with it, but not before the owner had seen him; the old man evidently knew him, for he called out, "Put down my bread, Hlakanyana." Hlakanyana only ran the faster, the old man after him, till, finding that the latter was gaining on him, he crawled into a snake's hole. The old man put in his hand and caught him by the leg. Hlakanyana cried, laughing, "*He! He!* you've caught hold of a root!"[2] So the old man let go, and, feeling about for the leg, caught a root, at which Hlakanyana yelled, "Oh! oh! you're killing me!" The old man kept pulling at the root till he was tired out and went away. Hlakanyana ate the bread in comfort, and then crawled out and went on his way once more.

He nurses the Leopard's Cubs

In the course of his wanderings he came upon a leopard's den, where he found four cubs and sat down beside them till the mother leopard came home, carrying a buck with which to feed her little ones. She was very angry when she saw Hlakanyana, and was about to attack him, but he disarmed her by his flattering tongue, and finally persuaded her to let him stay and take care of the cubs, while she went out to hunt. "I will take care of them, and I will build a beautiful house, that you may lie here at the foot of the

---

[1] *Isinkwa.* Though now used for 'bread' in our sense (which was unknown to the Bantu before they came in contact with Europeans), this word really means steamed dumplings of maize or *amabele* (millet).

[2] So Brer Tarrypin says to Brer Fox, "Tu'n loose dat stump-root an' ketch hold o' me!" This incident occurs over and over again in Bantu folklore.

rock with your children." He also told her he could cook—
a somewhat unnecessary accomplishment, one would think,
in this case; but it would seem that he had his reasons. The
leopard having agreed, Hlakanyana brought the cubs, one
by one, for her to suckle. She objected, wanting them all
brought at once, but the little cunning fellow persisted
and got his way. When they had all been fed she called on
him to make good his promise and skin the buck and cook it,
which he did. So they both ate, and all went to sleep. In
the morning, when the leopard had gone to hunt, Hlakanyana
set to work building the house. He made the usual round
Zulu hut, but with a very small doorway; then, inside, he
dug a burrow, leading to the back of the hut, with an opening
a long way off. Then he took four assagais which he had
carried with him on his travels, broke them off short to
rather less than the width of the doorway, and hid them in
a convenient place. Having finished, he ate one of the cubs.
When the mother came home he brought them out as before,
one by one, taking the third twice, so that she never missed
any of them. He did the same the next day, and the next.
On the fourth day he brought out the last cub four times,
and at length it refused to drink. The mother was naturally
surprised at this, but Hlakanyana said he thought it was not
well. She said, " Take care of it, then," and when he had
carried it into the house called him to prepare supper. When
she had eaten Hlakanyana went into the house, and the
leopard called out that she was coming in to look after the
child. Hlakanyana said, " Come in, then," knowing that
she would take |some time squeezing herself through the
narrow entrance, and at once made his escape through the
burrow. Meanwhile she had got in, found only one cub,
concluded that he must have eaten the rest, and followed
him into the burrow. By this time Hlakanyana was out at
the other end; he ran round to the front of the house, took
his assagais from the hiding-place, and fixed them in the
ground at the doorway, the points sloping inward. The
leopard found she could not get very far in the burrow, so
she came back into the hut, and, squeezing through the

HUT-BUILDING IN NATAL

doorway to pursue Hlakanyana into the open, was pierced by the assagais and killed.

Hlakanyana and the Ogre

Hlakanyana now sat down and ate the cub; then he skinned the leopard, and gradually—for he remained on the spot for some time—ate most of the flesh, keeping, however, one leg, with which he set out once more on his travels, " for he was a man who did not stay long in one place." Soon after he met a hungry ogre, with whom he easily made friends by giving him some meat, and they went on together. They came across two cows, which the *izimu* said belonged to him. Hlakanyana suggested that they should build a hut, so that they could slaughter the cows and eat them in peace and comfort. The ogre agreed; they killed the cows and started to build. As rain was threatening Hlakanyana said they had better get on with the thatching.

This is done by two people, one inside the hut and the other on the roof, passing the string with which the grass is tied backward and forward between them, pushing it through by means of a pointed stick. Hlakanyana went inside, while the ogre climbed on the roof. The latter had very long hair (a distinguishing feature of the *amazimu*), and Hlakanyana managed to knit it, lock by lock, into the thatch, so firmly that he would not be able to get off. He then sat down and ate the beef which was boiling on the fire. A hailstorm came on, Hlakanyana went into the house with his joint, and the ogre (who seems to have been a harmless creature enough) was left to perish. " He was struck with the hailstones, and died there on the house "—as anyone who has seen an African hailstorm can readily believe.

Having caused the death of another *izimu* in a way which need not be related here, as the same thing occurs (with more excuse) in a different story, Hlakanyana took up his abode for a time with yet another, who seems to have had no reason to complain of him. As usual, when no ill fortune befell him he became restless, and took the road once more, directing his steps towards the place on the river where the iguana had robbed him of his whistle. He found the iguana on his tree, called him down, killed him, and recovered the whistle. Then he went back to the ogre's hut, but the owner had gone away, and the hut was burned down. So he said, " I will now go back to my mother, for, behold, I am in trouble."

He goes Home

But his return was by no means in the spirit of the Prodigal Son, for he professed to have come back purely out of affection for her, saying, " Oh, now I have returned, my mother, for I remembered you ! " and calmly omitting all mention of his exploits during his absence. She believed this, being only too ready to welcome him back, and he seems to have behaved himself for a time. Nothing is said of his father's attitude, or of that of the clansmen.

The next episode is a curious one : it is told all over Africa in connexion with different characters—the hare, the jackal, a man, an old woman, a girl, a boy. The attraction evidently lies in the repeated enumeration of objects, adding one every time, after the fashion of *The House that Jack Built*.

The day after his return home Hlakanyana went to a wedding, and as he came over a hill on the way back he found some *umdiandiane*—a kind of edible tuber, of which he was very fond. He dug it up and took it home to his mother, asking her to cook it for him, as he was now going to milk the cow. She did so, and, tasting one to see if it was done, liked it so much that she ate the whole. When he asked for it she said, " I have eaten it, my child," and he answered, " Give me my *umdiandiane*, for I dug it up on a very little knoll, as I was coming from a wedding." His mother gave him a milk-pail by way of compensation, and he went off. Soon he came upon some boys herding sheep, who were milking the ewes into old, broken potsherds. He said, " Why are you milking into potsherds ? You had better use my milk-pail, but you must give me a drink out of it." They used his milk-pail, but the last boy who had it broke it. Hlakanyana said, " Give me my milk-pail, my milk-pail

my mother gave me, my mother having eaten my *umdiandiane*"—and so on, as before. The boys gave him an
assagai, which he lent to some other boys, who were trying
to cut slices of liver with splinters of sugar-cane. They
broke his assagai, and gave him an axe instead. Then he
met some old women gathering firewood, who had nothing
to cut it with, so he offered them the use of his axe, which
again got broken. They gave him a blanket, and he went
on his way till nightfall, when he found two young men
sleeping out on the hillside, with nothing to cover them.
He said, " Ah, friends, do you sleep without covering?
Have you no blanket?" They said, "No." He said,
"Take this of mine," which they did, but it was rather
small for two, and as each one kept dragging it from the
other it soon got torn. Then he demanded it back. " Give
me my blanket, my blanket which the women gave me,"
and so on. The young men gave him a shield. Then he
came upon some men fighting with a leopard, who had no
shields. He questioned them as he had done the other
people, and lent one of them his shield. It must have been
efficient as a protection, for they killed the leopard, but the
hand-loop by which the man was holding it broke, and of
course it was rendered useless. So Hlakanyana said:

> " Give me my shield, my shield the young men gave me,
> The young men having torn my blanket,
> My blanket the women gave me,
> The women having broken my axe,
> My axe the boys gave me,
> The boys having broken my assagai,
> My assagai the boys gave me,
> The boys having broken my milk-pail,
> My milk-pail my mother gave me,
> My mother having eaten my *umdiandiane*,
> My *umdiandiane* I dug up on a very little knoll,
> As I was coming from a wedding."

They gave him a war-assagai (*isinkemba*).

Here the story as given by Bishop Callaway breaks off,
the narrator saying, " What he did with that perhaps I may
tell you on another occasion." But a Xosa version recorded

by McCall Theal,[1] which gives the series of exchanges rather differently, puts this episode before that of the ogre's traps (also quite different in detail) and that of the leopard's cubs, and follows it up with two more incidents. One (relating to the tree belonging to the chief of the animals, of which no one knows the name) is much better told elsewhere, as an adventure of the hare; the other recalls an exploit of the hare in providing food for the lion, which is told by the Pokomo on the Tana river, and by many other people besides. But in this case Hlakanyana made provision only for himself. He came to the house of a jackal and asked for food. Being told there was none, he said, "You must climb up on the house and cry out with a loud voice, ' We are going to be fat to-day, because Hlakanyana is dead!'" When the jackal did so all the animals came running to hear the news, and, finding the door open, went in. Hlakanyana, hidden inside, shut the door, killed them at his leisure, and ate. We hear no more about the jackal.

Then he returned home for the last time, and his story reaches its conclusion. He went out to herd his father's calves—no doubt seized by a sudden impulse to make himself useful—and found a tortoise, which he picked up and carried home on his back. His mother said, "What have you got there, my son?" And he answered, "Just take it off my back, Mother." But that she could not do, however hard she tried, for the creature held fast. So she heated some fat and poured it on the tortoise, which let go only too quickly, "and the fat fell on Hlakanyana and burned him, and he died. That is the end of this cunning little fellow."

But I suspect that this is only a late version, and that the real Hlakanyana never came to an end in that sense, any more than Huveane. Has anyone ever heard the end of Jack the Giant-killer?

Though Hlakanyana is not, so far as one knows, associated with any such traditions, however dim, as those told of Huveane, it is by no means impossible that he may, in the far-off origins of myth, have played a similar part.

[1] *Kaffir Folklore*, p. 96.

Huveane was really a benefactor, as well as a trickster, though in the popular tales the latter aspect has tended to predominate, and we may even discover traces of such a character in Hlakanyana, as when he supplies the herd-lads with a milk-pail, the women with an axe, and so forth, though the emphasis is certainly laid on the way in which he invariably got back his own with interest.

This union of apparently incompatible characteristics does not seem to strike the primitive mind as impossible. Wundt, in his *Völkerpsychologie*,[1] points out that legendary heroes are of three kinds, the deliverer and benefactor, the malignant, hurtful demon, and the mischievous jester, who stands midway between the two. And in the imagination of very primitive people we not infrequently find " these qualities united in one and the same being. Thus Manabozho of the Algonkin is both demiurgus (creator) and deliverer, but at the same time he plays the part sometimes of a harmful demon, sometimes of a tricksy, humorous sprite," the hero of innumerable popular jests.

[1] Vol. v, Part II, p. 47.

CHAPTER XII : THE AMAZIMU

THE word *izimu*, in the Zulu tales, is usually, as by Callaway and Theal, translated 'cannibal.' But this word, with us, is ordinarily applied to people who, for one reason or another, are accustomed to eat human flesh. As Callaway pointed out long ago, however, " it is perfectly clear that the cannibals of the Zulu legends are not common men ; they are magnified into giants and magicians." Perhaps it might also be said that the attributes of the legendary *amazimu* were transferred to the abhorred beings, who, driven to cannibalism by famine, kept up the habit when it was no longer needed and, as Ulutuli Dhladhla told the bishop, " rebelled against men, forsook them, and liked to eat them, and men drove them away . . . so they were regarded as a distinct nation, for men were game (*izinya-mazane*) to them." [1] In fact, he distinctly says that " once they were men," and implies that they were so no longer.

Cannibals

The practice of cannibalism undoubtedly exists in Africa, though it is much less common than is sometimes supposed ; and it is usually of a ceremonial character, which is a different matter from using human flesh as ordinary food. This last seems to be—or to have been—done by some tribes in West Africa—*e.g.*, the Manyema—but one need not accept all the sensational statements that have been published on this subject. So far as there is any truth in these, the custom probably originated in famine times, as it did with the people referred to by Bishop Callaway's informant. Thus, it is said, in Natal, after a long drought, a certain chief of the Abambo, named Umdava, " told his people to scatter themselves over the veld and catch all the people they came upon in the paths to serve as food . . . and those people lived on human flesh till the time for the crops came round." [2] The dwellers on Umkambati (the Table Moun-

---

[1] *Nursery Tales*, p. 156.
[2] Colenso, *Zulu-English Dictionary*, p. 705.

tain near Pietermaritzburg) were more than once attacked by these cannibals.

The old chief Nomsimekwana, who died less than thirty years ago, had a narrow escape from them in his childhood. They seized his whole family and drove them along, making the boy carry on his head the pot in which, so they told him, he was to be cooked. Watching his opportunity, at a turn in the path hidden by the tall grass he slipped into the Umsunduzi river, and lay concealed under the bushes which overhung the bank—the spot was pointed out to me in 1895. Failing to find him, the enemy came to the conclusion that he had been killed by the hippopotami, who at that time abounded in the river, and passed on their way. Nomsimekwana's sister and the other captives were ultimately killed and eaten.

Those man-eaters who refused to give up the practice when the necessity for it had passed fled to the mountains, pursued by universal execration, and eked out a wretched existence in dens and caves, sallying forth, when occasion offered, to attack lonely travellers. Moshesh, paramount chief of the Basuto, spared no pains in putting an end to these horrors, though he refused to exterminate the criminals, as his councillors advised, provided they would turn from their evil ways. He gave them cattle, and encouraged them to till the soil, and when that generation had died out cannibalism was a thing of the past.

Ulutuli Dhladhla, whom we quoted in a previous paragraph, said that " the word *amazimu*, when interpreted, means to gormandize—to be gluttonous." But the word exists in so many Bantu languages, with (as far as one can discover) no such connotation, that I cannot help thinking him mistaken. Moreover, it has, distinctly, some relation to *mzimu* (of a different noun class), which means ' a spirit ' —in the first instance an ancestral spirit. It is not used in Zulu, where the ancestral spirits are called *amadhlozi*, or *amatongo*, save in the phrase *izinkomo ezomzimu*, " cattle of the spirits "—i.e., slaughtered as a sacrifice to them. Here *umzimu* seems to be " a collective name for *amatongo*."

Ogres

The Basuto use the word *madimo* (singular *ledimo*) for 'cannibals,' *badimo* for 'spirits' or 'gods.' *Zimwi* is the Swahili word for a being best described as an ogre; the word occurs in old, genuine Bantu tales, and I have heard it used by a native; but most Swahili nowadays seem to prefer the Arabic loan-words *jini* and *shetani*. A ghost is *mzuka*; but the stem *-zimu* survives in the expression *kuzimu*, " the place of spirits "—thought of as underground —and *muzimu*, a place where offerings are made to spirits. The Wachaga and the Akikuyu have their *irimu*, the Akamba the *eimu* (the Kamba language is remarkable for dropping out consonants), and the Duala, on the other side of Africa, their *edimo*. Other peoples in West Africa, while having a notion of beings more or less similar, call them by other names. The *makishi* of the Ambundu in Angola play the same part in folk-tales as the *amazimu*—their name may perhaps be connected with the Kongo *nkishi* (*nkisi* in some dialects), which meant originally 'a spirit,' but now more usually 'a charm,' or the object commonly called a 'fetish.' The Aandonga (in the Ovambo country south of Angola), strangely enough, tell the usual ogre tales of the *esisi* 'albino.' Albinos are found, occasionally, in all parts of Africa; they are not, as a rule, so far as one can learn, regarded with horror, though the Mayombe of the Lower Congo think that they are spirit children, and observe particular ceremonies on the birth of such a one.

The appearance of the *izimu* is variously described, but it seems to be agreed that he can assume the appearance of an ordinary human being, if it is not his usual guise. The Zulus and the Ambundu say they may be recognized by their long, unkempt hair—a noticeable point among people who either shave off their hair frequently for reasons of cleanliness, or build it up into elaborate structures, like the conical *coiffures* of Zulu wives or the head-rings of their husbands.

The *makishi* are sometimes said to have many heads; in one story when the hero cuts off a *dikishi's* head he imme-

diately grows a second; in another a *dikishi* carries off a
woman and makes her his wife; when her child is born and
found to have only one head the husband threatens to call
" our folk " to eat her if she ever has another like it.   As
the second baby appears with two heads the threat was not
fulfilled.   But, thinking it best to be on the safe side, the
wife took the elder child and ran away, hid for the night in a
deserted house, was surprised when asleep by a wandering
dikishi, and eaten after all.

Other accounts of the *amazimu* are still more weirdly
sensational.   The *irimu* of the Wachaga is said to be a 'were-
leopard '—that is, a man who is able at will to change himself into a leopard.   But in one story this *irimu*, or leopard,
is described as having ten tails; in another he presents
himself in human shape at a homestead, as a suitor to the
daughter, but is detected when she catches sight of a second
mouth on the back of his head.[1]   In the Ronga story of
" Nabandji " [2] the people of the cannibal village whence the
young man takes a wife all have this peculiar feature.   It
may not be out of place here to mention a Hausa (Nigeria)
belief that a witch has mouths all over her back.   It is not
easy to see what can have suggested this notion.

The Chaga idea of the *irimu* seems to be a fairly compre-
hensive one.   An unfortunate man, who broke a *tabu*, was
turned into an *irimu*, with the result that thorn-bushes grew
out of his body, and he wandered about the country,
swallowing everything that came in his way.   His brother,
whom he had considerately warned to keep his distance,
consulted a diviner and, by his advice, set the thorns on fire.
When they were all burned away the *irimu* returned to his
own proper shape.[3]

Sometimes the *amazimu* are said to have only one leg, or
only half a body; one story of a Kikuyu *irimu* describes him
as having one leg, but two heads, one of which was stone;
one-half of his body was human, but the other half stone.
The Basuto speak of a set of beings with one leg, one arm,

[1] Gutmann, *Volksbuch*, p. 75.   [2] Junod, *Chants et contes*, p. 246.
[3] Gutmann, *Volksbuch*, p. 73.

one ear, and one eye, but these are called *matebele* [1] (it is not quite clear why), not *madimo*. They carry off a chief's daughter, though it is not suggested that she is to be eaten. In the story of "The Mothemelle" [2] we hear of cannibals (*madimo*) "hopping on one leg." But these half-bodied beings, while appearing in folklore all over Africa, are, as a rule, quite distinct from the *amazimu*. They are not invariably malignant; often, indeed, very much the reverse. They will be discussed later on.

The Little People

Chatelain thought that the *makishi* were the aboriginal inhabitants of the country, the 'Batua' (Batwa) Pygmies, "not as they are now, but as they appeared to the original Bantu settlers." But there is no evidence that the Pygmies or the Bushmen (whom the Zulus call Abatwa) were ever regarded as cannibals. Callaway's Zulu informants were very emphatic about " the dreadfulness of the Abatwa," who, if offended, as by a reference to their small stature, about which they were especially sensitive, would shoot you with a poisoned arrow as soon as look at you. But there is no reference to their eating human flesh.

There is a distinct body of tradition about these 'little people,' who are nowhere confused with the *amazimu*; they may be dangerous if irritated, as stated above, but are otherwise inoffensive, and even helpful, when approached in the right way. The Wachaga have tales about the Wakonyingo, supposed to live on the summit of Kilimanjaro (formerly believed inaccessible to human feet), which show them in quite an amiable light. Even the man who insulted them by taking them for children and asking when their parents were coming home met with no worse fate than waiting dinnerless till nightfall, and then going home as he

---

[1] This name is applied by the Basuto not only to the Zulus of Rhodesia (Amandebele), but to the Zulus and Xosa in general. Their relations with these people have so often been hostile that their name may have been given for this reason to the monsters in question.

[2] Jacottet, *Treasury of Ba-Suto Lore*, p. 224,

had come, whereas his more tactful brother was presented with a fine herd of cattle.

Dr Doke,[1] writing about the Lamba people, also distinguishes between ogres (*wasisimunkulu* or *wasisimwe*[2] and dwarfs (*utuchekulu*), whom he calls 'gnomes.' These, however, differ from the other 'little people' in one important respect—they eat people. The gnome "is renowned for the one long tooth, blood-red and sharp, with which it kills its victims. Moreover, the Lamba people recognize the existence of pygmies (*utunyokamafumo*), distinct from the gnomes. In the one story in which they figure they come much nearer the character of the *wakonyingo*. Yet in "The Choric Story[3] of the Lion" a gnome shows himself helpful in saving a man and his sister from an ogre.[4] And in another tale a gnome who has been robbed of his drums by the chief's orders sprinkles 'medicine' over the men carrying them off, whereupon they all fall down dead, and he recovers his property. But, having done so, he sprinkles them again, and they return to life. And the matter was arranged amicably in the end.

The Kamba Aimu

A different origin for the *amazimu* has been suggested by others—*viz.*, that they are the ghosts of evil-disposed persons. This is expressly affirmed by the Akamba about some spirits called *Aimu ya kitombo*. They

> haunt woods and waste places . . . they are evil spirits and are supposed to be the disembodied relics of people who have killed their neighbours by the help of black magic. . . . God has banished them to the woods, where they wander about without anyone to care for them by sacrificing to them. . . . A man who lived at Kitundu went out one night about midnight to look at a maize-field

[1] *Lamba Folklore*, pp. 385–386.
[2] This word contains the same root (*-simwe*) as *-zimu*.
[3] Dr Doke uses this expression to translate *ulusimi*, "a prose story interspersed with songs," in which the audience join. See also Steere, *Swahili Tales*, Preface, p. vii.
[4] This belongs to the type of story labelled "Robber Bridegroom" in the Folk-Lore Society's classification.

some distance away. . . . On his way back he met a spirit in the
path ; it was of enormous size, and had only one leg . . . before
he could move he was struck down by a flash of fire, and the spirit
passed on its way.[1]

This may well have been the origin of the *amazimu*, but
I fancy that in most cases it has been forgotten, and they
are looked on as quite different from the ghosts, good or
bad. Another point to notice is that the ghosts are still
largely believed in and taken quite seriously, while the
amazimu proper occur only in stories related for entertainment (and, possibly, instruction), but not accepted as fact.
This fits in with Mr Hobley's account of the *aimu*, described
by the Akamba as wicked ghosts, and actually seen (and
even felt !) by people now living.

It will be noticed that the Akamba, like the Akikuyu, give
the *aimu*, or some of them, only one leg. Dr Lindblom also
mentions this characteristic. In addition he states that the
eimu is " a figure appearing in different shapes, sometimes
smaller than a dwarf, sometimes of superhuman size . . .
though, on the other hand, he also often appears as a wholly
human being . . . he is a gluttonous ogre, and kidnaps
people in order to eat them up." This writer refers to
several Kamba stories—unfortunately not yet published—
in one of which the *eimu* appears as a handsome young man
and lures a girl to his home ; in another a Kamba woman
turns into an *eimu* and eats her own grandchild.[2]

The idea of the *eimu* seems here to be mixed up, in some
cases, with that of the Swallowing Monster, in the peculiar
form in which it occurs in Basutoland and in Ruanda :

A favourite ending to many tales about the *eimu*, or nearly
related, more or less monstrous beings, is that the monster, now

---

[1] Hobley, *Bantu Beliefs*, pp. 89 and 91. It is curious that both this and other
authorities give the plural of *eimu* as *aimu*, which is properly a plural of the person
class, whereas the right form would be *maimu*, of the sixth noun class. *Aimu* is
also the Kamba word for the ancestral spirits, but this plural is seldom, if ever, used
for the ogres, while the singular of *aimu*, ' ghosts,' is equally rare, so that there is
not likely to be any confusion between the two. *Izimu* and all cognate words in
Bantu belong to the *li-ma* class (5–6), while the words for the ancestral ghosts
belong (with some exceptions, as *aimu*, above) to the *mu-mi* class (3–4).

[2] Lindblom, *Kamba Tales*, pp. viii and ix.

at length vanquished, tells his conqueror in his death-hour to cut off his little finger, and, this having been done, the people and cattle that he had devoured all come to life again.

Stories of Escape from Ogres

There are several stories which, in slightly differing shapes, are found probably in all parts of the Bantu area. Some of them are familiar to us from European analogues, though this does not necessarily mean that they have been imported. In one the ogre puts a girl into a bag and carries her about the country till she is rescued by her relations. Another tells how a party of girls or lads pass the night in an ogre's hut, and are rescued by the ready wit of the youngest. Then we have the girl forcibly married to an ogre who makes her escape in various ways. And, again, there is the theme, already referred to, of the " Robber Bridegroom," though he is more commonly a transformed animal (hyena, leopard, or lion) than an ogre properly so called. But, as the Chaga *irimu*, for instance, is also described as a 'were-leopard,' it is not always easy to keep the two notions distinct.

Some stories of escape from ogres employ the familiar device of obstacles created by the fugitives throwing various things behind them, which become a rock, a fire, a forest of knives, and a lake or river. This particular incident may not be indigenous to Africa ; it is not found in all the stories, and those which have it—*e.g.*, " Kibaraka," referred to in our concluding chapter—contain other foreign elements. There is no reason to suppose that most of the other incidents are not of home growth.

Of the type first mentioned there is a well-known example in the story of " Tselane," which (first published by Arbousset in 1842) was introduced to English readers by Sir James G. Frazer, under the title of "A South African Red Riding-hood." [1] The resemblance to the European Red Riding-hood is not very close, and applies chiefly to the opening incident, which is not found in most of the versions.

[1] *Folk-Lore Journal* (1889), vol. vii, p. 167.

Tselane, remaining behind in the hut from which her parents have migrated, is charged by her mother not to open the door to anyone but herself. The ogre, by imitating the mother's voice, gains admission and carries the girl off. The same opening is found in "Demane and Demazana" (where it is a brother, not the mother, whose voice is counterfeited), but in the Zulu "Usitungusobendhle" [1] and the Xosa "The Cannibal's Bird," [2] and in most, if not all, of the other stories, a party of girls go out to bathe, or to gather wild fruits, or for some other purpose, and one of them, either unwittingly, or even in wanton mischief, offends the ogre, who thereupon seizes her.

A curious point in the Sesuto, Xosa, and Zulu versions is that when the ogre has been (as they think) finally disposed of he is changed into a tree, which seems to have retained harmful powers, for when people tried to get honey out of the hollow trunk their hands stuck fast.[3] Something of the same notion appears in the Swahili tale I am about to relate. It is called "The Children and the *Zimwi*."

A Swahili Tale

Some little girls went out to look for shells on the sea-shore. One of them found a very beautiful shell and, fearing to lose it, laid it on a rock, so that she could pick it up on the way home. However, as they were returning she forgot it till they had passed the place, and then, suddenly remembering it, asked her companions to go back with her. They refused, and she went alone, singing to keep up her courage,[4] and found a *zimwi* sitting on the rock. He said, "What do you want?" and she sang her song over again. He said, "I can't hear you. Come closer!" And when she

---

[1] Callaway, *Nursery Tales*, p. 74.   [2] Theal, *Kaffir Folklore*, p. 125.

[3] The same thing happens in a Ronga story to some women who had offended the ghosts by trespassing on their sacred grove.

[4] The words of the song are a mixture of Yao and Swahili (indicating a probable origin for the story). The meaning is not very clear, except for the two lines: "I have forgotten my shell; I said, Let me go back and pick it up." Neither is it clear from the text as it stands whether she began to sing before or after she had seen the *zimwi*. If the latter, the song may have been intended to propitiate him, though it seems to have had the opposite effect.

had done so he seized her and put her into a barrel (*pipa*) [1] which he was carrying.

He then set off on his travels, and when he came to a village made for the place of meeting [2] and announced that he was prepared to give a musical entertainment in return for a meal. "I have this drum of mine. I should like a fowl and rice." He beat the drum, and the imprisoned child sang in time to the rhythm, to the delight of every one. He was given plenty of food, but gave none to the girl. He went on and repeated his performance at the next village, which happened to be the girl's own home. The report of his music seems to have preceded him, for the people said, "We have heard, O *zimwi*, that you have a most beautiful drum; now, please, play to us!" He asked for *pombe* (native beer), and, being promised that he should have some, began to beat the drum, and the girl sang. Her parents at once recognized her voice, and when the performance was over supplied the drummer with all the liquid refreshment he required. He soon went to sleep, and they opened the drum, released their daughter, and hid her in the inner compartment of the hut. They then put into the drum a snake and a swarm of bees and some biting ants, and fastened it up again.

In the Sesuto and Xosa versions the parents, instead of making the ogre drunk, induce him to go to the stream for water, and give him a leaky pot in order to delay his return as long as possible. In one case they put in a dog as well as the venomous ants, in the other snakes and toads, the latter being supposed poisonous.

After a while they awakened him, saying, "Ogre, wake up! Some strangers have arrived, and they want to hear

[1] Later on it is called a drum (*ngoma*), as it is in Dudley Kidd's story of "The Child in the Drum," in *Savage Childhood*, p. 233. In this the child is said to be a boy; but I cannot help thinking this is a mistake. Europeans seem to take for granted that a child is masculine unless otherwise specified.

[2] Called by Duff Macdonald the 'Forum'; in Chinyanja *bwalo*; in Swahili *baraza*. It is sometimes merely an open space under the village fig-tree, sometimes an erection like a bandstand, sometimes a more ambitious structure, with seats for the elders, who hold their discussions there. Strangers arriving at a village always make for this place.

your music." So he lifted his drum and began to beat it, but the voice was silent. He went on beating, but no other sound was heard, and at last he took his leave, and was not pressed to stay.

When he had gone a certain distance and was no longer in sight of the village he stopped and opened his drum. Immediately the snake shot out and bit him, the bees stung him, and he died.

The Baleful Pumpkin

But that was not the end of him. On the spot where he died there sprang up a pumpkin-vine, which bore pumpkins of unusual size. One day some small boys passing by stopped to admire them, and, prompted by the destructive instinct which seems to be inherent in the very young of all climes, exclaimed, " Jolly fine pumpkins, these ! Let's get father's sword and have a slash at them ! "

The largest of the pumpkins waxed wroth and chased the children—breaking off its stem and rolling over and over, one must suppose—and they took to their heels. In their headlong flight they came to a river, and saw the old ferry-man sitting on the bank by his canoe.

" You, Daddy, ferry us over ! Take us to the other side ! We are running away from a pumpkin."

The old man, without waiting for explanations, took them across, and they ran on till they came to a village, and found all the men sitting in the *baraza*, to whom they appealed : " Hide us from that pumpkin ! The *zimwi* has turned into a pumpkin. You will just have to take it and burn it with fire."

No doubt this version has lost some particulars in transmission ; the whole neighbourhood must have known the story, and been aware that the pumpkin-plant had grown out of the *zimwi's* remains ; one may guess that the boys had, over and over again, been told not to go near it, and, boylike, were all the more attracted to the forbidden thing.

The men seem at once to have appreciated the danger ;

they hurried the boys off into a hut and told them to keep quiet behind the partition at the back. Presently the pumpkin arrived. It is not explained how it had crossed the river, but in such a case one marvel the more is easily taken for granted. It spoke with a human voice, saying, " Have you seen my people [*i.e.*, my slaves] who are running away?"

The village elders, who by this time had returned to their seats and were deliberately taking snuff, asked, " What are your people like? We don't know anything about them." But the pumpkin was not to be put off. " You have them shut up inside the hut ! "

Then the old headman gave the word, two or three strong men seized the pumpkin, chopped it to pieces, and built a roaring fire, in which it was consumed to ashes. They scattered the ashes, and then released the boys, who went home to their mothers.

We have already referred to versions in which the dead ogre turns into a tree; in a Kiniramba story [1] collected by Mr Frederick Johnson a porcupine, which seems to partake of the nature of an ogre or some other uncanny being, is killed and buried under the fireplace. " In the morning they found a pumpkin growing." This began by speaking, repeating everything that was said in its presence, and ended by swallowing all the people in the village. The Shambala people also have a story in which a pumpkin figures as the Swallowing Monster—but here nothing is said about its origin.

To return to the story of the ogre, some other versions give it a more dramatic ending. In these he reaches his home, hands the bag to his wife, and tells her to open it and cook the food. She refuses, on finding that " the bag bites "; so, in turn, do his daughter and his son. He shuts himself into the hut and opens the bag, with the result already related; but instead of expiring on the spot he forces his way out, and throws himself head first into a pool, or a marsh, out of which a tree subsequently grows.

[1] *Kiniramba Folk-tales*, p. 334.

The Magic Flight

The second of the types mentioned above is well exemplified by the story of Sikulumi, which is told, without much variation in its main features, by Zulus, Xosas, Basuto, and Baronga.

One day a number of men seated by the fence of the chief's cattle-fold saw several birds of a kind they had never seen before perched on a tree not far off. The chief's son, Sikulumi, said, " These are indeed beautiful birds. I want to catch one and make a plume for my head [*isidhodhlo*] of his feathers."

So he and some friends set off in pursuit of the birds, which had already flown away while they were seizing their knobkerries. They followed them across country for a long time, and at last succeeded in knocking down several. By this time the sun had set, and they were far from home; but as darkness fell they perceived the glimmer of a distant fire, and made for it straightway. When they came up with it they found it was burning in an empty hut, which, though they could not know it, belonged to some *amazimu*. They went in and made themselves at home, plucked their birds, roasted, and ate them, after cutting off the heads, which Sikulumi arranged all round the ledge of the hut. Then they made plumes out of the feathers, and when they had done so went to sleep—all but Sikulumi.

In the middle of the night an ogre arrived, having left his fellows at a distance, and Sikulumi heard him muttering to himself, " Something smells very good here in my house ! "[1] He looked at the sleepers, one by one—Sikulumi, of course, pretending to be asleep—and said, " I will begin with this one, I will eat that one next, and then that one, and finish up with him whose little feet are white from walking through the sand ! "[2] He then caught sight of the birds' heads, crunched them up, and swallowed them, before starting off to call the other ogres to the feast.

---

[1] *Endhlini yami lapa kwanuka 'zantungwana !* Some versions make him say, " I smell human flesh."

[2] In the Ronga version he says, " . . . I shall get fat right down to my little toe ! "

THE AMAZIMU

Sikulumi at once roused his friends and told them what had happened, and they, picking up their plumes and their sticks, set off for home, running for all they were worth. They had gone quite a long way when Sikulumi remembered suddenly that he had left his plume behind. His friends said, " Don't go back. Take one of ours. Why should you go where cannibals are? " But he persisted. He took his stick, rubbed it with ' medicine,' and planted it upright in the ground, saying, " If this stick falls over without rising again you will know that I am dead, and you must tell my father when you get home. As long as it stands firm I am safe; if it shakes you will know that I am running for my life."

Meanwhile the ogre had come back with his friends, and when they found no one in the hut they were furious with him for cheating them, so they killed and ate him.

On his way back to the hut Sikulumi saw an old woman sitting by a big stone beside the path. She asked him where he was going, and he told her. She gave him some fat, and said, " If the ogres come after you put some of this on a stone." He reached the hut, and found a whole party seated round the fire, passing his plume from hand to hand. On the fire a large pot was boiling, in which they were cooking toads.[1] Sikulumi sprang in among them, snatched his plume from an old hag who happened to be holding it at that moment, and at the same time shattered the pot with a blow of his knobkerrie, scattering the toads all over the floor. While the ogres were occupied in picking them up he made his escape. They were not long, however, in following him, and when he saw them he did as the friendly old woman had told him and threw some of the fat on a stone. When the ogres came up to this stone they began (it is not explained why) to fight for the possession of it. One of them swallowed it, whereupon the others killed and ate him. Sikulumi thus

---

[1] Is this significant? I do not remember to have seen it noticed by any writer on folklore; but a Nyasaland native told me that witches, at certain seasons, eat frogs (or toads) as a part of their magical practices. The incident of the stone, a little farther on, is not easy to understand.

gained some advantage, but soon they had nearly come up with him again. He threw some more fat on a stone, and the same thing happened as before. Again they started after him, and this time he threw down his skin cloak, which began to run off by itself. The ogres ran after it, and were so long catching it that he was able to rejoin his friends, and they all made their way home.

Here, properly, the story comes to an end, but the Baronga add another adventure at a cannibal village, and the Xosa version [1] gives the further incident of the ogres again nearly coming up with them and being baffled by a " little man " (not accounted for by the narrator) who turned a large stone into a hut. They took refuge in it, and the ogres, to whom the outside still looked like a stone, tried to bite it, till they broke all their teeth and went away.

The young men then reached their own village, and found that it had been swallowed up, with all its inhabitants, except one old woman, by a monster called an *inabulele*. This episode really belongs to another story, which will be dealt with in a later chapter. The tale then goes on to relate Sikulumi's courtship and marriage to the daughter of Mangangezulu. It is not said that her family are cannibals, though " no one ever leaves the place of Mangangezulu," as they seem to be in the habit of killing strangers. By the help of a friendly mouse Sikulumi escapes with the girl, and she takes with her " an egg, a milksack, a pot, and a smooth stone." When she throws down the first it produces a thick mist, the milksack becomes a lake, the pot darkness, and the stone a huge rock. Thus the pursuers are baffled, and he reaches his home in safety.

The Ogre Husband

From the Duruma, a tribe living inland from Mombasa to the west and north-west, comes the story of " Mbodze and the *Zimwi*," which forms a good illustration of our third type.

There was a girl named Mbodze, who had a younger

[1] Theal, *Kaffir Folklore*, p. 78.

sister, Matsezi, and a brother, Nyange. She went one day, with six other girls, to dig clay—either for plastering the huts or for making pots, which is usually women's work. There was a stone in the path, against which one after the other stubbed her toes; Mbodze, coming last, picked up the stone and threw it away. It must be supposed that the stone was an ogre who had assumed this shape for purposes of his own; for when the girls came back with their loads of clay they found that the stone had become a huge rock, so large that it shut out the view of their village, and they could not even see where it ended. When they found that they could not get past it the foremost in the line began to sing:

> "Stone, let me pass, O stone! It is not I who threw you away, O stone!
> She who threw you away is Mbodze, Matsezi's sister,
>   And Nyange is her brother."

The rock moved aside just enough to let one person pass through, and then closed again. The second girl sang the same words, and was allowed to pass, and so did the rest, till it came to Mbodze's turn. She, too, sang till she was tired, but the rock did not move. At last the rock turned into a *zimwi*—or, rather, we may suppose, he resumed his proper shape—seized hold of Mbodze, and asked her, "What shall I do with you? Will you be my child, or my wife, or my sister, or my aunt?" She answered, "You may do what you like with me." So he said, "I will make you my wife"; and he carried her off to his house.

There was a wild fig-tree growing in front of the *zimwi's* house. Mbodze climbed up into it, and sang:

> "Matsezi, come, come! Nyange, come, come!"

But Matsezi and Nyange could not hear her.

She lived there for days and months, and the *zimwi* kept her well supplied with food, till he thought she was plump enough to be eaten. Then he set out to call the other ogres, who lived a long way off and were expected to bring their own firewood with them. No sooner had he gone than there appeared a *chitsimbakazi*,[1] like the friendly gnome in the Lamba story, who, by some magic art, put Mbodze into a hollow bamboo and stopped up the opening with wax. She then collected everything in the house except a cock, which she was careful to leave behind, spat in every room, including the kitchen, and on both the doorposts, and started.

Before she had gone very far she met the ogres, coming along the path in single file, each one carrying his log of wood on his head. The first one stopped her, and asked, "Are you Marimira's wife?"—Marimira being the ogre, Mbodze's husband.

She sang in answer, "I am not Marimira's wife: Marimira's wife has not a swollen mouth [like me [2]]. *Ndi ndi!* this great bamboo!"

At each *ndi* she struck the bamboo on the ground, to show that it was hollow, and the ogre, seeing that the upper end was closed with wax, suspected nothing and passed on.

The other ogres now passed her, one after another. The second was less easily satisfied than the first had been, and insisted on having the bamboo unstopped, but when he heard a great buzzing of bees [3] he said hastily, "Close it! Close it!" The same happened with all the rest, except the last, who was Marimira himself. He asked the same question as the others, and was answered in the same way, and then said, "What are you carrying in that stick? Unstop it and let me see!" The sprite, recognizing him, said to herself, "Now this is the end! It is Marimira; I must be very cunning," and she sang:

> "I am carrying honey, *ka-ya-ya!*
> I am carrying honey, brother, *ka-ya-ya!*
> *Ndi ndi!* this great bamboo!"

[1] This sprite will come into the next chapter. There is usually no indication as to its sex, unless we can infer it from the termination *-kazi*, which in some languages is a feminine suffix. But in a Swahili story very like this one the helpful being is expressly said to be "a little old woman."

[2] The appearance of the *chitsimbakazi* is not described, but one may assume that it had some sort of a snout, like an animal.

[3] These bees are not accounted for; the text says simply: "The bees buzzed at him—*who-o-o-o!*" Perhaps we are to suppose that the sprite had filled up the top end of the bamboo with honeycomb, and that the bees hatched out inside!

But he kept on insisting that he must see, and at last she took out the wax: the bees swarmed out and began to settle upon him, and he cried in a panic, *"Funikia! funikia!* Shut them up!"

So he passed on with his guests, and the sprite went on her way.

The ogres reached Marimira's house, and he called out, *"Mbodze!"* The spittle by the doorposts answered, *"He-e!"* He then cried, "Bring some water!" and a voice from inside answered, "Presently!" He got angry, and, leaving the others seated on the mats, went in and searched through the whole house, finding no one there and hearing nothing but the buzzing of flies. Terrified—and, as will be seen, not without reason—at the thought of the guests who would feel themselves to have been brought on false pretences, he dug a hole to hide in and covered himself with earth—but his one long tooth projected above the soil.

It will be remembered that a cock had been left in the house when everything else was removed; and this cock now began to crow, *"Kokoikoko-o-o!* Father's tooth is outside!"

The guests, waiting outside, wondered. "Hallo! Listen to that cock. What is he saying?" "Come! Go in and see what Marimira is doing in there, for the sun is setting, and we have far to go!" So they searched the house, and, coming upon the tooth, dug him up and dragged him outside, where they killed, roasted, and ate him—all but his head. While doing so they sang:

"Him who shall eat the head, we will eat him too."

After a while one of them bit off a piece from the head; the others at once fell upon him and ate him. This went on till only one was left. He fixed up a rope to make a swing and climbed into it, but the rope was not strong enough; it broke, and he fell into the fire. "And he began to cry out, *'Maye! Maye!* [Mother!] I'm dying!' And he started to chew himself there in the fire," and so perished.

This incident is somewhat puzzling; it may be a

misunderstood report of an episode in another story [1] in which the ogre tries to trick his victim by inducing him to get into a swing fixed above a boiling cauldron, but is caught in his own trap. The swing is quite a popular amusement in Africa, wherever children can get a rope fixed to a convenient branch of a tree.

Meanwhile the *chitsimbakazi* had reached Mbodze's home. A little bird flew on ahead, perched outside the house, and sang :

> " Mother, sweep the yard! Mbodze is coming! "

The mother said, " Just listen to that bird! What does it say? It is telling us to sweep the yard, because Mbodze is coming." So she set to work at once, and presently the sprite arrived and said, " Let me have a bath, and then I will give you your daughter."

She gave her a bath and rubbed her with oil and cooked gruel for her. The sprite said, " Don't pour it into a big dish for me ; put it into a coconut shell," which the woman did. When the *chitsimbakazi* had eaten she unstopped the bamboo and let Mbodze out, to the great joy of the whole family, who could not do enough to show their gratitude.

The Were-wolf Husband

The ogre as bridegroom appears in a Chaga story, of a kind found all over Africa,[2] and told to warn girls against being overhard to please in the choice of a husband. But the wooer is not so often called an ogre, as such, as a lion, a hyena, or a leopard, who has assumed a man's shape for the time being. Some of these stories are more detailed than the one I am about to give, and will come better into the next chapter.

There was once a girl who refused to marry.[3] Her

---

[1] Steere, *Swahili Tales*, p. 383 : " The Spirit and the Sultan's Son."

[2] Thus by the Ewe on the Gold Coast, the Ikom, the Hausa, and others. English-speaking people in Sierra Leone call the ogre the Devil (the story is headed " Marry the Devil, there's the Devil to pay "), but such a person is not known to Africans, unless they have heard of him from white people.

[3] Gutmann, *Volksbuch*, p. 75.

PREPARATIONS FOR A ZULU WEDDING
Photo Mariannhill Mission

parents, too, discouraged all wooers who presented themselves, as they said they would not give their daughter to any common man. (This is an unusual touch: in most tales of this kind it is the parents who remonstrate and the girl who is wilful.)

On a certain day the sword-dance was going on at this girl's village, and men came from the whole countryside to take part in it. Among the dancers there appeared a tall and handsome young man, wearing a broad ring like a halo round his head, who drew all eyes by his grace and noble bearing. The maiden fell in love with him at first sight, and her parents also approved of him. The dancing went on for several days, during which time she scarcely took her eyes off him. But one day, as he happened to turn his back, she caught sight of a second mouth behind his head, and said to her mother, " That man is a *rimu*! " They would not believe it. " That fine fellow a *rimu*! Nonsense! Just you go with him and let him eat you, that's all ! "

The suitor presented himself in due course, and the marriage took place. After spending some days with the bride's parents the couple left for their home. But her brothers, knowing the husband to be a *rimu*, felt uneasy, and followed them, without their knowledge, keeping in the bushes alongside the path. When they had gone some distance the husband stopped and said, " Look back and tell me if you can still see the smoke from your father's hut." She looked, and said that she could. They went on for another hour or two, and then he asked her if she could see the hills behind her home. She said yes, and again they went on. At last he asked her again if she could see the hills, and when he found that she could not said, " What will you do now? I am a *rimu*. Climb up into this tree and weep your last tears, for you must die ! "

But her brothers, watching their chance, shot him with poisoned arrows, and he died. She came down from the tree, and the brothers took her home.

CHAPTER XIII: OF WERE-WOLVES, HALF-MEN, GNOMES, GOBLINS, AND OTHER MONSTERS

WERE-WOLVES is a term used for convenience, as being most familiar, but there are no wolves in Africa, at any rate south of the Sahara. It is the hyena (called 'wolf' by South Africans), the lion, and the leopard who have the unpleasant habit of assuming at will the human form or, which comes to the same thing, sorcerers have the power of turning themselves into these animals; and some tribes even have the strange notion that a course of treatment with certain medicines will enable a person to take after his death the shape of any animal he wishes.

I have already referred to the numerous stories of which the theme is the "Robber (or Demon) Bridegroom." In one collected by R. E. Dennett on the Lower Congo the original idea seems to have dropped out of sight: the chief character is simply called a 'robber' (*mpunia*); and in Dr Doke's book [1] he is a *chiwanda*,[2] which this writer translates 'devil'—a word I prefer to avoid in discussing African beliefs.

"The Choric Story of the Lion," also given by Dr Doke,[3] is a fairly good specimen of this type, but is without the usual opening. Most stories of this kind begin by saying that a girl refused every offer of marriage, sometimes imposing a difficult, or even impossible, condition on her suitors.

The Girl who married a Lion

A lion "went to a village of human beings and married." It is not expressly said that he changed his shape, but this seems to be implied in the following sentence: "And the

---

[1] *Lamba Folklore*, p. 85.

[2] The Balamba distinguish between *chiwanda* ('demon or evil spirit'), *sisimwe* ('ogre'), *mukupe* ('goblin,' 'half-man,' also called *mupisi* and *chinkuwaila*), and *akachekulu* (pl. *utuchekulu*) ('gnome').

[3] *Lamba Folklore*, p. 107.

people thought that maybe it was but a man and not a wild creature."

In due course the couple had a child. Some time after this the husband proposed that they should visit his parents, and they set out, accompanied by the wife's brother. In several parallel stories a younger brother or sister of the bride desires to go with her, and when she refuses follows the party by stealth, but there is no indication of this here.

At the end of the first day's journey they all camped in the forest, and the husband cut down thorn-bushes and made a kraal (*mutanda*), after which he went away, saying that he was going to catch some fish in the river. When he was gone the brother said to his sister, " He has built this kraal very badly," and he took his axe and cut down many branches, with which to strengthen the weak places.

Meanwhile the husband had gone to seek out his lion relations, and when they asked him, " How many animals have you killed? " he replied, " Two and a young one." When darkness fell he " had become a huge male lion," and led the whole clan (with a contingent of hyenas) to attack his camp. Those inside heard the stealthy footfalls and sat listening. The lions hurled themselves on the barrier, trying to break through, but it was too strong, and they fell back, wounded with the thorns. He who by day had been the husband growled : "*M* . . .," and the baby inside the kraal responded : "*M* . . ." Then the mother sang :

> " The child has bothered me with crying; watch the dance!
> Walk with a stoop; watch the dance! "

The were-lion's father, quite disgusted, said, " You have brought us to a man who has built a strong kraal ; we cannot eat him." And as day was beginning to break they all retired to the forest.

When it was light the husband came back with his fish, and said that he had been detained, adding, " You were nearly eaten," meaning that his absence had left them exposed to danger. It seems to be implied that the others were taken in by his excuses, but the brother, at any rate, must have had his suspicions. When the husband had gone off again, ostensibly to fish, he said, " See, it was that husband of yours who wanted to eat us last night." So he went and walked about, thinking over the position. Presently he saw the head of a gnome (*akachekulu*) projecting from a cleft in a tree; it asked him why he had come, and, on being told, said, "You are already done for; your brother-in-law is an ogre that has finished off all the people in this district." The creature then asked him to sweep out the midden inside his house [1]—and after he had done so told him to cut down the tree, which it then hollowed out and made into a drum, stretching two prepared skins over the ends. It then slung the drum round the man's waist, and said, " Do as if you were going to do this "—that is, raise himself from the ground. And, behold, he found himself rising into the air, and he reached the top of a tree. The gnome told him to jump down, and he did so quite easily. Then it said, "Put your sister in the drum and go home." So he called her, and, having stowed her in it, with the baby, rose up and sat in the tree-top, where he began to beat the drum. The lion, hearing the sound, followed it, and when he saw the young man in the tree said, " Brother-in-law, just beat a little "; so the man beat the drum and sang:

> " *Boom, boom* sounds the little drum
>   Of the sounding drum, sounds the little drum!
> Ogre,[2] dance, sounds the little drum
>   Of the sounding drum, sounds the little drum! "

The lion began to dance, and the skins he was wearing fell off and were blown away by the wind, and he had to go back and pick them up. Meanwhile the drum carried the fugitives on, and the lion pursued them as soon as he had recovered his skins. Having overtaken them, he called up into the tree, "Brother-in-law, show me my child!" and the following dialogue took place:

" What, you lion, am I going to show you a relation of mine? "

[1] Meaning, evidently, the hollow tree!
[2] It is noticeable that the name *sisimwe* is here applied to the lion.

" Would I eat my child? " conveniently ignoring the fact that he had himself announced the killing of " the young one."

" How about the night you came? You would have eaten us ! "

Again the brother-in-law beat the drum, and the lion danced (apparently unable to help himself), and as before lost his skins, stopped to pick them up, and began the chase again, while the man went springing along the tree-tops like a monkey. At last he reached his own village, and " his mother saw as it were a swallow settle in the court-yard " of his home. She said, " Well, I never ! Greeting, my child ! " and asked where his sister was. He frightened her at first by telling her that she had been eaten by her husband, who was really a lion, but afterwards relented and told her to open the drum. Her daughter came out with the baby, safe and sound, and the mother said, praising her son, " You have grown up ; you have saved your sister ! " She gave him five slave-girls—a form of wealth still accepted in Lambaland not so very long ago.

The lion had kept up the pursuit, and reached the out-skirts of the village, but, finding that his intended victims were safe within the stockade, he gave up and returned to the forest.

The Hyena Bridegroom

A story from Nyasaland is different enough from the above to be interesting. I was told it, many years ago, by a bright little boy at Blantyre ; but, as might be expected, he did not know it perfectly, and very likely I missed some points in writing it down from his dictation. I have therefore pieced it out from another version, written out much later by a Nyanja man, Walters Saukila, which clears up several difficult points.

There was a girl in a certain village who refused all suitors, though several very decent young men had presented them-selves. Her parents remonstrated in vain ; she only said, " I don't like the young men of our neighbourhood ; if one came from a distance I might look at him!" So they left off asking for her, and she remained unmarried for an unusually long time.

One day a handsome stranger arrived at the village and presented himself to the girl's parents. He had all the appearance of a rich man; he was wearing a good cloth, had ivory bracelets on his arms, and carried a gun and a powder-horn curiously ornamented with brass wire. The maiden exclaimed, on seeing him, "This is the one I like!" Her father and mother were more doubtful, as was natural, since no one knew anything about him; but in spite of all they could say she insisted on accepting him. He was, in fact, a hyena, who had assumed human shape for the time being.

The usual marriage ceremonies took place, and the husband, in accordance with Yao and Nyanja custom, settled down at the village of his parents-in-law, and made himself useful in the gardens for the space of several months. At the end of that time he said that he had a great wish to visit his own people. His wife, whom he had purposely refrained from asking, begged him to let her accompany him. When all was ready for the journey her little brother, who was suffering from sore eyes, said he wanted to go too; but his sister, ashamed to be seen in company with such an object, refused him sharply. He waited till they had started, and then followed, keeping out of sight, till he was too far from home to be sent back.

They went on for many days, and at last arrived at the hyenas' village, where the bride was duly welcomed by her husband's relations. She was assigned a hut to sleep in, but, to keep her brother out of the way, she sent him into the hen-house.

In the middle of the night, when she was asleep, the people of the village took their proper shape and, called together by the hyena husband, marched round the hut, chanting:

"*Timdye nyama, sananone!*"
["Let us eat the game, but it is not fat yet."]

The little boy in the hen-house was awake and heard

them; his worst fears were confirmed. (W. Saukila says: "Though that one was small as to his size, he was of surpassing sense.") In the morning he told his sister what he had heard, but she would not believe him. So he told her to tie a string to her toe and put the end outside where he could get it. This he drew into the hen-house, and that night, when the hyenas began their march, he pulled the string, and awakened his sister. She was now thoroughly frightened, and when he asked her next morning, "Did you hear them, sister?" she had nothing more to say.

The Magic Boat

The boy then went to his brother-in-law and asked him for the loan of an axe and an adze. The man (as he appeared to be), who had no notion that he was detected and every reason to show himself good-natured, consented at once, and watched him going off into the bush, well pleased that the child should amuse himself.

The latter soon found and cut down a tree such as he needed, and then began to shape a thing which he called *nguli* [1]—something in the nature of a small boat. When he had finished it he got into it and sang:

> " *Chinguli changa delu-delu!*
> *Chinguli changa delu-delu!* "
> [" My boat! swing! swing!"]

And the *nguli* began to rise up from the earth. As he went on singing it rose higher and higher, till it floated above the tops of the tallest trees. The hyena-villagers all rushed out to gaze at this wonder, and the boy's sister came with them. Then he sang once more:

> " *Chinguli changa, tsikatsika de-de, tsikatsika!* "
> [" My boat! come down! down, *de-de!* [expressive of descending] come down! "]

---

[1] *Nguli* is properly a spinning-top—a toy very popular in African villages. *Chinguli*, the word used later on, means a large *nguli*. This object has hitherto been a great puzzle. The Rev. H. B. Barnes (*Nyanja-English Vocabulary*) says, " *Chinguli* in a native story apparently plays the part of the ' magic carpet ' in the *Arabian Nights*." The explanation that it was " like a canoe to look at " is due to Walters Saukila.

And it floated gently down to the ground. The people were delighted, and cried out to him to go up again. He made some excuse for a little delay, and whispered to his sister to get her bundle (which, no doubt, she had ready) and climb in. She did so, and when both were safely stowed he sang his first song once more. Again the vessel rose, and this time did not come down again. The spectators, after waiting in vain, began to suspect that their prey was escaping, and shouted to the boy to come back, but no attention was paid to them, and the *nguli* quickly passed out of sight. Before the day was out they found themselves above the courtyard of their home, and the boy sang the words which caused them to descend, so that they alighted on their mother's grain-mortar. The whole family came running out and overwhelmed them with questions; the girl could not speak for crying with joy and relief, and her brother told the whole story, winding up with: " Look here, sister, you thought I was no good, because I had sore eyes—but who was it heard them singing, 'Let us eat her !' and told you about it? " The parents, too, while praising the boy, did not fail to point the moral for the benefit of their foolish daughter, who, some say, had to remain unmarried to the end of her days.

Anyone who has heard a native story-teller chant *Chinguli changa* cannot help wondering whether we have a far-off echo of it in Uncle Remus's " Ingle-go-jang, my joy, my joy ! " though it occurs in an entirely different story.

The Half-men

Some of the *amazimu*, as stated in the last chapter, are described as having only half a body, but this by no means applies to all of them, and there is a distinct set of half-beings who cannot be classed as ogres.

In Nyasaland a being called Chiruwi is, or was, believed to haunt lonely places in the forest, carrying an axe. He has one eye, one arm, one leg, the other half of his body being made of wax. He challenges any man he meets to wrestle with him; if the man can overcome him he offers

POUNDING MAIZE
Photo Dr Clement M. Doke

to show him "many medicines" if he will let him go, and tells him the properties of the various trees and herbs. But if the man is thrown " he returns no more to his village; he dies."

A little boy at Ntumbi, in the West Shire district, told me a curious story in which " a big bird," with one wing, one eye, and one leg, carried some children across a flooded river.

In a tale of the Bechuana, which is something like this, the children are pursued by an ogre, take refuge up a tree, and are rescued before he is able to cut it down by a " great thing called *Phuku-phuku*," which is not further described. What seems to be a parallel version attributes the rescue to " a great bird," which " hovered over them and said, ' Hold fast to me.' " There is no indication that this bird was without the usual number of wings and legs ; but it is quite evident that he is, as the editor of the South African *Folk-Lore Journal* [1] remarks, "a personage worth studying."

A fuller form of the story, however, was obtained by the Rev. C. Hoffmann among the Bapedi in the Transvaal. But even this throws no light on the bird's nature ; he is simply called *nonyana votze*, " a beautiful bird," and carries the children home under his wings. In retelling it in a more popular form for young readers [2] Mr Hoffmann calls him a peacock, and represents him as such in his illustration ; but this must be a picturesque addition of his own, for the peacock was quite unknown in South Africa till introduced by Europeans, and it is very unlikely that the original narrators had ever heard of it.

The Baronga tell of a village of "one-legged people" (*mangabangabana*), who also possess wings, or, at any rate, the power of flying. They seem to be quite distinct from ogres—called in Ronga simply "eaters of men," though they sometimes have another name, *switukulumukumba*. A girl who escapes from the cannibals' village is, later on, carried off by the flying half-men ; but there is no suggestion that they intend to eat her.

[1] Vol. i, Part I, January 1879, p. 16.   [2] *Afrikanischer Grossvater*, p. 5.

In the story of Namachuke, however, the one-legged beings are certainly cannibal ogres. Part of this story is much like that given in the last chapter, of the girl escaping from the ogre's house; but the opening is different, and there is also an unexpected sequel: Namachuke and her co-wives are beguiled by curiosity into leaving their home and following the monsters, and are devoured, together with the unfortunate children who have come to look for them.

Similarly, the Zulu *amadhlungundhlebe*, who had only one leg, were said to be man-eaters.

But these are exceptions: the genuine half-men are more akin to Chiruwi, though their character varies; some are merely terrifying, like the one formerly believed to haunt the Cameroons Mountain, to see whom was death.

Sechobochobo of the Baila is " a kind of wood-sprite, described as a man with one arm and one eye, living in the forest; he brings good luck to those who see him; he takes people and shows them trees in the forest which can serve as medicines.

But the accounts of this being would seem to vary, for elsewhere we read, " If one chances to see it he will die."

Sikulokobuzuka

The Basubiya say that Sikulokobuzuka is wax on one side of him; the leg on the other is like that of an animal. Some say that he has a wife and children, in form like himself. He lives on wild honey, and is reported to have a hut made of elephants' tusks and python skins, but his village, where are stored many pots of honey, meat, and fat, is invisible to human eyes. His axe and spears are made of wax. The account given to M. Jacottet by Kabuku, a young man of the Subiya tribe, scarcely bears out the statement made by some that it is death to meet Sikuloko-buzuka—fortunately, he has a shorter name, Chilube, which will be more convenient to use. A certain man, Mashambwa,[1] told Kabuku that while looking for honey in

---

[1] " Textes Subiya," No. 47, p. 138.

200

the forest he heard a honey-guide calling; he whistled to it, and it led him to a tree containing a bees' nest. He lit a torch, climbed the tree, smoked the bees out, and had just taken the honey, when he saw Chilube approaching. He came down, carrying his honey on a wooden platter, and met Chilube, who at once demanded it. Mashambwa refused, and Chilube said, "Come, then, let us wrestle." They did so, Mashambwa taking care to get his opponent off the grass and on to a sandy place, where, after a long struggle, he succeeded in throwing him. He said, "Shall I kill you?" and Chilube replied, "Don't kill me, my chief, and I will get you the medicine for bewitching people and killing them." Mashambwa said, "I don't want that," and Chilube said, "There is another, which helps you to get plenty of meat." He agreed to accept this, and Chilube said, "Let me go, and I will get it for you." So he showed him all the herbs and trees which possessed healing properties or were good as charms for luck in hunting, or finding food in other ways, or for gaining the favour of one's chief.

Mashambwa set off homeward, but soon lost his way and wandered about till he once more met Chilube, who guided him to his village, telling him that he must not speak to anyone or answer if spoken to. This seems to have been a recognized rule, for when Mashambwa reached home and the people found that he did not respond to their greetings they knew that he had met Chilube, and let him alone, but built a hut for him in a place apart.

Mashambwa lay ill in that hut for a whole year. Chilube arrived as soon as those who had built it had left, and thenceforth came regularly, bringing him food and medicine. At last he recovered, and, looking out over the forest one day, saw a number of vultures. This appears to have been the sign that his period of silence and seclusion was over, for he called out, "Look at my vultures over there!" and the villagers went to the spot and found a freshly killed animal. So they brought back the meat and gave him some, and he ate with them and took up his old life again.

After this it seems hardly fair to dismiss Chilube as "cruel

and wicked " or " a strange and maleficent being " (in
M. Jacottet's words, "*être étrange et malfaisant*"). Nor is it
apparent why an up-to-date hunter, meeting Chilube in the
forest, should, without provocation, have pointed his gun
at him and set his dogs on him. Chilube fled—he is said
(not unnaturally) to fear dogs and guns—and one would not
be surprised to learn that no more medicines were shown to
people in that neighbourhood.

In Angola [1] we find that Fenda Madia is helped by an
old woman with " one arm, one leg, one side of face, and
one side of body," and among the Wangonde a similarly
formed old woman takes some girls across a river.

There is a curious development of the same notion in
a story about a jealous woman who tricked her co-wife into
throwing away her baby. When she found out that the
mother had recovered her child and received rich gifts in
addition she threw her own baby into the river—and
recovered it, indeed, but only to find that it had but half
a body.[2]

There is a strange legend of the Wagogo to the effect
that the first heaven (there are four in all, one above the
other) is inhabited by half-beings of this kind ; I do not
know whether such a notion has been recorded elsewhere.

Perhaps the lake-god Mugasha, on the Victoria Nyanza,
who has only one leg, should be mentioned in this connexion ; and I recall a curious statement made by a Giryama,
Aaron Mwabaya, at Kaloleni in 1912 : " When the print
of a human foot is seen side by side with a hyena's spoor
the traces are those of a sorcerer who is on one side human,
on the other a hyena." This I have never heard elsewhere :
—people in Nyasaland had a different way of accounting
for human footprints beside a hyena's track, but that is
" another story."

Gnomes and Spirits

We have already come across Dr Doke's 'gnomes,'
fearsome beings called by the Balamba " little ancient ones,"

[1] Chatelain, *Folk-tales of Angola*, p. 32.   [2] See *ante*, p. 96.

who kill their victims with " one long tooth, blood-red and sharp." But, as we have seen in the story of the lion, they are by no means always malignant. They may be of either sex.

The *chitsimbakazi* of the Duruma perhaps belongs to the same family; their neighbours the Giryama have a *katsumbakazi*—no doubt the same word—of which W. E. Taylor remarks that it is " said to be seen occasionally in daylight. It is usually malignant." He does not describe its appearance, beyond saying that its stature is very low—a point on which it seems to be sensitive: " When it meets anyone it . . . asks him, ' Where did you see me?' If the person is so unlucky as to answer, ' Just here,' he will not live many days; but if he is aware of the danger and says, ' Oh, over yonder,' he will be left unharmed, and sometimes even something lucky will happen to him." [1]

A similar story used to be told by the Zulus of the Bushmen, only, instead of inflicting death by some occult means, they would retaliate on the spot with a poisoned arrow.

The " little people " in Nyasaland, known by a name which means " Where did you see me? " are similarly quick to resent this insult.

The forests of the Tana Valley are haunted by a thing which the Wapokomo call *kitunusi*, which behaves like Chiruwi or Chilube, though not shaped like them. As far as one can gather, its form is that of a normal human being, and it does not seem to be particularly small. There are two kinds: one walks about upright, " like a child of Adam," as my informant said, the other hitches itself about in a sitting position, though not devoid of legs. It wears a cloth of *kaniki* (dark blue cotton stuff): if anyone who wrestles with it can manage to tear off a bit of this his fortune is made: " he puts it away in his covered basket [*kidzamanda*] and becomes rich "; presumably the cloth multiplies itself, but this is not explained. Those who meet the *kitunusi* and do not stand up to it boldly are apt to

[1] *Giryama Vocabulary*, p. 32.

be stricken with paralysis in all their limbs, or with some other illness.

Two other creatures, classified by Professor Meinhof as "haunting demons" (*Spukdämonen*), are, or were some time ago, to be found in the Tana forests. One is the *ngojama*, in sight like to a man, but with a long claw (" an iron nail," say some) in the palm of his right hand. Other people, the Galla, for instance, say that the *ngojama* is simply a lion who has grown too old to hunt game and taken to eating men. This is curiously borne out by the very similar names for ' lion ' in Zulu, Herero, and Tswa[1]; in the last-named language, moreover, it is confined to man-eating lions. I was told, by Pokomo natives, a strange story about a man named Bombe, which to some slight extent resembles Mashambwa's adventure with Chilube. The *ngojama* came upon Bombe when he was up a tree taking honey, and waited to seize him when he came down, but Bombe handed him the best pieces of honeycomb, and made his escape while the monster lingered to eat them. When he saw Bombe in his canoe, half-way across the river, he stood on the bank, crying, "*Wai! wai!* If I had known I would not have eaten the honey ! " There is no suggestion of a contest (as with the *kitunusi*), and it is evident that the *ngojama* cannot swim. His last words to Bombe were, "Go! You are a man! But we shall meet another day."

The other forest-haunting bogy is the *ngoloko*, described to me as a huge serpent—so huge that when my informant's father saw him at night he took him for a great dead tree —a white bulk which would be clearly visible even without a moon. When he got nearer he saw that it was a monstrous snake, with luminous ears (a strange touch), which he had at first taken for flames. They were like the yellow flowers I had just picked from a bush—which, if I remember rightly, were something like the *Corchorus* of our gardens. This seems to have been all I could gather about the *ngoloko*. A writer in *Blackwood's Magazine*[2] some years ago

[1] The language of a tribe near Inhambane, in Portuguese East Africa.
[2] November 1917.

gave an account of what he had heard from the natives about this being, but his description rather fits the *ngojama*. He took it to be an anthropoid ape—hitherto unknown in Africa east of the Great Lakes. He was shown a print of its foot (which, in fact, seemed to show a long claw), and heard uncanny roarings at night, which people assured him were the voice of the *ngoloko*. But the print, of which a tracing was procured, was credibly pronounced to have been made by the foot of an ostrich; and the cry of the ostrich is powerful enough to be heard at a great distance, especially by night.

About the *kodoile*, also enumerated among the dangers of the Tana forests, I did not succeed in getting any information, beyond the fact that " the Swahili call it *dubu*," which is *dubb*, the Arabic name for the bear. In the Pokomo New Testament (Revelation xiii, 2) ' bear ' is translated *kodoile*, and *ngojama* is the rendering of ' dragon.' There are, so far as known at present, no bears in Africa south of the Sahara—the ' Nandi bear,' concerning which many reports have been in circulation, is now generally held to be a mythical animal. In fact, a Zanzibar man who saw a bear for the first time in his life in the London Zoo could only describe it as " the illegitimate offspring of a hyena " (*yule mwana haramu wa fisi*).

CHAPTER XIV: THE SWALLOWING MONSTER

THE legend of a monster which swallows the population of a village—or, indeed, of the whole country—and is subsequently slain by a boy hero seems to be current all over Africa. We have found part of it fitted into one of the ogre tales already dealt with, and we shall find some versions incorporating parts of stories which, strictly speaking, should be classed under other headings. McCall Theal[1] remarked:

> There is a peculiarity in many of these stories which makes them capable of almost indefinite expansion. They are so constructed that parts of one can be made to fit into parts of another, so as to form a new tale. . . . These tales are made up of fragments which are capable of a variety of combinations.[2]

This might be taken to imply that conscious invention was at work in so constructing the stories, but it is not necessary to assume that this was the writer's meaning. Classical mythology affords numerous examples of the way in which floating traditions attach themselves to each other without special intention on anyone's part. After writing has been introduced and poets have given literary form to these traditions the case is different. African folklore has not in general reached this stage.

The main points of the legend are these:

A whole population is swallowed by a monster.
One woman escapes and gives birth to a son.
This son kills the monster and releases the people.
They make him their chief.

Some versions add that the people in time become envious and plan his destruction (here the incidents resemble those of Huveane's story); and these, again, vary considerably. Some say that he triumphed over his enemies in the end; others that he was slain by them.

[1] The historian of South Africa, who also collected the folklore of the Xosas.
[2] *Kaffir Folklore*, p. vii.

In most of these legends the boy is miraculously precocious, like Hlakanyana and Kachirambe; but occasionally, like Theseus, he has to wait till he is grown up. In one his mother tells him to lift a certain stone, several years in succession, and when at last he is able to do it he is reckoned strong enough for the great enterprise.

The Whale and the Dragon

E. B. Tylor [1] was of opinion that this legend is a kind of allegorical nature-myth.

> Day is daily swallowed up by night, to be set free at dawn, and from time to time suffers a like but shorter durance in the maw of the Eclipse and the Storm-cloud. Summer is overcome and prisoned by dark Winter, but again set free. It is a plausible opinion that such scenes from the great nature-drama of the conflict of light and darkness are, generally speaking, the simple facts which in many lands and ages have been told in mythic shape, as legends of a Hero or Maiden devoured by a monster and hacked out again or disgorged.

The point is illustrated by examples from the myths of the Burman Karens, the Maoris, and the North American Indians, as well as by the stories of Ditaolane and Untombinde, about to be related here. Tylor traces to the same origin the legends of Perseus and Andromeda (ultimately modernized and Christianized as St George and the Dragon), Herakles and Hesione, and Jonah's 'whale.' This last introduces a different element, which finds a parallel in some African stories we shall have to consider in a later chapter.

But such allegorizing, as Wundt [2] has shown, is foreign to the thought of primitive people. They may think that the lightning is a bird and that an eclipse is caused by something trying to eat up the sun or moon; but this myth of day and night is too abstract a conception for them.

It may be worth noting that a Christian writer of Basutoland has made use of the Swallower legend as a dim

[1] *Primitive Culture*, vol. i, p. 334 *sqq.*
[2] *Völkerpsychologie*, vol. v, Part II, p. 268.

foreshadowing of the promise of a Redeemer.[1] In his some-what mystical story *Moeti oa Bochabela* (*The Traveller to the East*) the old men relate it to Fekisi, the young dreamer, tormented by the " obstinate questionings " of ' whence ' and ' whither.' And, indeed, it might well lend itself to such an interpretation.

Khodumodumo, or Kammapa

The Basuto tell the legend as follows.

Once upon a time there appeared in our country a huge, shapeless thing called Khodumodumo (but some people call it Kammapa). It swallowed every living creature that came in its way. At last it came through a pass in the mountains into a valley where there were several villages ; it went to one after another, and swallowed the people, the cattle, the goats, the dogs, and the fowls. In the last village was a woman who had just happened to sit down on the ash-heap. She saw the monster coming, smeared herself all over with ashes, and ran into the calves' pen, where she crouched on the ground. Khodumodumo, having finished all the people and animals, came and looked into the place, but could see nothing moving, for, the woman being smeared with ashes and keeping quite still, it took her for a stone. It then turned and went away, but when it reached the narrow pass (or *nek*) at the entrance to the valley it had swelled to such a size that it could not get through, and was forced to stay where it was.

Meanwhile the woman in the calves' pen, who had been expecting a baby shortly, gave birth to a boy. She laid him down on the ground and left him for a minute or two, while she looked for something to make a bed for him. When she came back she found a grown man sitting there, with two or three spears in his hand and a string of divining-bones (*ditaola* [2]) round his neck. She said, " Hallo, man !

---

[1] Thomas Mofolo, who has more recently written an historical romance, *Chaka*, introduced to English readers through the medium of Mr Dutton's translation.

[2] So in some versions of the story he is called Ditaolane ; in others he is merely Moshanyana, which means ' little boy.'

"He built himself a Fine Kraal"

The lower picture is from a photo by A. M. Duggan-Cronin, and is reproduced by permission of the McGregor Museum, Kimberley

Where is my child?" and he answered, "It is I, Mother!" Then he asked what had become of the people, and the cattle, and the dogs, and she told him.

"Where is this thing, Mother?"

"Come out and see, my child."

So they both went out and climbed to the top of the wall surrounding the calves' kraal, and she pointed to the pass, saying, "That object which is filling the *nek*, as big as a mountain, that is Khodumodumo."

Ditaolane got down from the wall, fetched his spears, sharpened them on a stone, and set off to the end of the valley, where Khodumodumo lay. The beast saw him, and opened its mouth to swallow him, but he dodged and went round its side—it was too unwieldy to turn and seize him—and drove one of his spears into it. Then he stabbed it again with his second spear, and it sank down and died.

He took his knife, and had already begun to cut it open, when he heard a man's voice crying out, "Do not cut me!" So he tried in another place, and another man cried out, but the knife had already slashed his leg. Ditaolane then began cutting in a third place, and a cow lowed, and some one called out, "Don't stab the cow!" Then he heard a goat bleat, a dog bark, and a hen cackle, but he managed to avoid them all, as he went on cutting, and so, in time, released all the inhabitants of the valley.

There was great rejoicing as the people collected their belongings, and all returned to their several villages praising their young deliverer, and saying, "This young man must be our chief." They brought him gifts of cattle, so that, between one and another, he soon had a large herd, and he had his choice of wives among their daughters. So he built himself a fine kraal and married and settled down, and all went well for a time.

Ingratitude of the Tribe

But the unintentionally wounded man never forgot his grudge, and long after his leg was healed began, when he noticed signs of discontent among the people, to drop a cunning word here and there and encourage those who were secretly envious of Ditaolane's good fortune, as well as those who suspected him because, as they said, he could not be a normal human being, to give voice to their feelings.

So before long they were making plans to get rid of their chief. They dug a pit and covered it with dry grass—just as the Bapedi did in order to trap Huveane—but he avoided it. They kindled a great fire in the courtyard, intending to throw him into it, but a kind of madness seized them ; they began to struggle with each other, and at last threw in one of their own party. The same thing happened when they tried to push him over a precipice; in this case he restored to life the man who was thrown over and killed.

Next they got up a big hunt, which meant an absence of several days from the village. One night when the party were sleeping in a cave they induced the chief to take the place farthest from the entrance, and when they thought he was asleep stole out and built a great fire in the cave-mouth. But, less successful than the MacLeods in the case of the MacDonalds of Eigg, when they looked round they saw him standing among them.

After this, feeling that nothing would soften their inveterate hatred, he grew weary of defeating their stratagems, and allowed them to kill him without offering any resistance. Something of the same kind is told of Chaminuka, the Prophet of the Mashona, as will be seen in due course. Some of the Basuto, when relating this story, add, "It is said that his heart went out and escaped and became a bird."

The Guardian Ox

The legend of Ditaolane, however, does not always end like this, on a bitter note of sorrow for human ingratitude. One version makes him escape from his enemies, like Hlakanyana, by turning himself into a stone, which one of them throws across a river; but this, somehow, does not seem quite in character.

THE SWALLOWING MONSTER

A Sesuto variant [1] ascribes his safety to a favourite ox, which warns him of danger, cannot be killed without its own consent, and returns to life after being slaughtered and eaten. The peculiar relationship between Ditaolane and this ox is not explained : but in a Zulu tale which resembles this episode (though it has no reference to the Swallowing Monster) the ox is said to have been born shortly before the boy and to have been brought up with him.[2] The latter, with two others of the same kind, being quite distinct from the subject of this chapter, will not be dwelt on here. In this version the conclusion is so well worked out in connexion with the earlier part that it does not strike one as a mere accidental mixing up of two stories. It seems, however, to stand alone among the many variants of the Khodumodumo legend.

A notable point is that the young man's own mother, frightened by the neighbours' talk, turns against him and tries to poison him. Warned by the ox, he refuses the bread she gives him ; his father afterwards takes it by accident and dies. The ox said : " You see, you would have died yourself ; your mother does not love you." Here, as in the case of Huveane, we see natural affection overcome by the fear of one who is regarded as an uncanny being. The circumstances of his birth would have become known, and, the villagers would argue, a being so powerful for good would be equally capable of doing harm, quite regardless of the fact that he had never given them cause to distrust him.

Untombinde and the Squatting Monster

In the Zulu tale of Untombinde the *isiququmadevu* [3] lives in the Ilulange, a mythical river not to be located nowadays. The names applied to this monster in the course of the story show that it is looked upon as a female.

A chief's daughter, Untombinde, goes, with a number of

---

[1] Jacottet, *Treasury of Ba-Suto Lore*, p. 76.
[2] Callaway, *Nursery Tales*, p. 221 : " Ubongopa ka' Magadhlela."
[3] Callaway explains this word to mean " a bloated, squatting, bearded monster."

other girls, to bathe in the Ilulange, against the warnings
of her parents : " To the Ilulange nothing goes and returns
again ; it goes there for ever." The girls found, on coming
out of the water, that the clothes and ornaments they had
left on the bank had disappeared ; they knew that the
isiququmadevu must have taken them, and one after another
petitioned politely for their return. Untombinde, however,
said, " I will never beseech the *isiququmadevu*," and was
immediately seized by the monster and dragged down into
the water.

Her companions went home and reported what had
happened. The chief, though he evidently despaired of
recovering her ("Behold, she goes there for ever ! "), sent
a troop of young men to " fetch the *isiququmadevu*, which
has killed Untombinde." The warriors found the monster
squatting on the river-bank, and were swallowed up, every
one, before they could attack her. She then went on to
the chief's kraal, swallowed up all the inhabitants, with
their dogs and their cattle, as well as all the people in the
surrounding country.

Among the victims were " two beautiful children,[1] much
beloved." Their father, however, escaped, took his two
clubs and his large spear, and went his way, saying, " It is
I who will kill the *isiququmadevu*."

By this time the monster had left the neighbourhood,
and the man went on seeking her till he met with some
buffaloes, whom he asked, " Whither has Usiququmadevu [2]
gone? She has gone away with my children ! " The
buffaloes directed him on his way, and he then came across
some leopards, of whom he asked the same question, and
who also told him to go forward. He next met an elephant,

[1] The narrator says they were twins, but nothing in the story turns on this,
which is remarkable, as twins are usually considered by the Bantu either as extremely
unlucky (in former times one of them was frequently killed) or as possessed of
abnormal powers and bringing a blessing to the family and the village.

[2] Note the different initial. *U-* is the prefix for personal names, which has not
hitherto been considered necessary ; it is used only by the father of the twins. The
buffaloes, the leopards, and the elephant, in replying, call her by three elaborate
"praise-names," with which the reader need not be troubled. The father as
deliverer is an important variation.

A Swahili and a Shehri

Photos Alice Werner

who likewise sent him on, and so at last he came upon the monster herself, and announced, " I am seeking Usiququmadevu, who is taking away my children ! " Apparently she hoped to escape recognition, for she directed him, like the rest, to " go forward." But the man was not to be deceived by so transparent a device : he " came and stabbed the lump, and so the *isiququmadevu* died."

Then all the people, cattle, and dogs, and, lastly, Untombinde herself, came out unharmed, and she returned to her father.

Her story is by no means finished, but the rest of it belongs to an entirely different set of ideas, that which is represented in European folklore by the tale of " Beauty and the Beast."

The same monster figures in the story of " Usitungusobenhle," [1] but only as the final episode. Here it is a girl who effects the deliverance. Nothing is said of her subsequent career, only : " Men again built houses and were again happy ; and all things returned to their former condition."

The Family swallowed by the Elephant

Another story,[2] which treats the theme after a somewhat different fashion (though agreeing in one point with the last), is that of a woman who rashly built her house " in the road," and left her children there while she went to look for firewood. An elephant came by and swallowed the two children, leaving a little girl who happened to be staying with them and who told the mother, on her return, what had happened. The woman (like the father in the previous tale) set out to look for the elephant, carrying provisions (a large pot containing ground maize and *amasi* [3]) and a knife. She went on her way, asking all the animals she met where she could find an elephant with one tusk, which had eaten her children. They told her to go on till

---

[1] Callaway, *Nursery Tales*, p. 84.   [2] *Ibid.*, p. 31 : " Unanana-bosele."
[3] Sour milk, a staple article of diet with the pastoral tribes of Africa. Fresh milk is not, by the Zulus at any rate, drunk by grown-up people ; but it is given to children.

she came to a place where there were white stones on the ground under some high trees. She found the elephant in the place indicated, and asked it the same question : it also told her to go on, and, when she persisted, swallowed her. Inside it " she saw large forests and great rivers and many high lands ; on one side there were many rocks ; and there were many people who had built their villages there, and many dogs and many cattle ; all were there inside the elephant ; she saw, too, her own children sitting there."

The elephant thus comes into line with Kammapa and the other monsters, though we are not in their case told anything about the country inside them. This is quite natural, as the deliverer, coming from outside, would not, of course, see anything of the interior. Tylor says that the description of the country in the elephant's stomach " is simply that of the Zulu Hades " ; but I have hitherto failed to come upon any other evidence for the country of the dead being so located.

The mother gave her children some *amasi*, and, finding that they had eaten nothing since they had been parted from her, said, " Why do you not roast this flesh ? " They said, " If we eat this beast, will it not kill us ? " She reassured them : " No, it will itself die."

She made a great fire—how we are not told ; but as she had been gathering wood she may have had some sticks of the right kind for producing sparks by friction. She then took her knife and cut pieces off the elephant's liver, which she roasted and gave to the children. The other people, who had never thought of this expedient and had likewise eaten nothing, soon followed her example, with the result that " the elephant told the other beasts, saying, ' From the time I swallowed the woman I have been ill ; there has been pain in my stomach.' " The animals could do nothing to help him, merely suggesting that the pain might be caused by his having so many people inside him, and he soon afterwards died. The woman then began to cut her way out, and before long a cow came out, saying, " *Moo, moo* ; at length we see the country ! " followed by a goat, a dog, and the people, who all, in their several ways, said the same thing. "They made the woman presents: some gave her cattle, some goats, and some sheep," and she set out for home with her children, rich for life. There she found the little girl who had been left behind and who had given her up for dead.

There is an important difference here, in that the deliverance is effected from inside, by one of the persons swallowed. In the story of "Little Red Stomach" ("Siswana Sibomvana"[1]) the boy is swallowed by a monster called "the owner of the water," but not further described, and when it died in consequence (nothing is said of his inflicting any further injury) cut his way out, and was none the worse.

But in the great majority of Bantu stories the Swallower is cut open, as by Ditaolane, and usually (though not always) by a small boy. The Zulu story last mentioned has points of contact with a curious and rather repulsive incident occurring in some of the animal tales, in which the tortoise, or some other creature, gains entrance to the body of some large animal and proceeds to eat it from the inside. We find this outside the Bantu area, among the Malinke of French West Africa and the Temne of Sierra Leone,[2] and Dr Nassau has recorded[3] from the Bantu-speaking Benga of Spanish Guinea the story of the giant goat, who was done to death through the greed of the tortoise and the leopard.

The Devouring Pumpkin

In the story of Tselane[4] it was seen that the slain ogre was changed into a tree. In "The Children and the Ogre [zimwe]"—told in Swahili, but apparently coming from the Yao tribe—a pumpkin-vine springs up on the spot where he died. This in due course produces pumpkins, and one of these, apparently offended by the remarks of some passing children, breaks off its stem and rolls after

---

[1] Theal, *Yellow and Dark-skinned People of Africa*, p. 227. Also in South African *Folk-Lore Journal*, March 1879, p. 26.

[2] Cronise and Ward, *Cunnie Rabbit*, p. 231.

[3] *Where Animals Talk*, p. 202.

[4] See *ante*, p. 180.

them. In Usambara a gourd or pumpkin appears as the
Swallowing Monster. Nothing is said as to its origin, but
a comparison with the Swahili story suggests that it may have
been the reincarnation of some ogre or wicked magician.[1]

Some little boys, playing in the gardens outside their
village, noticed a very large gourd, and said, "Just see how
big that gourd is getting!" Then the gourd spoke and
said, "If you pluck me I'll pluck you!" They went home
and told what they had heard, and their mother refused
to believe them, saying, "Children, you lie!" But their
sisters asked to be shown the place where the boys had seen
the talking gourd. It was pointed out to them, and they
at once went there by themselves, and said, as their brothers
had done, "Just see how big that gourd is getting!" But
nothing happened. They went home, and, of course, said
that the boys had been making fun of them. Then the
boys went again and heard the gourd speak as before. But
when the girls went it was silent. It would probably have
been contrary to custom for all to go together.

The gourd continued to grow: it became as big as a
house, and began swallowing all the people in the village.
Only one woman escaped—we are not told how. Having
swallowed every one within reach, the gourd made its way
into a lake and stayed there.

In a short time the woman bore a boy, and, apparently,
they lived on together on the site of the ruined village.
When the boy had grown older he asked his mother one
day where his father was. She said, "He was swallowed
up by a gourd which has gone into the lake." So he went
forth, and when he came to a lake he called out, "Gourd,
come out! Gourd, come out!" There was no answer,
and he went on to another lake and repeated his command.
He saw "one ear of the gourd" come out of the water (by
which it would appear that the gourd had by this time
assumed some sort of animal shape), and climbed a tree,
where he kept on shouting, "Gourd, come out!" At last
the gourd came out and set off in pursuit of him; but he

[1] Seidel, *Geschichten und Lieder der Afrikaner*, p. 174.

ran home and asked his mother for his bow and quiver. He hastened back, and when he came in sight of the monster loosed an arrow and hit it. He shot again and again, till, wounded by the tenth arrow, it died, roaring " so that it could be heard from here to Vuga." [1]   The boy then called to his mother to bring a knife, and the usual ending follows. It may be worth while to remark that the young chief seems to have lived out his life without further trouble.

Another Talking Pumpkin

The pumpkin-monster who swallowed up a whole population is also found, but in a totally different setting—in a Kiniramba story collected by Mr Frederick Johnson.[2] Here the first part, relating how Kiali left her husband because he had murdered her sister, and was thrown into a hole and left for dead by a porcupine on her way to her mother's village, has very little to do with the episode which mainly concerns us. The connecting-link is the porcupine, which assumed Kiali's shape and took her place in her home, till exposed by the recovery of the real Kiali. They threw it on the fire, and " it died, and they buried it in the fire-place." Next morning a pumpkin was seen growing on the spot, and, some one remarking on it, it repeated the words. Everything that was said before it it repeated, and when they brought an axe to make an end of this uncanny growth " they were swallowed, and it swallowed all the people in the land, except a woman who was with child and had hidden herself in some cave." The child, when born, asked, " Where are the people? " and, on being told, went off to forge a weapon. This boy, Mlilua, is the hero of another story where, in somewhat different circumstances, people who have been swallowed are restored to life. In this one he set out to seek the giant (*lintu*) of whom

[1] The old capital of the Shambala paramount chiefs, distant about twenty-five miles from the mission station where one gathers that the story was told.

[2] The Aniramba are to be found in the central districts of Tanganyika Territory (*Kiniramba Folk-tales*, p. 334).

his mother had told him, and brought her one animal after another (beginning with a grasshopper!), only to be told every time that this was not the right one. In the same way the lad in the Swahili tale of " Sultan Majnun " brought his mother the various animals he had killed, hoping that each one was " the Nunda, eater of people." [1]

At last Mlilua found the monster bathing, and shot an arrow at it. He went on shooting, while his mother sang, " My son, throw the spines, Kiali, hundred spines [of the porcupine]! If you do not throw to-day we shall be finished completely ! " (It is not clear whether this is a figurative expression for arrows, or whether Mlilua really shot the spines of the porcupine at the monster. The mention of the name Kiali refers to the fact that the pumpkin took its origin from the porcupine which had personated the woman Kiali.)

At last the giant's strength was exhausted, and he said to Mlilua, " When you begin cutting me begin at the back. If you cut me in front you will kill your people." Having said this, he died. Mlilua took the hint, and the people, cattle, goats, and fowls came out safely, all except one old woman, who, being in an awkward place, had her ear cut. She apparently accepted his apologies, and made some beer, which she invited him to drink. But she bewitched (poisoned?) him, and Mlilua died.

Three Variants

In the Delagoa Bay region the ' Swallowing ' (or ' Engulfing ') Monster theme is represented, in a somewhat different form, by two tales [2] : in one a little herd-boy, swallowed by a cannibal ogre, made him so uncomfortable that the ogre's own companions, with his consent, cut him open and thus released—not only the boy, but all the people and cattle previously swallowed.

In the other tale the giant Ngumbangumba is killed by the boy Bokenyane, who, like Kachirambe, is produced from an abscess on his mother's leg, but, unlike him, is followed

[1] See *infra*, p. 220.   [2] Junod, *Chants et contes*, pp. 198 and 200.

by two younger brothers. Bokenyane first hit the ogre with an arrow, and the other two went on shooting at him till he died. It was the mother who cut the body open—in this case with an axe. The conclusion is somewhat unusual. After the people had begun rebuilding their villages they asked who was their deliverer; the mother answered, " It is Bokenyane." They gave the three brothers five wives apiece, and then chose Bokenyane for their chief, because it was he who had shot the first arrow.

The other two were not pleased with this decision, and Bochurwane, the second, said, " Let me reign ! " Bokenyane refused absolutely, but his brothers dispossessed him by force, and he fled into the bush, where, in the end, he went mad.

Mrs Dewar's Chinamwanga collection[1] contains two very different versions of the same tale—one, certainly, incomplete. This one opens like " Tselane," but, as a brother and sister are concerned, it also recalls " Demane and Demazana " and the almost too well known parallel in Grimm. It begins by saying that " Once upon a time a goblin [*ichitumbu*] ate up all the people in the world. Only two remained—Nachiponda and Changala."

But when Changala had killed the goblin with his spear nothing further is recorded. When first wounded he said, " A hippo-fly has stung me "—just as Ngumbangumba, as each arrow hit him, remarked, " The mosquitoes are biting me."

The second story, called " Ichitumbu," begins and ends like most of the others, but the mother is shut up in a hut by her two sons (as Tselane is by her parents) while they go to hunt, and foolishly opens the door to the goblin. He suggests ' playing '; she wrestles with him, but is overcome and carried off. The boys come up in time, set their dogs on the goblin, and rescue her. Next day (in spite of the sons' warning) the same thing happens, and again on the day after that; but this time she is killed and eaten. The sons bring about the usual ending, and so " became chiefs, and the people honoured them."

[1] See Chapter VII, p. 106.

Yet another version has been obtained from the Duala people, in the far north-west, but quite sufficient have already been given.

The Nunda

Quite a different line of thought, which may or may not have developed out of the " Swallowing Monster " idea, is that connected with " the Nunda, eater of people." This is found in the story of " Sultan Majnun," [1] but has little if any connexion with the first part of the story, which relates how a bird year after year stole the dates from the sultan's garden, till defeated by his youngest son. This may be of exotic origin, but the Nunda, whether under this name or another, is not confined to Swahili-speaking Africans. The peculiarities of this particular version seem to be : the Nunda begins as an ordinary cat, which, being left unmolested when catching and eating the chickens, grows in size and fierceness with each successive year, till it ends as a monstrous creature larger than an elephant. Secondly, though it has devoured everything it came across, nothing is ever recovered. The youngest son, who kills the Nunda in the end, does so only after bringing in a succession of animals, each larger than the last, and ending with an elephant. He is told by his mother, on every occasion, " My son, this is not he, the Nunda, eater of people."

This "method of trial and error" is that followed by Mlilua in the Kiniramba tale, which, however, in what follows is true to the main type of the ' Swallower ' stories.

Jonah's Whale, the Frog, and the Tortoise

Both Tylor and W. A. Clouston (though the latter does not mention the African legend we have been discussing in the pages he devotes to " Men swallowed by Monster Fish "[2]) associate the Biblical story of Jonah with the same class of ideas. Whether or not one can suppose any original connexion, there is this important difference that Jonah was

---

[1] Steere, *Swahili Tales*, pp. 199 and 247.
[2] *Popular Tales and Fictions*, vol. i, pp. 403–411.

returned to the upper air unharmed, and (so far as one knows) without injury to the whale. But in all but one of the examples he quotes as parallels the fish is cut open. In these two cases we have a link with a curious incident which occurs more than once in African ogre-tales: a frog, or in some cases a tortoise, swallows some children in order to save them from the ogre, and produces them safe and sound at their home. A good, typical instance of this class of tale is that given by M. Junod[1] under the title of "L'Homme-au-Grand-Coutelas." We have the usual set of incidents— girls passing the night in the ogre's hut and saved by the wakefulness of one among them; the friendly frog is less frequently met with, but Dr Doke has a similar ending to the story of "The Great Water-snake and the People."[2] A man of the Luo tribe (a non-Bantu-speaking people commonly called 'Kavirondo' in Kenya Colony) told me much the same story, in which the girls were swallowed by a tortoise.

Those of us who have been brought up on Grimm will easily remember "The Wolf and the Kids," which, like "Red Riding-hood," if not springing from the same root, must have originated in a similar stratum of thought. The differences of background and colouring are as interesting as the resemblance persisting through the long course of development which has separated the European stream of tradition from the African.

---

[1] *Chants et contes*, p. 144.
[2] *Lamba Folklore*, p. 247. See *infra*, p. 300.

CHAPTER XV: LIGHTNING, THUNDER, RAIN, AND THE RAINBOW

IT is only natural that lightning and thunder should power-fully affect the human imagination all the world over. Even when their causes are more or less understood there are few or none but must feel a peculiar thrill at sight of the flash and sound of the answering roar. To the primitive mind lightning is a living thing, instinct with destructive power, thunder the voice of some angry spirit or supra-mundane animal. Lightning is, perhaps, most often con-ceived of as a bird, and there seems no reason to doubt the good faith of those who declare they have actually seen it.

Various descriptions are given of it: sometimes it be-comes identified with an actual bird; thus the Amandebele give the name of *isivolovolo* both to the 'bird of heaven' (*inyoni yezulu*) and to the white-necked fish-eagle, which flies at a great height and whose droppings possess magical properties.

Dudley Kidd, in Bomvanaland, had a brown bird pointed out to him as the lightning-bird. He was about to shoot it, but was dissuaded, and therefore presumably was unable to determine its species, as he gives no further information. The bird known to Afrikanders as 'hammerkop' (the tufted umber) seems in some way to be associated with lightning as well as rain; to destroy its nest is to bring down a storm.

The Lightning-bird described

One of Bishop Callaway's informants had seen a feather of the lightning-bird, which may very possibly have been a peacock's feather, as it is a fact that peacocks' feathers were sold in Natal about 1860 by some enterprising person who declared that they had been obtained from the 'heaven-bird.'[1] According to this man, the bird " is quite peculiar, for its feathers glisten. A man may think it is red; again he sees that it is not so—it is green." [2] This suggests a kind

[1] *Amazulu*, p. 119.   [2] *Ibid.*, p. 383.

of metallic iridescence, so that it is not surprising if peacocks' feathers were accepted as being the genuine article. Another account says that it has a red bill, red legs, and a short red tail, like fire; "its feathers are bright and dazzling, and it is very fat."

The Xosas call this bird *impundulu*—a name nowadays adopted for an electric tram-car! It is said to "appear as such"—that is to say, in its proper form as a bird—only to women, but Dr Hewat[1] does not mention what women, if any, have ever seen it. When it darts down as lightning people only see the flash.

> It lays a big egg where it strikes, which eggs bring ill-luck to the neighbourhood where laid. The only way to circumvent the bird is to stand ready with a kerrie and hit right through the flash. . . . No one has ever succeeded in killing one yet.

He goes on to say that the doctor[2] is supposed to dig up the egg in order to destroy it; but it is somewhat inconsistent with this to be told in the next sentence that "the possession of the egg would bring great good fortune."

The Lightning-bird's Nest found in Mashonaland

The destruction of the egg seems elsewhere to be considered essential, as would appear from a very interesting account by a magistrate in Mashonaland, writing under the name 'Mbizo.'[3] He says that, the lightning having struck a tree near the native messengers' camp at his station, a woman doctor was called in. After examining the place she ran to and fro, round and round, and at last fixed on a spot, which she marked by sticking a horn into the earth, and said that the eggs would be found there. (It seems that none but natives were present at this ceremony.) "Digging operations followed"; but it is not said who dug, which is not without importance. The three Government messengers who were looking on reported that not far from the surface a small round hole was found, very smooth, as if plastered; digging down from this, at a depth of some two

---

[1] *Bantu Folklore*, p. 91.   [2] *Isanusi*; in Natal he is *inyanga yezulu*.
[3] *Nada* (1924), p. 60.

feet they found a nest with two eggs—quite ordinary-looking eggs apparently. The magistrate, on examining the spot, could find no trace of the smooth hole, nor any reason to doubt that the woman had placed the nest in the excavation herself, probably diverting the spectators' attention, as conjurors know how, at the critical moment. When he dropped the eggs on the ground and broke them (they were unmistakably addled) all the people present fled in real terror; but some one must have returned later—perhaps the doctor herself—for " all particles of the eggs were carefully gathered, doctored, and thrown into a deep pool in the Sebakwe River."

This was done to prevent the lightning striking again in the same spot, which, as a matter of fact, it never did, in this instance, up to the time of writing, though fifteen years had passed since the incident took place. If these precautions are omitted it is believed that the bird will come back to pick up its eggs, " with probably fatal results."

Mr Guy Taylor, the editor of *Nada*, has in his possession a curious earthenware object, turned up by the plough near the Chikuni Mission,[1] which the natives declare is "an egg laid by lightning." None of the local natives (Batonga and Baila) had ever seen anything like it.

Heaven-doctors

The Natal ' heaven-doctors ' are more concerned with the bird itself than with its eggs. They set a bowl of *amasi* mixed with various medicines in the place where they wish the lightning to strike, and when they see the flash rush forward and kill the bird. It seems to have been believed that this had repeatedly happened. The bird was boiled down for the sake of its fat, which was a very precious medicine, used, among other purposes, for anointing the sticks held by the ' heaven-herds ' in the ceremony of conjuring the lightning, to be described presently. The Bomvanas, it would seem, do not recognize the possibility of this procedure, if Dudley Kidd was correct in stating it

[1] In Northern Rhodesia.

as their belief that " the bird sets its own fat on fire and throws it down."

Chimungu of the Baronga

The Baronga identify the lightning-bird with a hawk called *chimungu*, which is believed to bury itself in the ground where it strikes. These people credit the 'medicine' prepared from it with the peculiar virtue of enabling its possessor to detect thieves. One has not heard of this use of it among the Zulus, with their well-known character for honesty. When lightning has struck any spot of ground and burnt up the grass on it the Ronga chief " casts the bones," and then sends for the professional expert. This man arrives, with a long black stick in his hand, digs at the spot indicated, and finds the bird, alive or dead; one supposes that in the former case he kills it, but this is not specified. He then carefully measures the depth of the hole, making a notch on his stick for future reference, takes the bird home, roasts it, and grinds it to powder. What is done when a case of theft is reported may be read in M. Junod's book.[1]

The Girl who saw the Lightning-bird

A Tumbuka native told the Rev. Donald Fraser that he had never seen the lightning-bird, " but a girl of our village saw it not long ago." It was a large black bird, with " a big, curling tail, like a cock's." It seems to have splashed into a pool of water near where she was hoeing in her garden, and then to have " run up her hoe and scratched her," after which it flew back into the clouds. As the narrator had seen " the marks of its claws on her body " it is probable that the girl had really been struck by lightning, which has been known to leave curious scars. Further, it is believed that " those little scarlet insects you see on the path during the rains are the children of the lightning."[2]

The lakeside people of Buziba (on the eastern shore of Lake Victoria) think lightning and thunder are caused by

---

[1] *The Life of a South African Tribe*, vol. ii, pp. 403–404.
[2] *Winning a Primitive People*, p. 65.

flocks of small, glittering red birds, which nest in the rocks near the lake. When Kayura, ruler of the storm (he is the son of the one-legged lake-god Mugasha), is so disposed he sends these birds out: the flashing of their feathers is the lightning and the rushing sound of their wings the thunder. During a thunderstorm Mugasha's missing leg is said to be seen in the clouds—a phenomenon of which, so far as I am aware, no explanation has been offered.

Other Embodiments of Lightning

But birds are not the only creatures held responsible for, or supposed to be connected with, the lightning. The Lambas [1] say that with the flash an animal like a goat, but with the hind legs and tail of a crocodile, descends to earth, let down by a cord like a "strong cobweb." Ordinarily it is drawn up again, but should the 'cobweb' break the animal would be heard crying like a goat, "and the people run together to kill and burn it." They cannot do this without being protected by special 'medicine,' as it is highly dangerous to approach the creature.

No one will use for firewood a tree which has been struck by lightning, while the Zulus (and other cattle-breeding peoples) will never eat the flesh of an animal so killed, unless it has been 'doctored' and they themselves have been washed with the proper 'medicines.' It is a world-wide notion, quite easy to understand, that any person or thing marked for destruction by this mysterious power must be *tabu*. So the Romans used to sacrifice a sheep on the spot where anyone had been struck by lightning, and made it a sacred place for ever. The Bushongo people of the Kasai suppose lightning to be an animal something like a leopard, but black. It is called "Tsetse Bumba," and is the subject of a curious legend.[2] Bumba, the creator, after producing nine creatures, of which Tsetse was one, and, subsequently, the human race, imposed on them various *tabus*, which are observed to this day. But Tsetse refused to obey these

---

[1] Doke, *The Lambas of Northern Rhodesia*, p. 225.
[2] Torday and Joyce, *Les Bushongo*, p. 20.

rules, and began working mischief; so Bumba drove her [1] from the earth, and she took refuge in the sky, where she has dwelt ever since. But when people began to suffer because they could not get fire Bumba allowed her to return now and then, and, though every one of these occasions was marked by disaster, men were able to light their fires from trees which had been struck, and thenceforth carefully kept them burning in their huts.

The Lightning-dog of the Congo

The people of the Lower Congo call lightning Nzazi (or Nsasi); with them it takes the form of a kind of magic dog, either red or black, with shaggy hair and a curly tail. When he comes down he gives one sharp bark—*ta !*—and with the second bark he goes up again. No charm can avail against him, and neither wizard nor witch-doctor has power to avert his attacks. The Zulus, however, know better, as we shall see.

R. E. Dennett was told this story by a Luangu man :

A man met a beautiful dog, and was so pleased with its appearance that he determined to take it home with him. As it was raining heavily he took it with him inside his *shimbec* (hut) and, lighting a fire, proceeded to dry and warm his pet. Suddenly there was an explosion, and neither man, dog, nor *shimbec* were ever seen again. This dog was Nsasi, so Antonio told me.[2]

This same man, Antonio Lavadeiro (the Lower Congo people very often have Portuguese names), had a strange experience on his own account, which seems to imply that Nzazi is not himself a dog, but hunts with twelve couple of hounds. Here Nzazi is the thunder, and his dogs the lightning. Antonio was playing at marbles under a shed with some friends during a heavy shower of rain, when "it thundered frightfully, and Nzazi sent his twenty-four dogs down upon them. They seized one of the party who had left the shed for a moment, and the fire burnt up a living palm-tree."[3]

---

[1] Torday, writing in French, made Tsetse feminine, but this may only have been because of the gender of *la foudre*.

[2] *The Black Man's Mind*, p. 138.   [3] *Folk-lore of the Fjort*, p. 7.

But Antonio also told of a man, still living when he spoke, who had been caught up to heaven by a flash of lightning and had a very good time there for two or three weeks. He was then asked by Nzambi (God) himself whether he would rather stay for ever or return to earth. He said he wanted to return, as he missed his friends and relations. So he was sent back to them.

Dudley Kidd mentions, somewhat vaguely, "a fat baby"[1] said by the people of Mashonaland to cause the thunder when it crawls on the ground after descending from the sky at the spot where the lightning struck the earth. No further details are given about this infant, which seems to have been reported at second or third hand, or even less directly. We have already seen that some, at least, of the Mashona believe in the lightning-bird.

The Balungwana

But one wonders whether there may be some obscure connexion with the *balungwana* of the Baronga. These are tiny beings, sometimes called 'dwarfs' (*psimhunwanyana*), but more often by the name which seems to mean 'little Europeans.'[2] They are said to come down from the sky when heavy rain is falling; if there is thunder without rain people say, "The *balungwana* are playing up there." Nothing is said about lightning in connexion with them, and they sometimes appear before a great disaster, such as the locust visitation of 1894, when "a little man and a little woman" fell from the sky and said to the people, "Do not kill the locusts; they belong to us!" In 1862, just before the war between two rival Gaza chiefs, a *mulungwana* alighted on a hill at Lourenço Marques, and was seen by many people. M. Junod's informant had not himself seen him: he was "too little" at the time, and his parents would not let him go and look. He added, surprisingly, that "the white men

[1] *The Essential Kafir*, p. 121.
[2] Junod, *Life of a South African Tribe*, vol. ii, p. 405. Possibly the name is not, as one thinks at first, a diminutive of the Ronga word for 'white men' (perhaps borrowed from Zulu), but of a plural of *Mulungu*, as used by many East African tribes, though not by the Baronga. In that case it would mean 'little gods.'

INYANGA YEZULU WARDING OFF A HAILSTORM
Photo Mariannhill Mission

seized him and took him to Mozambique." It does not appear that any inquiries were made of the Portuguese authorities concerning this extraordinary capture.

Heaven-herds, or Heaven-doctors

Thunderstorms being exceedingly frequent and violent in tropical and sub-tropical Africa, more particularly, perhaps, in the south, where the abundance of ironstone in the hills may add to the danger from lightning, the art—or science—of averting them, or, at any rate, of preventing damage, has been developed in great detail. The Zulus have their 'heaven-herds' (who shepherd the thunder-clouds), or 'heaven-doctors.' They instinctively feel a storm coming on, a faculty acquired by what is called 'eating the heaven'—that is, eating the flesh of a beast killed by lightning—they also make cuts in their bodies and rub in a 'medicine' compounded from this flesh, with, in addition, that of the lightning-bird, scrapings from the 'thunderbolt,' and, perhaps, certain herbs. The 'thunderbolt' may be a meteorite; it is said to be "a thing like the shank of an assagai," which buries itself in the ground where the lightning strikes, the spot being marked by "a heap of jelly-like substance." The 'doctor,' who has been watching the flash, at once digs here and finds the object.

These experts are supposed to turn back hail and lightning, but not rain, which, in a land of frequent and disastrous droughts, is a blessing anxiously awaited. They have to undergo a special initiation and observe certain *tabus*, which do not, to our thinking, seem to have much point: for instance, they must never drink from a cup of beer unless it is quite full, or eat *izindumba* beans unless given to them. But if these and other prohibitions are infringed the 'doctor' loses his power, and if he is unsuccessful in averting a storm it is at once attributed to his not having 'fasted'—a term which includes other matters besides abstinence from food.

When a storm is coming on the *inyanga yezulu* seizes his sticks, which have been rubbed with the proper 'medicines,' and takes up his station outside the house—sometimes on the wall of the cattle-fold, if this is of stone. He brandishes his sticks, and shouts, 'scolding the heaven,' ordering the storm to depart, and whistling to it as herd-boys do to their cattle. While this goes on no one in the house is supposed to speak; and if it is hailing people do no work, for this, it is believed, would attract the lightning.

Birds which bring Rain

Rain, of course, is a pressing preoccupation for many natives of Africa, and the professional rain-doctor is an important person. He will be more fitly treated in the next chapter; but there are also rain-rites in which all the people take part, and rain-charms which may be used by individuals. Thus the ground hornbill (*insingizi* [1]) is a bird intimately associated with rain. When there has been no rain for some time they catch an *insingizi*, kill it, and throw it into a pool, when, "if it rains"—for it seems as if this result were by no means certain—"it is said it rains for the sake of the *insingizi* which has been killed: the heaven becomes soft; it wails for it by raining, wailing a funeral wail." [2] If a number of these birds are seen gathered together in one place, uttering their cries, it is supposed that they are calling for rain, and that it will soon follow.

The Bateleur eagle (*ingqungqulu*) is looked to for omens of various kinds; among others it announces the coming of rain. But it is not, like the other bird, used as a rain-charm.

Shouting for Rain

The feast of first-fruits (*ukutshwama*) was formerly, perhaps is still, held in or about the month of January, when the new crops begin to be fit for use. But it sometimes happens that the rains have been late in coming, and consequently there is no 'new food' to be eaten. On such occasions the assembled people intone 'magical songs,'

[1] The dictionaries give both 'ground hornbill' and 'turkey-buzzard' as equivalents for *insingizi*. There is no clue as to which is meant here, but I imagine the former.

[2] Callaway, *Amazulu*, p. 407.

which are believed to produce the desired effect. These same songs may also be used with the opposite intention— *viz.*, to stop excessive and long-continued rain when an army is on the march.

I have heard people 'shouting for rain' on the slopes of Mount Bangwe, in the Shire Highlands, with weird, wailing cries—perhaps calling on the spirit of the old chief Kankomba, who used to be invoked for the same purpose in Duff Macdonald's day.[1] But this is straying too far from our proper subject, and it is time to consider the myths of the rainbow.

The Rainbow

Africans have been struck not so much by the beauty of the rainbow as by its strangeness, and they nearly always look on it as malignant and dangerous. This may seem unaccountable to us, accustomed to think of it as the symbol of hope, and familiar with the lovely figure of Iris, the messenger of the gods. But it is a common belief that it stops the rain, and this is quite enough to constitute it an enemy. Its colours are sometimes said to be the glow of a destroying fire : " If it settles on the trees," said a Luyi man to Émile Jacottet, "it will burn all the leaves." It is curiously associated with ant-heaps, in which it is supposed to live. Anyone who sees it—that is, sees the place where its end seems to rest on the earth—runs away as fast as he can : " if he sees you he will kill you." It is described—one cannot see why—as an animal as big as a jackal, with a bushy tail. Others say it is like a many-coloured snake,[2]

---

[1] *Africana*, vol. i, p. 70.

[2] Virgil, in the fifth book of the *Æneid* (84–93), tells how, when Æneas had made offerings at his father's tomb, a snake came out from " the foot of the shrine " and glided round it seven times. Its scales were blue and gold, and glittered in many colours like the rainbow. It tasted the food and drink there set out, and then crept back into the earth whence it came. Æneas did not know whether to think it " the genius of the place " or an attendant on his father : an African would never have doubted that it was Anchises himself. The reference to the rainbow is curious, but must not be pressed as indicating that in ancient Italy it was thought of as a snake ; while in Africa the rainbow snake has no connexion with the ancestral ghost.

which is more intelligible. Some Zulus say that it is a sheep, or lives with a sheep. The common Zulu expression for it, however (the only one I remember to have heard), is *utingo lwenkosikazi*, 'the Queen's arch'—that is, one of the arched wattles forming the hut of that mysterious being the Queen of Heaven, concerning whom it is difficult to obtain exact information.

The Kikuyu [1] say it is a 'wicked animal,' which lives in the water, comes out at night, eats goats and cattle, and has even been known to eat people. There was one which lived in Lake Naivasha and swallowed the cattle of the Masai, but was at last killed by the young warriors. This, it seems, was related as an actual occurrence.

It is worth noting that the Kikuyu say, " the rainbow in the water [in the spray from a waterfall] and the sky is not the animal itself, but its picture," because in a very distant region of West Africa the Ewe (in Togo) say the same thing : the rainbow is the reflection of the snake in the clouds. These people also think that it hides in an ant-hill, whence it rises up after rain.

One of the Kikuyu stories of the rainbow (" The Giant of the Great Water ") could really be classed with those about the Swallowing Monster, recounted in a previous chapter.

The Baganda are perhaps exceptional in their way of regarding the rainbow, whom they call Musoke ; he is the patron of fishermen. It is wrong, by the by, to point at the rainbow, so they say: anyone who does so will find his finger become stiff. The Baila,[2] on the contrary, point at the rainbow to drive it away, not with the finger, but with the pestle used for pounding grain. They call it the bow of Leza (God), but none the less credit it with preventing the fall of rain.

Where the Rainbow ends

" They have a curious idea that just below where the bow touches earth there is a very fierce goat-ram, which burns

---

[1] W. S. and K. Routledge, *With a Prehistoric People*, pp. 307–314.
[2] Smith and Dale, *The Ila-speaking Peoples*, vol. ii, p. 220.

THE RAINBOW LIVES IN AN ANT-HILL!

Photo Motor Tours, Ltd., Nairobi

like fire." But here and there one comes upon traces of the notion—familiar to us in Europe—that some treasure would be found at the point where the rainbow touches the ground, if one could only reach it. The Ewe (who, however, need not concern us here) think this is where the valuable 'Aggrey beads' are to be found. A Chaga story told by Dr Gutmann [1] relates how a needy Dorobo set out from his home to ask Iruwa for cattle. When he came to the "rainbow's end" he stood still and uttered his prayer. And this he did for many days. But no cattle appeared. Then he was seized with rage (the story-teller says, " his heart rose up "); he drew his sword and cut the rainbow in two. Half of it flew up to the sky; the other half fell to the ground and sank in, making a deep hole. Nothing more is said about the Dorobo; one would not be surprised to learn that he perished miserably as a punishment for his presumption. Later on some people came upon the hole and, climbing down, found " another country." They came back and reported what they had seen: those to whom they told it would not believe them. So they went down again, and returned with vessels full of milk, which convinced the sceptics. But some lions had followed them down, and the next time any people descended they found no one there, the inhabitants having emigrated. (It is not actually stated that the first explorers found any people in the underground region, but it must be understood that they are implied in the mention of milk.) They heard the growling of the lions, and made the best of their way back, as they had come. Since then no one has ventured down the pit. Frankly, I do not know what to make of this.

Rainbow Snakes

The people of Luangu hold, if Dennett was correctly informed, that there are two rainbows, a good and an evil one. But the rainbow snakes, which seem to be distinct from these two, are six, and not one. They correspond to the colours of the rainbow, which are counted as six, not seven—perhaps

[1] *Volksbuch*, p. 153.

CHAPTER XVI: DOCTORS, PROPHETS, AND WITCHES

THE term 'witch-doctor' is often loosely used, as if it were synonymous with 'witch' or 'sorcerer.' This is something like putting the policeman and the detective in the same category as the criminal. There *may* be witch-doctors who are scoundrels, as there *may* be unjust magistrates or corrupt policemen; but, on the whole, the witch-doctor is a force on the side of law and justice, and one does not see how, where a belief in witchcraft is firmly rooted in the minds of the people, he could well be dispensed with. His office is to detect and prevent crime and bring offenders to justice, and his methods are on the whole less barbarous than those of Matthew Hopkins, the witch-finder.

No African would ever confuse these two personages: the 'doctor' is *inyanga* (*mganga*, *sing'anga*), the witch *mchawi*, or *mfiti*, or *umtagati*.

But the Zulu word *inyanga*, like our 'doctor,' covers a variety of meanings; properly it denotes a person skilled in any art or knowledge: a blacksmith, for instance, is *inyanga yensimbi*, " a doctor of iron." So the *inyanga* may be either a diviner or a herbalist, or both at the same time; possibly, also, a seer or prophet.

The Doctor's Training

The diviner and the herbalist learn their business in the ordinary way, being trained by a professional, to whom they act as assistants till duly qualified. The rules of the diviner's art have been carefully studied by M. Junod, and fully described in his book *The Life of a South African Tribe*.[1] The seer is usually a man of a peculiar, nervous temperament, either known as such from childhood or seeming to

[1] Vol. ii, pp. 493–519. Smith and Dale (*The Ila-speaking Peoples*, vol. i, pp. 265–272) enumerate nine methods of divination, all different from that of the 'divining-bones' used by the Baronga, Zulus, and others. An interesting point is the statement of a diviner, apparently made in all good faith, that the spirits of his father and mother were contained in his " medicine gourd," and it was they who gave the answers to the questions put.

develop special powers after a dangerous illness. He has to undergo a severe initiation, spending a great deal of time alone in the wilds. Some say that this condition is brought about through possession by a spirit. The Lambas[1] think there are certain goblins (*ifinkuwaila*, already mentioned in Chapter XIII) with only half a body who wander about, invisible, in troops, hopping along on their one leg. Sometimes the fancy takes one of them to possess a human being, and then he or she (for they are of both sexes and all ages) hits some passer-by in the face. It is not clear whether the man feels anything at the time, but after reaching his home he is taken ill, and begins to see visions—perhaps a procession of " beings in endless march across the heavens, going westward, arrayed in feather headdresses and carrying their sleeping-mats."[2] He has then to be treated by some person already initiated, and is thenceforward known as a *mowa*. He can always see the one-legged goblins, which are invisible to other people; he becomes peculiarly skilled in dancing, and acquires the power of composing special songs and singing them. These people are called in to sing and dance at funerals and other ceremonies, and, being paid for their services, make quite a good thing of it.

Prophets

The prophet is able to see what is happening at a distance, to predict the future, and to receive and deliver messages from spiritual beings, whether the ghosts of ancestors or others. The immense influence wielded by such men has been proved over and over again by such incidents as the " cattle-killing " of 1856, when Umhlakaza, passing on the messages received in trance by his niece (some say his daughter) Nongqauze, prophesied that when the people had slaughtered all their cattle and emptied their grain-bins, so as to leave themselves no store of food, the old dead chiefs would come back, bringing with them huge herds of splendid beasts, and the white men would leave the country, never to return. The sun would rise blood-red, and

---

[1] Doke, *The Lambas of Northern Rhodesia*, p. 251.   [2] *Ibid.*, p. 253.

SPIRIT-HUT OF THE ŴAMOŴA

Photo late Rev. J. J. Doke

236

the pits would be miraculously filled to overflowing with food. All this was firmly believed by many people, and the resulting tragedy is only too well known. About twenty-five thousand lives are thought to have been lost in the famine.

Umhlakaza had an official standing as a doctor, and is said to have himself seen visions confirming what his niece had told him. The girl used to sit by a pool, where she saw faces of people and other images in the water—in fact, practised what is known as crystal-gazing, though she seems to have been subject to trances as well.

Trances

The trance is a familiar phenomenon among the Bantu tribes. Doctors induce it in themselves, or others, by means known to themselves, probably chewing certain herbs or inhaling the smoke of them when burned. The practitioners of the Wakuluwe [1] prepare a drink known as *Lukansi*, which gives the drinker " invulnerability, superhuman strength, and the power to know and see things withheld from ordinary people."

But trances also occur spontaneously. The Rev. Donald Fraser [2] heard of a man who had himself seen the abode of the spirits.

> He was supposed to have died, and his body was tied up in a mat and prepared for burial, but . . . signs of returning life were seen. On his recovery he told how he had gone by a narrow road until he came to a great village where the people lived without marriage. He had spoken to them, but none would hold conversation with him. They told him to be gone, for he was not wanted there. He tried to tell his story, but no one would listen to him. They beat irons together and tried to drown his words, for he was too uncanny.

This is much the same as the tale of Mpobe and others like it, where people had similar experiences during their waking hours. But these are usually related as legends, not as having happened to people known to the narrators. There

---

[1] Melland and Cholmeley, *Through the Heart of Africa*, p. 21.
[2] *Winning a Primitive People*, p. 126.

is a novel touch here in the behaviour of the dead people. As a rule they are more civil, and, instead of silencing their visitor, content themselves with telling him not to talk about them on his return to the upper world.

Probably what happened to the man whose story was told by Antonio Lavadeiro [1] might also be described as a trance. He was either struck by lightning or stunned by a clap of thunder, and remained unconscious for two or three weeks, during which, according to his own account, he was caught up to the sky and very hospitably entertained by Nzambi Mpungu.

'Possession'

This trance state may be caused, according to African ideas, either by the person's spirit leaving his body and travelling off into unknown regions or by ' possession.' A Lamba man or woman may be possessed, as we have seen, by an *ichinkuwaila* goblin, but also by the ghosts of deceased human beings. There is quite an influential order of people in this tribe who are possessed by spirits of Lenje chiefs, never by chiefs of their own tribe. The first sign of possession is a serious illness, for which no remedy seems to avail, and which brings on a state in which he " begins to speak in a weird way, using the most extravagant language, telling of wonderful things he says he has seen." [2]

It is the possessing spirits who enable such persons to prophesy. Sometimes their prophecies are said to have been fulfilled, as, for instance, that of those who told the people, long, long ago, " You will all drink out of one well," meaning that tribal differences would be disregarded, which was held to have come true when white men came into the country and put a stop to inter-tribal warfare.

Possibly some of these people are clairvoyants ; others may have built up a reputation by means of some lucky guesses ; but many, in Lambaland, at any rate, would appear to be unscrupulous impostors, who travel from place

---

[1] See *ante*, p. 228.
[2] Doke, *The Lambas of Northern Rhodesia*, pp. 258–267.

to place and charge substantial fees for their services. They deliver oracles from deceased chiefs, whose 'mediums' they are; they profess to bring rain in time of drought and to keep the birds from the crops; they practise incantations warranted to ensure luck in hunting and administer medicine to childless couples. Dr Doke knew a lazy ne'er-do-well who made quite a comfortable living in this way.

These *ŵamukamwami* are readily distinguished by their appearance; they never cut their hair, but wear it plaited in long tails, smeared with oil and red ochre and (in former times, at any rate) adorned with the white shell-disks which are the insignia of chieftainship. The 'ecstatic' seer of the Zulus seems always to have a more or less unkempt appearance—which is only in character—but I do not know that he adopts any distinctive fashion. The get-up of the witch-doctor proper is a different matter; of course, it varies locally, but an essential part of it is usually the tail of a zebra fitted into a handle and waved about in performing exorcisms or other operations. Bishop Peel of Mombasa used to carry a fly-whisk of this kind when on tour, and it was a favourite joke with his carriers to declare that he was a *mganga*.

The Lamba doctors proper, *aŵalaye*, are herbalists and diviners, and provide charms of all sorts, for protecting the crops and for other purposes. Charms of this kind are also supplied by the *ŵamukamwami*, a fact which illustrates the overlapping of functions already referred to.

Predictions fulfilled

More than one prophet is said to have foretold the coming of the Europeans—among others one Mulenga in Ilala (Northern Rhodesia). He said, "There will arrive people white and shining, their bodies like those of locusts!" Whether this description was recognized as fitting the first white explorers when they made their appearance does not seem to have been recorded. Ilala is the scene of Livingstone's last journey and death, but the prediction was probably made after his time. Mulenga also foretold the cattle plague of the early nineties and the locust invasion of 1894.

Podile, a chief of the Bapedi " in old times " (but unfortunately there is no clue to his date: 'old times' might mean in the time of the speaker's grandfather), prophesied the coming of the Boers by saying that " red ants will come and destroy the land "; and another wise man, about the same time, said, " I see red ants coming. They have baskets on their heads [hats]. Their feet are those of zebras [the impression produced by boots]. Their sticks give out fire [guns]. They travel with houses; the oxen walk in front. Receive them kindly." This was supposed to be fulfilled when Trichard's party arrived in 1837.[1] If the prediction was really made at the time stated it may be a genuine case of what is known in the Scottish Highlands as 'second sight.'

Chaminuka

A famous seer in Mashonaland was Chaminuka, of Chitungwiza, in the Hartley district. He is called a 'wizard' by Mr Posselt,[2] but he seems really to have been a man of high character and unusual, perhaps abnormal, gifts. Lobengula used frequently to consult him, and for many years treated him with great consideration. He had remarkable power over animals, not necessarily of an occult nature: he kept tame pythons and other snakes; antelopes gambolled fearlessly about his hut, and his celebrated bull, Minduzapasi, would lie down and rise up, march and halt, at the word of command. He was believed to be the medium of the spirit called Chaminuka; his real name was Tsuro. He was credited with the power to bring rain and to control the movements of game; Frederick Courteney Selous, when hunting in that part of the country, was told by his followers that they would never succeed in killing an elephant unless they first asked Chaminuka's permission. When this was done he gave the messenger a reed which was supposed " to bring the elephants back on their tracks

---

[1] Hoffmann, *Afrikanischer Grossvater*, p. 285.   [2] *Nada* (1926), p. 85.

PLAYING THE KAFIR PIANO

Photo A. M. Duggan-Cronin. By permission of the McGregor Museum, Kimberley

by first pointing the way they had gone and then drawing it towards him." [1]

In 1883 a man who believed Chaminuka to have been responsible for the death of his wife went to Lobengula with a false accusation of witchcraft against him. The king may or may not have believed this, but in any case he resolved on Chaminuka's destruction. He sent him a message, inviting him to Bulawayo on a friendly visit, but the old man was not deceived. He said, " I go to the Madzwiti [the Amandebele], but I shall not return ; but, mark you, some eight years hence, behold ! the stranger will enter, and he will build himself white houses."

The prophecy was fulfilled before the eight years were out, for the Chartered Company's pioneer expedition entered Mashonaland in 1890.

He set out, accompanied by his wife and two of his sons, and met Lobengula's war-party near the Shangani river. Most of the warriors kept out of sight ; only a few headmen came to meet him. His wife, Bavea, who had been a captive of the Amandebele (she was sent to Chaminuka by Lobengula), said, " They are going to kill you ! I know the Amandebele ; I see blood in their eyes ! Run ! Run ! " He refused, saying he was too old to run. " If his day has come Chaminuka does not fear to die ; but bid my son, who is young and swift of foot, creep away in the bushes while there is yet time and carry the news to my people."

The little party were soon surrounded and all killed, except Chaminuka himself, Bavea, and his other son, Kwari, who was wounded in the leg, but got away. The old chief sat on a rock, calmly playing on his *mbira*. [2] His assailants tried to stab him with their spears, but could not even wound him. Some of them had rifles and fired at him, but the bullets fell round him like hailstones, without touching

---

[1] *A Hunter's Wanderings*, p. 331.

[2] An elementary kind of piano, with a set of wooden or iron keys fixed over gourd resonators on a semicircular hoop, which the player carries suspended round his neck by a strap.

him.   At last he told them that he could be killed only by
an innocent young boy, and such a one, being fetched,
dispatched him unresisting.   The *impi*, having cut up his
body in order to get the liver and heart, which were held to
be powerful 'medicines,' went on to Chitungwiza, in order
to exterminate Chaminuka's whole clan, as Lobengula had
commanded.   But Bute, the son who had been sent away,
was fleet of foot, and reached the village in time, and when
the warriors arrived they found only empty huts and such
stores and cattle as the people had been unable to take with
them.   Bavea was taken back to Bulawayo, but escaped,
and in 1887 told the story to Selous,[1] who saw her in
Lomagundi's country (North Mashonaland).

The Rev. Arthur Shearly Cripps, who had abundant
opportunities of hearing the stories about Chaminuka on the
spot, has woven them into what might be called a beautiful
prose poem,[2] treating his material very freely, but never, one
feels, departing from the spirit underlying the cruder native
tradition.   This, of course, has not been drawn upon here.

Mohlomi of the Basuto

I cannot pass on without a reference to another seer,
Mohlomi, whom the Rev. E. W. Smith has called " the
greatest figure in Basuto history."   He died in 1815, long
enough ago for legends to have gathered about his name,
as, in fact, they have done, but not sufficiently so to have
obscured the real facts to any great extent.   Though in the
royal line and called to be chief through the incapacity of
his elder brother, he cared nothing for power, and much
preferred to travel about in quest of knowledge, more
particularly knowledge of medicinal herbs.   He was renowned both as a physician and a rain-maker.   There is no
reason to suppose him an impostor in the latter capacity;
he evidently believed in his powers, and his belief must

---

[1] *Travel and Adventure in South-east Africa*, p. 113.   The account in the text
is taken partly from this book and partly from Mr Posselt's article.   Selous does
not mention Kwari or the only way in which Chaminuka (whom he calls Chameluga)
could be killed.
[2] *Chaminuka*.

have been confirmed by the cases in which, if tradition is
to be believed, he was (possibly owing to some fortunate
coincidence) successful. His prophetic career began at an
early age, when, in the course of his puberty initiation-
ceremonies,[1] he felt himself, in a dream or trance, carried
up to the sky, and heard a voice saying, " Go, rule by love
and look on thy people as men and brothers." He had a
strong influence over Moshesh, who, like other chiefs, frequently came to him for advice and, unlike them, often
followed it. The mythical element in his story comes out
in the assertion that he was " able to transport himself from
one place to another in a supernatural way." In his last
illness he prophesied a famine and a cattle plague; and
when dying, on coming out of a kind of trance, he said,
" After my death a cloud of red dust will come out of the
east and consume our tribes. The father will eat his
children." This has been taken to refer to the series of
wars and migrations which began shortly afterwards and
continued till the middle of the nineteenth century.

Only One Way of Death

It will have been noticed that, as in the cases of Liongo,
Chikumbu and Chibisa, there was only one way in which
Chaminuka could be killed. The usual account given of
this is that the person in question had charms against every
possible weapon, or other cause of death, but one, which,
of course, had to be kept secret.

At Kolelo, in Nguu, Tanganyika Territory, there is a
cave haunted (almost within living memory, if not still) by
the spirit of a great *mganga* who in his lifetime was a chief
in Ukami. In time of drought the headmen of the Wadoe
and neighbouring tribes would come there to pray for rain.
When they greeted him on their arrival they would hear
a rushing sound, like that of an approaching rainstorm.
Then, in some cases, a voice would be heard, saying,
" There is an evil man among you," and would go on to
describe one member of the party by his clothes. If such

---

[1] Ellenberger, *History of the Basuto*, p. 90.

a one was indeed present he was at once driven away. Then they put up their prayer, and if they heard the rushing sound a second time they knew that their request was granted, and went away happy. If there was silence in the cave, it was a sign that the spirit was angry, and they had to "go back in the sun," instead of being refreshed by a shower even before they had reached their homes.

This rain-doctor—his name has not been recorded—was reckoned invulnerable during his lifetime; none of his enemies could succeed even in wounding him, with arrow, sword, or gunshot. But unfortunately he happened to quarrel with his wife when a raiding-party was close at hand, and she got into communication with the raiders and, like Delilah, though not for the same reason, betrayed her husband's secret. His *tabu* (*mwiko* or *mzio* in Swahili) was to be struck with the stalk of a pumpkin: if this was done he would die immediately.

The enemies at once procured a pumpkin-stalk, and threw it so as to hit him. It did, in fact, kill him, but the manner of his death was not seen, for a mighty wind arose and carried him off to the cave of Kolelo, "where he is to this day," and no one could tell whither he went. After some days his clothes and weapons were found in the cave, but he was never seen again.

The woods near this cave are uncanny: drums are occasionally heard there, though no drummers are to be seen, also the trilling cry made by women at weddings. Sometimes the traveller comes on an open space among the trees, where the ground is clean white sand, smooth as if just swept for a dance: this is where the ghosts hold their revels.

Kolelo and the Majimaji Rising

The name Kolelo attained a certain publicity about 1905, but not in connexion with the haunted cave in Nguu. This Kolelo was a huge serpent, living in a cave in the mountains of Uluguru.[1] The Zaramo people tell how, once upon a time, two women went into the forest to dig up roots.

[1] Klamroth, in *Zeitschrift für Kolonialsprachen*, p. 139.

SWAZI WITCH-DOCTOR

Photo A. M. Duggan-Cronin. By permission of the McGregor Museum, Kimberley

Suddenly they heard a rumbling underground, but could see nothing to cause it. One woman ran back to the village; the other, known as Mlamlali,[1] stayed. Presently a great snake appeared, took the woman into its cave, and said, "The High God has sent me. I am to take you to wife so that you can carry my message to mankind. And you of the Mlali clan shall be my people and serve me for ever in this cave. I have two companions, and we are commissioned to restore everything which has been spoiled or ruined on earth."

Mlamlali was long sought for by her friends, but no trace of her was found, till suddenly she came home wearing beautiful ornaments and none the worse for her experience.

The message she brought was mainly concerned with directions for cultivation; but in 1905 occurred the rising (known as the " Majimaji Rebellion "[2]) with which Kolelo's name is chiefly associated. Two prophets appeared, who foretold that the sun and moon would rise in the west and set in the east, and other wonders would be seen. They forbade the people to pay taxes to the Government, and won over the adherence of a certain chief by showing him, as he was persuaded to believe, his deceased father in the flesh. It appears that they were able to produce a person with a striking resemblance to the dead man. The tribesmen were to arm themselves with millet-stalks, which would turn to rifles in their hands; they would be supplied with a certain medicine which would have the effect of turning the enemy's bullets to water (*maji* in Swahili). The failure of the rising did not put an end to the Kolelo cult; but his oracles from thenceforth seem only to have concerned themselves with agricultural matters. For instance, his

---

[1] Women's names are that of their clan, with the prefix *Mla*.

[2] The rising was known as the " Majimaji Rebellion " on account of the belief in a certain sacred water, stated to have been obtained from the Sudan through Uganda, which was said to confer invulnerability in battle and to protect the user against every sort of evil. An account of the whole movement and of the secret society which is supposed to have originated it was contributed by Mr J. H. Driberg to the *Journal of the Royal Anthropological Institute*, vol. lxi, under the title " Yakañ."

medium, Kiganga, forbade people to eat the leaves of the manioc plant (elsewhere a popular vegetable), perhaps because it is of comparatively recent introduction into Uzaramo. All Wazaramo know the name of Kiganga, but no one professes to have seen her. Two men, however, have met Mlamlali, who acts as caretaker to Kolelo's cave, and would not allow them to enter it. Another medium in residence at the cave is Mhangalugome, who interprets Kolelo's oracles, given in the same way as those of the Nguu spirit, by a rushing noise in the depth of the cavern, perhaps caused by an underground river. It is true that it appears to be intermittent, but this might be accounted for by varying currents of air.

Witches and 'Voodoo'

As to the activities of the witch proper, which it is the business of the *mganga* to check, very strange things are related. Some level-headed missionaries have witnessed occurrences which they could attribute only to unseen agencies. Bishop Weston, at Weti, in the island of Pemba, saw and felt lumps of clay thrown by invisible hands, one falling through the iron roof of the hut in which he stood, another thrown upward from outside. Pemba is a well-known centre of witchcraft; anyone curious about such matters can find a detailed account of the witch-guilds and their horrible sacrifices in Captain Craster's book *Pemba, the Spice Island of Zanzibar*.

The doings of the *wachawi* (or *wanga*) there related are not unlike those we hear of in the island of Hayti—and we may be sure they lose nothing in the hands of romancers—under the names of Obeah and Voodoo (or Vaudoux). The subject hardly comes within the scope of this book, but one thing may be pointed out: it is too commonly assumed that these doings are typical of African mentality in general, and constitute an essential part of African religion. But it is a very suggestive fact that the Pemba witch-guilds and those described by Dr Nassau in West Africa are recruited from the slaves, and the same is obviously the case in the West

Indies. It should be remembered that many, if not most, of these people had been sold into slavery for their crimes, perhaps for this very crime of witchcraft. Dr Nassau says, in fact, that the Benga and neighbouring tribes credited the slaves as a body with addiction to unlawful arts, and if a free man died

> suspicion almost always located itself on the slave community, for the reason that it was known that slaves did practise the Black Art, and partly because it was safer to make an accusation against a defenceless slave than against a free man. It resulted, therefore, that, just because they were defenceless, the slaves actually did practise arts in their supposed self-defence that gave justification for the charge that they were witches and wizards.[1]

I have been assured, quite seriously, by more than one person in the coastal region of Kenya Colony, that certain sorcerers, whom they called *wanga*,[2] were in the habit of coming to your door in the night and calling the occupant of the house. If you came out and followed them into the forest it was implied, rather than stated, that it was all up with you. It also seemed to be implied that once the intended victim had answered the call he had no choice but to go and, presumably, be killed and eaten.

The Resuscitated Corpse

Another belief, held strongly in practically every part of Africa, is that witches hold their revels at the graves of those recently dead, digging up and reanimating the corpse, and then killing it again, eating the flesh, and taking some of the parts as ingredients of the most powerful charms.

But this is not their only reason for resuscitating corpses. There is a strange and horrible superstition, widely distributed, with considerable local variations, to the effect that it is done in order to obtain a familiar, who can be sent about

---

[1] *In an Elephant Corral*, p. 155. The Benga live near Corisco Bay, in Spanish Guinea.

[2] It is not clear what is the exact difference between *wanga* and *wachawi*. W. E. Taylor derived the former word from *anga*, ' to float in the air,' and seems to have believed seriously that these persons have the power of ' levitation.' But probably the word comes from the same root as *mganga* and (Lamba) *ubw-anga*, ' charm.'

on the warlock's evil errands. The Zulus call such a creature *umkovu*; it is supposed to be like a child in stature and to be unable to speak except in an " inarticulate, confused " sort of way, expressed by the word *ukutshwatshwaza*. This is because the owner has cut off the tip of its tongue, to prevent its betraying his secrets; he also, for what purpose is not stated, runs a red-hot needle up the forehead. It is employed, among other things, to place poison, or what is believed to have the same effect, in the kraals, and also acts the part of the Irish banshee, as a death is believed to occur when it has been seen in a kraal, and should anyone happen to be ill at the time the relatives would give up all hope of his recovery.[1] Another account says that they can make the grass trip up a belated traveller by twining round his legs, and (a touch recalling the *wanga* I was warned against at Jomvu) if anyone is foolish enough to answer when they call his name they cut his throat and, in some way, force him to become one of them.

The Yaos, and probably some other tribes, are terrorized by a thing called a *ndondocha*, of like origin with the *umkovu*, but in some ways very different. According to information kindly supplied by Dr Meredith Sanderson, on the day of burial, or within three days from that date, a wizard goes to the grave at night armed with a ' tail ' or a horn containing ' medicine '; with this he strikes the grave, uttering the words, " Arise; your mother summons you! " The earth in the grave heaves and ' boils,' and the corpse emerges without any visible passage having been made. The wizard then carries it on his back to a cave, or to his house, where he keeps it in the verandah-room (a compartment partitioned off under the broad eaves of the hut). Here other medicines are used, and the legs are amputated at the knee-joint. The corpse is now in a state of semi-animation; it is fed by the owner, but cannot move without his orders. If it is not fed it cries unceasingly; its cry is like the mewing of a cat. It cannot speak. It creeps along

[1] Bryant, *Zulu-English Dictionary*, p. 322. See also Colenso, *Zulu-English Dictionary*, p. 282.

the ground, propelling itself by means of the stumps of its legs and on its hands. The possession of a *ndondocha* gives supernatural power to its owner. It is usually employed for killing his enemies, and when people hear its cry they say, " It is ominous ; the banshee has wailed," meaning that by morning somebody will have died. Should the owner die the ' familiar ' will rot away for want of the necessary medicines to keep it alive.

The Tuyewera

Even queerer and more uncanny are the *tuyewera* of the Kaonde country, in Northern Rhodesia.[1] These are imps, having the figure of human beings, about three feet high—though the Lambas say they are like a kind of wild cat—and are made, for a consideration, by sorcerers, not professedly in order to kill people, but to get wealth for the purchaser. They do this by (invisibly) stealing the food of his neighbours and adding it to his store. After a while they tell him that they are lonely and want company, and if he does not name some one for them to kill they will kill him. He names a person, whom they kill by sucking his breath when he is asleep ; he then becomes one of them. The owner has to keep on supplying them with victims, and at last is himself killed, either by them or by his neighbours on discovering that he possesses *tuyewera*.

The Lambas occasionally procure these imps from the Kaonde practitioners, but for the purpose of counteracting witchcraft rather than of increasing their possessions. A man will come and tell the maker that he has lost a number of his relatives in suspicious circumstances, and wants some powerful *ubwanga* to put a stop to this. He is supplied with a pair, takes them home, and makes a sleeping-place for them in the bush, not far from his hut. The witches are soon got rid of, but the *tuyewera* are by no means satisfied. The man has to name one friend or kinsman after another, and at last his wife. When he really has no one left to give them he

---

[1] Melland, *In Witch-bound Africa*, p. 204, and Doke, *The Lambas of Northern Rhodesia*, p. 315.

picks them up and carries them back to the maker, saying,
" Here are your little things. The people are all finished."
But so long as one of his kin remains they will not go.[1]

The Baila call these creatures by a slightly different name,
tuyobela,[2] and say they are the ghosts of men and women
who have been killed by witches. These are said to raise
up the dead person " as an evil spirit "; but from the
accounts given it is not clear how this process differs from
that of restoring the corpse to life, since the *tuyobela* are
solidly material enough to bite people. Mr Smith's friend
Mungolo had seen them, and at first took them for children,
as they were only eighteen inches high, but " on looking
again he saw that they had the bodies of full-grown men,"
and their faces were turned round the wrong way. Their
activities are much the same as those already described :
" they are sent out to steal, to make people sick, and to kill."

A West African Parallel

The Mayombe, in French Congo, have a belief in some
gruesome beings which recall the above descriptions : they
are small in stature, have legs cut off at the knee, high
shoulders, and one remarkably long finger-nail ; their skin
is jet-black, and their hair long and tangled. They are called
nkuyu unana. But, instead of being fabricated by sorcerers
for their own evil purposes, they are the ghosts of witches
who rise from the grave of their own accord. They wander
about burial-grounds and deserted villages, approach people's
houses by night in order to steal chickens ; they frighten
children, and occasionally attack grown persons. They speak
through the nose, and may be heard moaning and com-
plaining of the cold. Sometimes they play tricks on people
by imitating children's voices. If a man should succeed in
shooting one of these creatures he ought to burn the body
—presumably to prevent its rising again. If he misses he

[1] Doke, *The Lambas of Northern Rhodesia*, p. 315.
[2] Smith and Dale, *The Ila-speaking Peoples*, vol. ii, p. 132. The name is
derived from *kuyobela*, ' to twitter,' because they chirp and twitter like birds.
Perhaps the word used in Kaonde is a corruption of this, as I cannot find an
etymology for it in that language.

Pa Shehe Jundani

should pour poison into the hole by which it has been in the habit of leaving and re-entering the grave.[1]

After these the more ordinary witches' familiars and messengers, such as baboons, hyenas, leopards, wild-cats, owls, seem quite commonplace.

Spells or Curses

The Swahili and some of the neighbouring coast tribes have, as might be expected, modified their beliefs to some extent under Moslem influence. The spirits of the dead are sometimes called *wazuka*, but more often spoken of by the Arabic names of *jini* and *shetani*, and though the *mganga* is still, if I mistake not, a power in the land, the charms he supplies are apt to be slips of paper with a verse of the Koran written on them, or a magic square bearing the names of the four angels (Michael, Gabriel, Azrael, Israfil), with other words of power. Women and children might often have been seen twenty years ago wearing the " amulet of seven knots," a cord of black wool over which the wise man, as he tied each knot, had repeated the *Sura Ya Sin* (the thirty-sixth chapter of the Koran).

One way of injuring an enemy is to get a duly qualified person to " read Hal Badiri " against him—that is, to intone the incantations contained in an originally harmless book of prayers offered in the names of those who fought at the battle of Badr (the Ahl Badri in correct Arabic). Again, the spiteful or vindictive person may go to the grave of a well-known saint (such as the site known as Pa Shehe Jundani at Mombasa) and leave an offering there, burning a little incense while uttering his or her desire. Not that all prayers put up at Shehe Jundani's tomb are necessarily malignant; no doubt there are many artless petitions akin in spirit to those one has seen pencilled on the walls of Saint-Étienne-du-Mont, in Paris—for children, for success in love, possibly (since the " march of progress " has not left Mombasa untouched) for success in examinations. These, of course, could hardly be classed as magic—black or white.

[1] Bittremieux, *Idioticon*, vol. ii, p. 510.

CHAPTER XVII : BRER RABBIT IN AFRICA

THE Uncle Remus stories, which suddenly became so popular about fifty years ago, not only delighted both young and old, but attracted the serious attention of folklore students. It is now generally recognized—though the point was hotly debated at first—that they originally came from Africa, brought by the Negro slaves, who, in the southern states, seem mostly to have belonged to Bantu-speaking tribes.[1] When it was discovered that the Indians of the Amazon had numbers of similar tales it was suggested by some that the Negro stories had been directly or indirectly borrowed from them; by others that the Indians had borrowed them from the Brazilian Negroes. Neither suggestion seems to fit the facts. On the one hand, every story in " Uncle Remus " can be shown to exist in a more primitive shape in Africa, and among people who cannot be suspected of having imported it from America or elsewhere. Thus the "Tar-baby" story is known, in slightly differing forms, to the Duala, the Sumbwa (a tribe to the south of Lake Victoria), the Mbundu of Angola, the Makua, the people of the Lower Congo, and several more.

On the other hand, the more we know of the folk-tales current in different parts of the world the less likely it seems that the Amazonian Indians should have borrowed their stories from the Negroes. In the Malay Peninsula, where the local equivalent for Brer Rabbit is the little mouse-deer, he figures in much the same incidents as the African hare and Hlakanyana. These incidents and the traits of character

[1] Most, as is generally supposed, from the Congo ; but there is evidence that slaves were frequently, during the first quarter of the nineteenth century, imported from Mozambique and other ports on the East Coast. " Mombasas " are mentioned among the Negro slaves in Cuba ; and many cargoes of slaves were smuggled from Havana into the southern states after the import trade had been declared illegal. This perhaps explains why the African hare (Kalulu of the Nyanja, Sungura of the Swahili) should be such a prominent figure in Negro folklore, while his place is taken on the Congo (where it appears there are no hares) by the little antelope known as the water chevrotain. The slaves of the British West Indies were chiefly West Africans (Yorubas, Ibos, Fantis, etc.), and their ' Nancy ' stories are mostly concerned with the spider (Anansi).

which they illustrate are common to human nature all the world over ; the animal actors, of course, vary locally.

The Jackal

In India it is the jackal who plays clever tricks on the stronger and fiercer animals ; in Europe the fox ; in New Guinea and Melanesia yet others. The tortoise, however, seems a universal favourite, except, perhaps, in North Germany, where one of his best-known adventures is ascribed to the hedgehog.

The jackal is the hero for the Hottentots, and also for the Galla and Somali of North-eastern Africa, who consider the hare a stupid sort of creature, and blame him (at least the Hottentots do) for—like the chameleon elsewhere— taking away men's hope of reviving after death. The Moon, angry with him for failing to deliver his message, threw a chunk of wood at him, which is why his lip is split to this day.

The Basuto have—apparently through contact with the Hottentots—confused the characters of the jackal and the hare, giving to the former the famous story of the Animals and the Well, which will be related presently, though the hare comes into his own on several other occasions.

Hare, not Rabbit

It is unfortunate that so many writers, no doubt influenced by " Uncle Remus," used the word ' rabbit ' in translating African stories. There are, I believe, no rabbits, properly so called, in Africa, and Sungura, Kalulu, Sulwe,[1] and Mutlanyana [1] undoubtedly represent what we mean by a hare. Uncle Remus would naturally speak of the more familiar animal, just as he makes Brer Wolf and Brer Fox take the place of the hyena.

Jacottet, in his translation of a Sesuto tale, speaks of a ' rabbit' victimized by Little Hare. This animal (*hlolo*) is, according to Mabille and Dieterlen's dictionary, the red hare (*Lepus crassicaudatus*). Whether this is the same as the ' March Hare ' of the Lalas and Lambas—the name literally

[1] The Shona and Sesuto names for the ' little hare.'

means the " Mad Big Hare "—it would be interesting to discover ; but I have nowhere met with a description of this latter creature.

Animals which figure in the Tales

The hare, then, we may say, is really the most prominent figure in the tales we are considering. Next to him —indeed, in some ways more successful in triumphing over his enemies, and once, at least, getting the better of the hare himself—is the tortoise.

The lion, the elephant, and, more frequently, the hyena are the foils and dupes, whose strength and fierceness are no match for the nimble wits of the little hare and the slow, patient wisdom of the tortoise. More inoffensive creatures, sad to say—the bush-buck, the duiker, and the monitor lizard—occasionally fall victims.

The crocodile is sometimes introduced, and not always in an evil aspect : for instance, a Tumbuka tale shows him helpful to the other animals and treated with gross ingratitude by the tortoise. The hippopotamus also makes an occasional appearance, and it would be possible to make a long list of animals and birds which are mentioned—some of them repeatedly—but play no very conspicuous parts.

The Animals and the Well

I will begin with the story of the Well, though I cannot pretend to arrange the hare's adventures (except for the final and fatal one) in chronological order. Some episodes are linked together in natural sequence, but such groups could, as a rule, be placed anywhere in the series without breaking the connexion.

It was a different matter when some unnamed Low German poet (or succession of poets) combined into the epic of *Reynard the Fox* (*Reinke Vos*) the scattered beast fables current in the Middle Ages. I have no doubt that one day a genius will arise in some Bantu tribe to perform the same service for Sungura.[1]

---

[1] It seems desirable to have a proper name for occasional use, and perhaps it is most convenient to keep to the Swahili form throughout.

I am not forgetting that the Mosuto Azariel Sekese has done something of the kind in his prose story *The Assembly of the Birds*. But this is rather a satire than the kind of epic that I have in mind, though it is a very remarkable work in its own way.

Now for the story.

Once upon a time there was a terrible drought over all the country. No rain had fallen for many months, and the animals were like to die of thirst. All the pools and water-courses were dried up. So the lion called the beasts together to the dry bed of a river, and suggested that they should all stamp on the sand and see whether they could not bring out some water. The elephant began, and stamped his hardest, but produced no result, except a choking cloud of dust. Then the rhinoceros tried, with no better success; then the buffalo; then the rest in turn—still nothing but dust, dust! At the beginning of the proceedings the elephant had sent to call the hare, but he said, " I don't want to come."

Now there was no one left but the tortoise, whom they all had overlooked on account of his insignificance. He came forward and began to stamp; the onlookers laughed and jeered. But, behold! before long there appeared a damp spot in the river-bed. And the rhinoceros, enraged that a little thing like that should succeed where he had failed, tossed him up and dashed him against a rock, so that his shell was broken into a hundred pieces. While he sat, picking up the fragments and painfully sticking them together, the rhinoceros went on stamping, but the damp sand quickly disappeared, and clouds of dust rose, as before. The others repeated their vain efforts, till at last the elephant said, "Let the tortoise come and try." Before he had been at work more than a few minutes the water gushed out and filled the well, which had gradually been excavated by their combined efforts.

The animals then passed a unanimous resolution that the hare, who had refused to share in the work, should not be allowed to take any of the water. Knowing his character, they assumed that he would try to do so, and agreed to take turns in keeping watch over the well.

The hyena took the first watch, and after an hour or two saw the hare coming along with two calabashes, one empty and one full of honey. He called out a greeting to the hyena, was answered, and asked him what he was doing there. The hyena replied, " I am guarding the well because of you, that you may not drink water here." " Oh," said the hare, " I don't want any of your water; it is muddy and bitter. I have much nicer water here." The hyena, his curiosity roused, asked to taste the wonderful water, and Sungura handed him a stalk of grass which he had dipped in the honey. " Oh, indeed, it is sweet ! Just let me have some more ! " " I can't do that unless you let me tie you up to the tree; this water is strong enough to knock you over if you are not tied." The hyena had so great a longing for the sweet drink that he readily consented; the hare tied him up so tightly that he could not move, went on to the well, and filled his calabash; then he jumped in, splashed about to his heart's content, and finally departed laughing.

In the morning the animals came and found the hyena tied to the tree. " Why, Hyena, who has done this to you ? " " A great host of strong men came in the middle of the night, seized me, and tied me up." The lion said, " No such thing ! Of course it was the hare, all by himself." The lion took his turn at watching that night; but, strange to say, he fell a victim to the same trick. Unable to resist the lure of the honey, he was ignominiously tied to the tree.

There they found him next morning, and the hyena, true to his currish nature, sneered : " So it was many men who tied you up, Lion ? " The lion replied, with quiet dignity : " You need not talk; he would be too much for any of us."

The elephant then volunteered to keep watch, but with no better success; then the rest of the animals, each in his turn, only to be defeated by one trick or another.

At last the tortoise came forward, saying, " I am going to catch that one who is in the habit of binding people ! " The others began to jeer: "Nonsense! Seeing how he has outwitted us, the elders, what can you do—a little one like you?" But the elephant took his part, and said that he should be allowed to try.

The Tortoise is too sharp for the Hare

The tortoise then smeared his shell all over with bird-lime, plunged into the well, and sat quite still at the bottom. When the hare came along that night and saw no watcher he sang out, "Hallo! Hallo! the well! Is there no one here?" Receiving no answer, he said, "They're afraid of me! I've beaten them all! Now for the water!" He sat down beside the well, ate his honey, and filled both his gourds, before starting to bathe. Then he stepped into the water and found both his feet caught. He cried out, "Who are you? I don't want your water; mine is sweet. Let me go, and you can try it." But there was no answer. He struggled; he put down one hand [1] to free himself; he put down the other; he was caught fast. There was no help for it: there he had to stay till the animals came in the morning.[2] And when they saw him they said, "Now, indeed, the hare has been shown up!" So they carried him to the *bwalo* for judgment, and the lion said, "Why did you first disobey and afterwards steal the water?" The hare made no attempt to plead his cause, but said, "Just tie me up, and I shall die!" The lion ordered him to be bound, but the hare made one more suggestion. "Don't tie me with coconut-rope, but with green banana-fibre; then if you throw me out in the sun I shall die very quickly."

They did so, and after a while, when they heard the banana-bast cracking as it dried up in the heat, they began to get suspicious, and some one said to the lion that the hare

---

[1] It is quite common for Africans to speak of the forefeet of a quadruped as 'hands.' But, in any case, animals in the stories are often spoken of as if they had human form. We find the same thing again and again in "Uncle Remus."

[2] In the Ila version he is killed on the spot; but I refuse to accept this. Even the tortoise, though more than once too much for the hare, could not bring him to his death; that had to come in the end from a quite unexpected quarter.

would surely break his bonds. The hare heard him and groaned out, as though at his last gasp, "Let me alone. I'm just going to die!" So he lay still for another hour, and then suddenly stretched himself; the banana-fibre gave way, and he was off before they could recover from their astonishment. They started in pursuit, but he out-ran them all, and they were nearly giving up in despair when they saw him on the top of a distant ant-hill, apparently waiting for them to come up. When they got within ear-shot he called out, "I'm off! You're fools, all of you!" and disappeared into a hole in the side of the ant-hill. The animals hastened up and formed a circle round the hill, while the elephant came forward and thrust his trunk into the hole. After groping about for a while he seized the hare by the ear, and the hare cried, "That's a leaf you've got hold of. You've not caught me!" The elephant let go and tried again, this time seizing the hare's leg. "*O-o-o-o-o!* He's got hold of a root."[1] Again the elephant let go, and Sungura slipped out of his reach into the depths of the burrow.

The animals grew tired of waiting, and, leaving the elephant to watch the ant-hill, went to fetch hoes, so that they might dig out the hare. While they were gone the hare, disguising his voice, called out to the elephant, "You who are watching the burrow open your eyes wide and keep them fixed on this hole, so that the hare may not get past without your seeing him!" The elephant unsuspectingly obeyed, and Sungura, sitting just inside the entrance, kicked up a cloud of sand into his eyes and dashed out past him. The elephant, blinded and in pain, was quite unaware of his escape, and kept on watching the hole till the other animals came back. They asked if Sungura was still there. "He may be, but he has thrown sand into my eyes." They fell to digging, and, of course, found nothing.

---

[1] Compare again Brer Tarrypin when caught by Brer Fox: "Tu'n loose dat stump-root an' ketch hold o' me!" This incident occurs in various connexions; it comes in quite appropriately here.

BRER RABBIT IN AFRICA

The Hare's Disguises

Meanwhile the hare had gone away into the bush, plaited his hair in the latest fashion, plastered it with wax [1] taken from a wild bees' nest, and whitened his face with clay, so that he was quite unrecognizable. Then he strolled casually past the place where the animals were at work, asked what they were doing, and offered to help. He was given a hoe, which he used with such vigour that it soon came off the handle. He asked the giraffe for the loan of his leg, used it as the handle of his hoe, and speedily broke it, whereupon he shouted, " I'm the hare ! " and fled, taking refuge in another ant-hill, which had more than one entrance. They started to dig; he escaped through the second hole, which they had not noticed, disguised himself afresh, and came back as before. This time, when his hoe came off the handle, he asked the elephant to let him hammer it in on his head ; and he did it with such good-will that he soon killed him. He ran away once more, shouting insults as he went, and the animals, having lost their two principal leaders, returned home, weary and discouraged.

The Hare nurses the Lioness's Cubs

The hare then went on his way quite happily, till, some time later, he met a lioness, who seized him and was about to kill him. But he pleaded so eloquently for his life, assuring her that he could make himself very useful if she would let him be her servant, that at last she relented and took him home to her den. Next day, when she went out to hunt, she left him in charge of her ten cubs.[2] While she

[1] Various disguises are mentioned as being used by the hare. At Delagoa Bay he makes himself a head-ring (like those worn by Zulu and Thonga men) ; elsewhere he plasters himself all over with mud, or shaves his head, or even takes off his skin (but I think this stratagem more properly belongs to another and clumsier character), or covers himself all over with leaves. In " Uncle Remus " Brer Rabbit, after spilling some honey over himself, rolls in the fallen leaves and becomes quite unrecognizable.

[2] The number of cubs varies in different versions of the story, but several agree in making them ten. The Basuto make the jackal the hero (if so he can be called), and the Akamba the hyena, perhaps thinking a carnivorous hare too great a strain on the probabilities ; but probabilities, as we have seen, count for nothing with the Bantu tale-teller.

was gone Sungura took the cubs down to the stream to play, and suggested that they should wrestle. He wrestled with one of them, threw it, and twisted its neck as they lay on the ground. Returning to the cave with the others, he skinned and ate the dead one at the first convenient opportunity. In the evening the mother came home and, staying outside the cave, told the hare to bring the children out for her to nurse. He brought one, and when she told him to bring the rest he objected, saying it was better to bring them out one by one. Having suckled the first, she handed it back, and he brought her the remaining eight, taking the last twice over.

Next day he did the same, bringing out the last cub three times, and so deceived the mother into thinking she had suckled the whole ten. This went on until he had eaten all but one, which he brought out ten times ; when it came to the tenth time the lioness noticed that the cub refused to suck. The hare explained that it had not been well all day, and the lioness was satisfied, and only told him to take good care of it.

The Hare and the Baboons

As soon as she was gone next day he killed, skinned, and ate the last cub, and, taking the other skins from the place where he had hidden them, set out on his travels. Towards evening he came to the village of the baboons, and found the 'men' playing with teetotums [1] in the 'forum.' He went and sat down in the usual place for strangers, and when some of them came to greet him said, " I have brought beautiful skins to sell. Does anyone want to buy them ? " The baboons crowded round, admiring the skins, and all ten were soon disposed of. They then returned to their game, and the hare sat watching them. Presently he said, " You are not playing right. Shall I show you how ? " They handed him a teetotum, and he began to spin it, singing all the time :

" We have eaten the lion's children on the quiet ! "

[1] Called in Nyasaland *nsika*, but found in many other parts of Africa ; made of a piece of gourd-shell, with a splinter of wood (the size of a match) stuck through it.

Two Zulus engaged in Wrestling

They listened attentively, and then said, "Let us learn this song"; so he taught them the words, and they practised for the rest of the evening. After which he shared their meal, and was given a hut to sleep in.

In the morning he was off before it was light, and made his way back to the lions' den, where he found the lioness distractedly searching for her missing cubs. On the way he had been careful to roll in the mud and get himself well scratched by the thorny bushes, so that he presented a most disorderly appearance. On seeing her he set up a dismal wail. "Oh! Oh! Some wild beasts came yesterday and carried off your children. They were too much for me; I could do nothing. See how they knocked me about and wounded me! But I followed them, and I can show you where they live. If you come with me you will be able to kill them all. But you had better let me tie you up in a bundle of grass and put some beans just inside, and I will carry you and tell them that I have brought a load of beans. They have the skins of your children, whom I saw them eating." The lioness agreed, and, having tied her up, the hare started with his load. Arriving at the village, he laid it down in the place for strangers. The baboons were so intent on their game that they hardly noticed him at first, and the lioness could hear them singing with all their might:

"We have eaten the lion's children on the quiet."

After a while they came up and greeted Sungura, and he said that he had brought them a load of beans in return for their hospitality of the day before. He loosened one end of the bundle, to show them the beans, and then eagerly accepted their invitation to join in the game. By the time it was once more in full swing the lioness had worked herself free, and sprang on the nearest baboon, bearing him to the ground. The others tried to escape, but the hare had run round to the gate of the enclosure, closed it, and fastened the bar. Then began "a murder grim and great"; not one of the baboons was left alive, and when

261

the hare had brought out the skins of the poor cubs and laid them before the lioness she knew for a certainty that she had but done justice, and was duly grateful to the hare. He, however, thought it just as well not to remain in her neighbourhood, so took his leave and resumed his wanderings.

The Hare and the Hyena

We may pass over two or three more of the exploits commonly attributed to him : how he treated an unoffending antelope as Hlakanyana treated the ogre's mother; how, again like Hlakanyana, he got a lion to help him thatch a hut and fastened his tail into the thatch; and how he killed another lion by getting him to swallow a red-hot stone wrapped in a quantity of fat. The Galla and, I think, the Hottentots attribute this exploit to the jackal.

Some of the most popular incidents arise out of his friendship with the hyena. How this friendship originated and why he should have chosen to ally himself with this most unattractive beast is not clear : the stories are apt to begin baldly with the statement that " the hare and the hyena (or the tortoise and the monitor, or various other pairs, as the case may be) made friendship with each other " (*anapalana ubwenzi*, in Nyanja), no explanation being offered. It will be seen that for any tricks played on the hyena the hare had ample provocation, and the final injury he suffered could by no means be condoned.

One very popular story tells how, being in want of food, they went to the chief of a certain village and offered to cultivate his garden. He agreed, and gave them a pot of beans as their food-supply for the day. When they reached the garden they made a fire and put the beans on to boil. By the time they knocked off for the midday rest the beans were done, and the hyena, saying that he wanted to wash before eating, went to the stream and left the hare to watch the pot. No sooner was he out of sight than he stripped off his skin and ran back. The hare, thinking this was some strange and terrible beast, lost his head and ran away;

the hyena sat down by the fire, finished the whole pot full of beans, returned to the stream, resumed his skin, and came back at his leisure. The hare, as all seemed quiet, ventured back, found the pot empty and the hyena clamorously demanding his food. The hare explained that he had been frightened away by an unknown monster, which had evidently eaten up the beans. The hyena refused to accept this excuse, and accused the hare of having eaten the beans himself. The unfortunate hare had to go hungry; but, finding denial useless, contented himself with remarking that if that beast came again he meant to shoot it; so he set to work making a bow. The hyena watched him till the bow was finished, and then said. " You have not made it right. Give it here ! " And, taking it from him, he pretended to trim it into shape, but all the while he was cutting away the wood so as to weaken it in one spot. The hare so far suspected nothing, and kept his bow handy against the lunch-hour on the following day. When the 'wild beast' appeared he fitted an arrow to the string and bent the bow, but it broke in his hand, and once more he fled.

By this time his suspicions were awakened, and when he had made himself a new bow he hid it in the grass when the hyena was not looking. On the next occasion when the hyena appeared he shot at him and wounded him, but not seriously, so that he ran back to get into his skin and returned to find the hare calmly eating beans.

In one Nyasaland version of this tale it was not the hyena but the elephant or the *dzimwe* (*zimwi, izimu*), a kind of bogy of whom it was difficult to get a clear account, who tricked the hare and was shot dead by him in the end; but the hyena fits in better (the poor, good elephant is more usually the dupe). And, according to some accounts, his end was to come otherwise.

The Roasted Guinea-fowl

Another time the hare and the hyena went into the bush together after game. They found a guinea-fowl's nest full of eggs,[1] and soon after trapped a guinea-fowl. They carried their spoils home, and the hare said to his friend, "You roast the fowl and the eggs. I'm tired; I want to go to sleep." The hyena made up the fire, spitted the bird on a stick, and put the eggs into the hot ashes. When the savoury steam filled the hut his mouth began to water, and when he had made sure that the guinea-fowl was done he ate it up, all but the legs, which he put into the fire. He then ate the eggs, carefully cleaned the shell of one and put it aside, together with one quill, threw the rest of the feathers into the fire, and lay down to sleep.

The smell of the burning feathers awakened Sungura, who started up, called the hyena, and then noticed that the guinea-fowl was missing. When asked where it was the hyena said he had fallen asleep while it was roasting, and it had got burned. The hare suspected the truth, but said nothing at the time. A little later he suggested that they should go to their respective relations and get some food; so they separated. The hyena went a little way, and as soon as he was out of sight lay down in the grass and slept. The hare, too, did not go far, but hid himself and waited awhile; then he gathered some banana-leaves and stealthily followed his partner. He tied him up and gave him a good beating, which effectually wakened him, so that he cried for mercy, though he could not see who was attacking him. The hare then went away, and a little later pretended to come upon his victim unexpectedly, kicked the supposedly unknown object in his path, and said, "What's this?"

"I'm here, your friend!"

"What's the matter?"

"Some man came along and tied me up and beat me."

"Do you know who it was?"

"No, I don't."

The hare condoled with the hyena, and they remained quiet for a few days, when the hyena heard that there was

---

[1] The Central and Southern Africans, as a rule, do not eat eggs (with some tribes they are *tabu* to young people only). If they ever do they do not seem to care whether, or how long, they have been sat on.

to be a dance at his village, and invited the hare to go with him. The hare accepted, but said he wanted to go home first: he would come in the afternoon.

The hyena went and had a bath, got himself up in his best clothes, complete with beads, for the dance, and, as a finishing-touch, put the egg-shell on his head and stuck the feather into it. When the hare arrived he welcomed him warmly, asked him to sit down, and thereupon took his *zomari* (a kind of clarinet) and played:

"The guinea-fowl and all! Put the blame on the fire! *ti! ti! ti!* "[1]

These are supposed to be 'riddling words,' *maneno ya fumbo*. They are explained to mean: "I've eaten up the guinea-fowl and all, though I pretended it had got burned!" The hare understood them well enough; he sprang up, seized a big drum, and fell to beating it and singing:

"I took him and bound him with banana-leaves and beat him! *pu! pu! pu!* "

Then ensued a free fight, which, strange to say, did not dissolve the partnership.[2]

The Hyena kills the Hare's Mother

There is a story, very variously told, of a visit paid by the two to the hyena's wife's relations, in which the hare defeats the hyena's tricks and finally turns the tables on him, but I hasten on to the final break.

In a time of famine, having exhausted every possible food-supply, the hyena proposed that he should kill and eat his mother, and the hare should do the same. The hare agreed, but kept his reflections to himself. The hyena went away, killed his mother, and ate her; the hare went, ostensibly for the same purpose, but hid his mother in a cave which could be reached only by climbing up the face of the

[1] In the original: *Kanga pia, singizia moto, ti! ti! ti!* As it is impossible to play a wind instrument and sing at the same time, it is perhaps implied that the notes conveyed the words, after the manner of the Ashanti drums.

[2] One Swahili version (Büttner, *Anthologie*, p. 95), which has in the main been followed here, as giving more detail, makes the greedy beast the mungoose (*cheche*), but the hyena, whom we find elsewhere, is the more probable.

cliff, and left with her a supply of wild herbs and roots, having first agreed on a signal to make his presence known. Next day, when the hyena had departed on his own business, the hare went to the cave and uttered the password. On hearing his mother's answer he called out to her to let down a rope, by which he climbed up into the cave. She had cooked sufficient food for herself and him, and after a hearty meal he returned to the place where he had left his friend. And this he did day by day.

The hyena, in the meantime, had finished his meat by the second day, and could not make out why the hare never seemed in want of food. So one day he followed him, and, hiding in the bushes, heard him give the password and the mother answer, and saw him drawn up into the cave. Next day he watched his opportunity, went to the cave, and called out the word, but there was no answer, the hare having warned his mother to take no notice should anyone else come. He saw that the hare had deceived him, and went away nursing his grievance, but at a loss what to do about it. He decided to consult the leopard, but got no help from him, only the suggestion that he had better go to the ant-eater.

The ant-eater, on hearing his story, said that there was no hope for him unless he could imitate the hare's voice so skilfully as to deceive his mother; and to make this possible he advised him to go to a nest of soldier-ants and put his tongue in among them; if he got it well stung his voice would be softened.[1] He did this, but was unable to endure the pain for more than a short time. He returned to the ant-eater, who desired him to try his voice, and found that it was not much improved. The ant-eater said, " My friend, you're a coward. If you want to eat the hare's mother you will have to go back and let the ants bite your tongue till it is half its present size ! "

The hyena's greed and resentment were stronger than his

---

[1] The ogre in the story of Tselane (and similar ones) softens his voice by swallowing red-hot iron. He does this on the advice of the witch-doctor. Brer Wolf, in like case, goes to the blacksmith.

dread of pain, so he went back and let the ants work their will on him till the desired result was obtained. In fact, when he went back to the cave the hare's mother was completely taken in and let down the rope at once—to her undoing.

The Hare's Revenge

When the hare went as usual on the following day he got no answer to his call, and, looking round, saw traces of blood on the grass. Then he guessed what had happened, and thought how he might be revenged. When he met the hyena again he said nothing, but went away and made his preparations.

He came forth in the evening most splendidly adorned— the details, of course, vary locally, from a wealth of brass and copper chains, pendants, rings, and ear-ornaments to the white shirt, embroidered coat, silver-mounted sword, and jewelled dagger of the coast men. Having thoroughly excited the hyena's admiration and envy, he showed him a mark on the top of his head, and told him that he had had a red-hot nail driven in there, and that if he, the hyena, would submit to the same operation he might be similarly adorned. The foolish beast was quite willing—the hare had the red-hot iron ready—and that, of course, was the end of Hyena.

In *Nights with Uncle Remus* this story is told (under the curious title "Cutta Cord-La") by an old man who, unlike Remus himself, had been brought from Africa in his youth. The hyena has become Brer Wolf, and Brer Rabbit hides his grandmother "in da top one big coconut-tree"—an African touch which puzzles the child listener. Brer Wolf has a red-hot poker thrust down his throat by the blacksmith, to soften his voice, or "mekky him talk easy."

The story is found in many different parts of Africa, though the actors in it are not always the same. This is also the case with the "Tar-baby" story, which is so well known that I need do no more than refer to it.

In spite of Sungura's pranks (some of them cruel enough, especially when played on the elephant, who, somewhat surprisingly, is not credited with much sense), he is always regarded with a certain affection. And it is only fair to recall one or two incidents which show him in a more amiable light than those hitherto given.

The Hare overcomes both Rhino and Hippo

The famous ' tug-of-war ' story sometimes (as in " Uncle Remus ") belongs to the tortoise, but quite as often the hero is the hare. So it is told by the Anyanja, the Baila, the Wawemba, the Ansenga (Northern Rhodesia), and probably many others.

The hare challenged the hippopotamus and the rhinoceros to a trial of strength,[1] going to each in turn and saying, " Take hold of this rope, and let us pull against each other. I am going to the bank yonder." He then disappeared into the bushes, carrying what purported to be his end of the rope, and calling out as he went, " Wait till you feel me pull at my end, and then begin." He had stationed the two on opposite sides of a bush-covered island, and when he reached a point midway between them he pulled the rope in both directions. Rhino and hippo both pulled with all their might; their strength being about equal, neither gave way to any extent, though the former, after a while, was dragged forward a little, and when he recovered himself went back with such a rush that he dragged the hippo out on to the bank, whereat they both ejaculated, " Stupendous !" and Hippo called, " Hare ! hare ! " but without receiving any answer. They went on pulling till they were both exhausted, and the rhino said, " I will go and see that man who is pulling me," and just then the hippo put his head out of the water, and said, " Who is that pulling me ? " And Chipembele (the rhino) said, " Why, Shinakambeza (one of Hippo's ' praise-names '), is it you pulling me ? " " It is I. Why, who was he that brought you the rope, Chipembele ? " " It was the hare. Was it he who gave it to you, Hippo ? " " Yes, it was he."

---

[1] The Ila version has in the main been followed. See Smith and Dale, *The Ila-speaking Peoples*, vol. ii, p. 377.

It seems that these two had previously been at enmity, and the rhino had vowed never to set foot in the river. But the fact that both had equally been made fools of disposed them more favourably towards each other.

> Thus they became reconciled, and that is why Rhinoceros drinks water to-day. Rhinoceros and Hippopotamus, when they do not see each other in the flesh, Rhinoceros will drink water in the river where Hippo lives, and Hippopotamus comes out to go grazing where Rhinoceros has his home.

This is the conclusion given by the Baila to the story; other people end it differently: either the rope breaks and both competitors fall backward, or the hare (or the tortoise) cuts it asunder in the middle, with the same result. In a Nyanja version it is the elephant who pulls against the hippopotamus; both are tired out, and the hare goes to each in turn and claims a forfeit, which he gets.

It is obvious that after the story had reached America the characters had to be changed. Brer Tarrypin challenged the bear, and, as no other animal of equal size was available, he fastened the other end of the rope to a tree.

The Hare decides a Case [1]

There is a very popular tale in which the hare shows himself both wise and helpful. There was a man who lived by hunting. One day, just as he was about to take a pig and an antelope out of his traps, a lion sprang upon him, and threatened to kill him unless he gave him a share of the meat. In fear of his life, he agreed, and allowed the lion to take out the hearts, livers, and such other titbits as he chose, while he himself carried the rest home. This happened every day, and the man's wife was consumed with curiosity, when she found that there was neither heart nor liver in any of the animals he brought home. She insisted, in spite of his denial, that he had given these to

---

[1] One version of this is to be found in Mr Posselt's *Fables of the Veld* (p. 51); another, which I have chiefly followed, I took down, in Pokomo, on the Tana river, in 1912. There is a similar story (Yao) in Duff Macdonald's *Africana* (vol. ii, p. 346), where the hare decides between a man and a crocodile.

some other woman, and so, one day, started early to look at his traps, and was herself caught in one of them. Presently the man and the lion arrived on the scene, and the latter demanded his share of the game. The man refused to kill his wife; the lion insisted on holding him to his bargain. The wretched man, driven to desperation, was about to give in, and the woman would have paid dearly for her suspicions, had the hare not happened to pass by. The husband saw him, and called on him to help; Mwakatsoo[1] said at first that it was no business of his, but, yielding at last to the man's entreaties, he stopped, and heard both sides of the story. He then ordered the man to release his wife, and set the trap again. This having been done, he asked the lion to show him how the woman had got into it. The lion fell into the trap, both figuratively and literally, " and got caught by the hand and foot." " So, this is the way it caught her. Now let me go!" But Mwakatsoo turned to the man and said, " You were a great fool to make such a promise. Now be off, you and your wife!" They did not wait to be told so twice, but hastened home, while the lion called on Mwakatsoo to release him, and received for answer: " I shall do no such thing. You are the enemy!"[2]

A Giryama story-teller remarks (but this was on a different occasion, when the hare had been supplying the lion with meat):

" So the Little Hare was on good terms with his neighbours and was a nice person in the Lion's opinion, and in the opinion of his neighbours also was he a nice person!"[3]

---

[1] So the hare is familiarly called by the Wapokomo.

[2] The Rhodesian hare was more ingenious. First he said he could not hear what they were saying for the wind, and they had better all come into a cave, the woman being released for the purpose. Then he called out that the cave was about to fall in, and they must hold up the roof. All four being so engaged, he sent off the man and his wife to get logs for propping it: he and the lion would hold it up till their return. The couple, of course, took the hint and made their escape. The hare ran away, and the lion, in terror lest the rock should fall, went on supporting it till he was tired, and then made a desperate leap to the mouth of the cave, hit his head against a rock, and crawled away half stunned. "Since that day lions have hunted their own game."

[3] Taylor, *Giryama Vocabulary*, p. 127.

A Rock at Esidumbini, Natal

BRER RABBIT IN AFRICA

The Hare's End

And now for Sungura's sad end, which was due not to force or fraud of an enemy, but to a friend's misplaced sense of humour.

He went one day to call on his friend the cock, and found him asleep, with his head under his wing. The hare had never seen him in this position before, and never thought of doubting the hens' word when they informed him (as previously instructed) that their husband was in the habit of taking off his head and giving it to the herd-boys to carry with them to the pasture. " Since you were born have you ever seen a man have his head cut off and for it to go to pasture, while the man himself stayed at home in the village ? " And the hare said, " Never ! But when those herd-boys come, will he get up again ? " And those women said, " Just wait and see ! " At last, when the herd-boys arrived, their mother said, " Just rouse your father there where he is sleeping." The cock, when aroused, welcomed his guest, and they sat talking till dinner was ready, and still conversed during the meal. The hare was anxious to know " how it was done," and the cock told him it was quite easy—" if you think you would like to do it." The hare confidently accepted the explanation, and they parted, having agreed that the cock should return the visit next day.

He was so greatly excited that he began to talk of his wonderful experience as soon as he reached his home. "That person the fowl is a clever fellow ; he has just shown me his clever device of cutting off the head till, on your being hit, you see, you become alive again. Well, to-morrow I intend to show you all this device ! "

Next morning he told his boys what to do. They hesitated, but he insisted, and when they were ready to go out with the cattle they cut off his head, bored the ears, and put a string through them, to carry it more conveniently. The women picked up the body and laid it on the bed, trusting, in spite of appearances, to his assurance that he was not dead.

By and by his friend arrived, and, not seeing him, inquired

271

for him; the women showed him the body lying on the bed. He was struck with consternation, and, let us hope, with remorse. " But my friend is a simpleton indeed! " They said, " Is not this device derived from you? " but he turned a deaf ear to this hint, and only insisted that the hare was a simpleton. He thought, however, he would wait and see whether, after all, he did get up. The boys came home when the sun declined; they struck their father, as he had told them, " but he did not get up. And the children burst out crying. And the mothers of the family cried. And folks sat a-mourning. And all the people that heard of it were amazed at his death: ' Such a clever man! And for him to have met with his death through such a trifling thing! ' " [1]

That was ' Harey's ' epitaph.

[1] Taylor, *Giryama Vocabulary*, p. 133.

CHAPTER XVIII: LEGENDS OF THE TORTOISE

NEXT to the hare the tortoise is the most conspicuous figure in Bantu folklore. In some parts, indeed, he is more so: of the sixty-one stories collected by Dr Nassau in the Corisco Bay district twenty have the tortoise as the principal character. There seem to be no hares in this part of the country; the animal who most frequently measures his strength and his wits against the tortoise is the leopard, and he is invariably defeated, though on one occasion his son avenges his death by killing the tortoise.

The African tortoise in the tales is usually of the land variety, though in one of the Benga stories [1] he is represented as taking to the water with his family, to escape the vengeance of the leopard. In Angola [2] they tell of a man who found a turtle (*mbashi*) and tried to drown him, as Brer Fox did "ole man Tarrypin," with the same result. The American terrapin is distinctly a water-tortoise, or turtle: there are various kinds of these in the African rivers and swamps, but, as might be expected from the immense extent of desert and forest country, the land ones are the commoner.

Uncle Remus's "Brer Tarrypin"

"Brer Tarrypin" figures in six of the earlier "Uncle Remus" stories; [3] one of these has already been mentioned; of the others the best are the "Tug of War" (the 'hare' version of which was given in the last chapter) and the famous race with Brer Rabbit, which he won, not (as in the later, moralized fable) through his own perseverance and the other's careless self-confidence, but by planting out his relatives at intervals all along the track.

In the later collection [4] we have him tricking the buzzard

[1] Nassau, *Where Animals Talk*, p. 158: "The Deceptions of Tortoise."
[2] Chatelain, *Folk-tales of Angola*, p. 153.
[3] The stories referred to are Nos. X, XII, XIV, XVIII, XXVI, and XXX.
[4] *Nights with Uncle Remus*, Nos. XIV, XV, and XLVI.

into getting burned to death, and then making the quills of his wing-feathers into a musical instrument, which is stolen from him by Brer Fox and recovered with difficulty. This recalls Hlakanyana killing a hare (not *the* hare !) and making a whistle out of one of his bones, which the ' iguana ' subsequently steals from him, and the Ronga hare, with his pipes made from the little horns of the gazelle he has treacherously done to death. Out of seventy stories in this book eleven introduce Brer Tarrypin ; the only one that need be noticed just now is where he rescues Brer Rabbit from the ungrateful wolf. Mr Wolf had got pinned under a falling rock ; Brer Rabbit, passing by, raised up the rock enough to release him, whereupon he found himself caught, and was about to be eaten when he suggests that they might "leave the whole case with Brer Tarrypin." His decision is the same as that of the hare against the crocodile in the Yao story, and Brer Rabbit escapes.

Character of the Tortoise

This, like some African examples one has met with, shows the tortoise in a kindly light ; but in general he appears to be less lovable than, with all his wicked tricks, we cannot help feeling the hare to be. The tortoise is slow, patient, vindictive, and, sometimes, cruel in his revenge ; but he never shows the inveterate and occasionally motiveless malignancy of the West African spider, the hero of the Anansi tales.

It is easy to see why the tortoise should get a reputation for uncanny wisdom. There is something mysterious about him. As Major Leonard says : [1]

Absolutely harmless and inoffensive in himself, the tortoise does not prey on even the smallest of insects, but subsists entirely on the fallen fruits of the forest. In the gloomy forests of the Niger Delta there are only two enemies capable of doing him any serious harm. The one is man, who is able to lift him up and carry him bodily away, which, however, he does not do, unless the creature is required in connection with certain religious

---

[1] *The Lower Niger and its Tribes*, pp. 314 and 315 (here somewhat condensed).

ceremonies. His other and most dangerous enemy is the python, who, having first crushed him, swallows him alive, shell and all. But pythons large enough to do this, unless the tortoise happens to be young and small, are very scarce. Thus the tortoise has been practically immune from attack—a fact that in a great measure explains his longevity. [His reputation has been enhanced by] the fact that he can exist longer without food than perhaps any other animal. . . . In process of time, the word which stood for ' tortoise ' became a synonym for cunning and craft, and a man of exceptional intelligence was in this way known among the Ibo as *Mbai* and among the Ibani as *Ekake*,[1] meaning a tortoise. Although slow, he was sure, and this sureness, in the native mind, implied doggedness and a fixed determination, while silence and secrecy implied mystery and a veiled purpose, behind which it is impossible to get.

The Race won by the Tortoise

The ' Race ' story is known in Africa to the Kamba, Konde,[2] Lamba, Ila, Duala, Bakwiri,[3] and, I believe, to many others. I have come across only two in which the one challenged is the hare, and one of these (the Ila) is curiously mixed up with the story of the Animals and the Well. The race is run by all the animals to the river, to get water in time of drought, and the youngest tortoise, who has been buried close to the bank, brings them a supply as they lie exhausted. In most cases it is an antelope who runs and loses—the duiker, the harnessed antelope, or some other kind—but the Kamba make the tortoise and the fish-eagle the competitors, and the Bondei the tortoise and the falcon; this last tortoise, strangely enough, turns into a fine young man.[4] And, finally, in Kondeland

---

[1] *Cf.* Mpongwe *ekaga*, ' tortoise.'

[2] Better, Ngonde, but their proper name appears to be Nyakyusa; they inhabit the northern end of Lake Nyasa, on its western side.

[3] Between the Wuri and Sanaga rivers, in the Cameroons. Their nearest neighbours are the Duala and the Isubu.

[4] See Woodward, "Bondei Folk-tales," p. 182. Here and in the Kamba story referred to the two are contending for the hand of the chief's daughter; but in general there is no inducement to the contest beyond the trial of strength. This Kamba story is given in Mr Hobley's book (*The Akamba*), but Dr Lindblom has another version, in which the tortoise races a young man.

the match is between the tortoise and the elephant.[1]   This
is as follows :

The tortoise one day met the elephant, and said, " Do
you think you are the greatest of all the beasts? "   The
conversation continued :

" Haven't you seen me, then? "

" Did you ever see your own head? "

" What of that? "

" Why, if I were to jump I could jump over it! "

" What, you? "

" Yes, I ! "

" Well, try it, then ! "

" Not to-day.   I'm tired.   I have come a long way."

The elephant thought this was a mere excuse, and told
the tortoise he was a liar ; but it was agreed that the trial
should take place next day.   The tortoise hastened away,
fetched his wife, and hid her in the bushes close to the spot
they had fixed on.

With daybreak the elephant arrived, and found the
tortoise already there.   He got the elephant to stand in the
middle of a clear space, and then took up his position on
one side of him, opposite to the point where his wife was
hidden in the grass.   The elephant said, " Jump away,
Tortoise! "   The tortoise cried, "*Hi-i !* " took off for the
high jump, and crept into the grass, while his wife, on the
other side, cried "*Ehe !*"   The elephant looked and found
the tortoise (as he thought) on the farther side, though he
had not seen the actual leap.   "*Joko !* [2]   Try it again, for
I couldn't see you doing it! "   This time the wife cried,
"*Hi-i !* " and the tortoise "*Ehe!* " and the elephant suspected nothing, thinking that the leap had been too swift
for his eye to catch, and acknowledged himself beaten, but
was sure that he would be the better in a foot-race.   The
tortoise was willing to try, " but not to-day, for my legs are
tired with the jumping.   But could you come to-morrow? "
The elephant agreed, and the same place was fixed for

---

[1] Schumann, *Grundriss einer Grammatik der Kondesprache,* p. 82.

[2] An exclamation expressive of surprise.

the starting-point of the course—the race to begin at sunrise.

The tortoise went home, called his children together, and spent the night in collecting the rest of the clan, stationing them at convenient intervals along the course and instructing them what to do.

The elephant appeared punctually in the morning, and after greetings started off at a trot—*ndi ! ndi ! ndi !* [1] When he had been running for some time he called out, " Tortoise! " thinking he must have left him far behind, but, to his consternation, he heard a voice in front of him : "*Yuba !* Why, I'm here ! " This happened again and again, till he reached the goal and found the original tortoise awaiting him there. " And so it befell that the elephant was defeated." (The original expresses this in three words.) The Benga wind up the story by saying, " So the council decided that, of all the tribes of animals Tortoise was to be held as greatest ; for that it had outrun Antelope. And the animals gave Tortoise the power to rule."

The Baboon invites the Tortoise to dine

Another favourite story is that of the friendship between the tortoise and the baboon, which ended (as in the case of Æsop's fox and crane) in consequence of their mutual invitations to dinner. The baboon, having brewed his millet-beer (*moa, pombe,* or *utshwala*), placed the pots up in a tree, and the tortoise, being, of course, unable to climb up, while his host offered no other accommodation, had to return home hungry and thirsty. The tortoise paid his friend out by inviting him at the end of the dry season (the time of the grass-fires) and preparing his feast on a spot which could be reached only by crossing a patch of burnt ground. When the baboon arrived he was politely requested to wash his hands. As he had to cross the burnt grass again to reach the stream in order to do so he came back with them as black as ever.[2]

---

[1] This is one of the famous 'descriptive adverbs,' or 'onomatopœias,' which abound in the Bantu languages. Cf. *kuputu kuputu,* of a horse galloping, etc.

[2] Baboons, of course, do not as a rule walk upright.

This went on so long—for the tortoise would not let him sit down till his hands were clean—that he was tired out, and went home in disgust.

The Tortoise and the Monitor

Still more spitefully vindictive is the character given to the tortoise in the Nyanja story which associates him with the *ng'anzi*, a large lizard, probably a species of *Varanus* (monitor). It opens, like many other tales of this kind, with the statement that these two " made friendship," by which we are to understand that they went through the ceremonies of the blood-covenant, binding themselves to help each other whenever called upon. One day the tortoise was in need of salt—well known to be a very precious commodity in certain parts of Africa—and set out to beg some from his friend. Having reached the *ng'anzi's* abode and got his salt, he next asked to have it tied up with string in a piece of bark-cloth. (Such bundles, each a man's load, used to be brought in to Blantyre by people who had been making salt on the shores of Lake Chilwa.) He passed the string over his shoulder, so that the parcel hung under his other arm, and started for home, dragging the salt after him—*gubudu gubudu!*[1] The *ng'anzi* came up behind him and seized the salt; the tortoise, pulled up short, *njutu njutu!* turned back to see what had caught his load. He found that the *ng'anzi* had seized the bundle of salt in the middle, and said to him, " Don't seize my salt. I have just brought it from my friend's house." The *ng'anzi* replied, " I've just picked it up in the path." " But you can see the string passing round my neck as we tied it. I, the tortoise, am the owner." But the *ng'anzi* insisted that he had found the parcel, and, as the tortoise would not give in, said, " Let us go to the smithy [this being the local gossip-shop or men's club of the village], that the elders may decide our case." The tortoise agreed, and they went to the smithy, where

---

[1] Intended to express the bumping of the parcel along the path as the tortoise makes his slow progress. When he is pulled up, *njutu njutu!* expresses the sudden stop which almost jerks him off his feet.

they found eight old men. The *ng'anzi* opened the case in proper form: " I have a suit against the tortoise." The elders said, " What is your suit with which you have come hither to us? " He stated his case, and they asked, " How did you pick up the tortoise's salt? " The tortoise replied, " Because I am short as to the legs I tied the salt round my neck, and it went bumping along, and then the *ng'anzi* took hold of it, and I turned back to see what had caught it, and there was my friend the *ng'anzi*, and he said, ' Let us go to the smithy,' and therefore we have come here." The elders suggested that they should compromise the case by cutting the bag of salt in two. The tortoise consented, though unwillingly, seeing that he had no chance, since the judges were all relatives of the *ng'anzi*, as he perceived too late. " Perhaps I have been wrong in taking to the road alone," was his reflection on finding that he had fallen among thieves. The bag was cut, and, of course, a great deal of salt fell out on the ground. The tortoise gathered up what he could, but it was only a little, " because his fingers were so short," and he failed to tie it up satisfactorily in the piece of barkcloth left to him. The *ng'anzi*, on the contrary, had his full half, and the elders scraped up what had been spilt, earth and all. So the tortoise went away, crying, " because my salt is spoilt," and reached his home with one or two tiny screws done up in leaves. His wife asked him what had become of the salt, and he told her the whole story, adding that he would go again to his friend and get a fresh supply. He rested four days, and then started once more.

On reaching the *ng'anzi's* burrow he found that the owner had entered it and was enjoying a meal of *lumwe* (the winged males of the termites, which are about an inch long and accounted a great delicacy). The tortoise came walking very softly, *nyang'anyang'a*, looked carefully about him, spied the *ng'anzi*, crept up to him without being seen, and seized him by the middle of his body. Thereupon he cried out, " Who has seized me by the waist? As for me, I am just eating white ants." The tortoise replied, " I have picked up. Yes, I have picked up. The other day you picked up my salt, and to-day I have picked you up! Well, let us go to the smithy, as we did the other day." The *ng'anzi* said, " Do you insist? " The tortoise answered, " Yes." So they came out of the burrow and went to the smithy, where they found nine old men. Having heard the case stated, these elders said, " You should do what you did the other day : you cut the salt in two." The tortoise cried in triumph, *"Ha! ha! ha! ha!*—it is good so," and rejoiced with his whole heart; but the *ng'anzi* said, " Are you absolutely resolved on killing me? " " You formerly destroyed my salt, and I, for my part, am going to do the same to you! " " Ha! This is the end of me! To want to cut me in half! . . . Well, do what you want to do. It's all over with me, the *ng'anzi*! " The tortoise leapt up, *tu!* and took a knife and cut the *ng'anzi* through the middle, and he cried, " Mother! Mother! I am dead to-day through picking up! " and died.

The tortoise took the tail and two legs and went on his way, and when he came to his wife's house he said, " We have settled the score : the *ng'anzi* ate that salt of mine, and to-day I have paid him back in his own coin, and he is dead." [1]

Perhaps he deserved it; but the tortoise reminds one of Shylock in his determination to get his pound of flesh.

This story may seem to have been related at unnecessary length (though in the original the speeches are repeated *verbatim*, over and over again); but it makes such a quaint picture of African life as it is, or was not so very long ago in Nyasaland, that the temptation to paraphrase it was irresistible : the journey for the salt, the covenant of friendship (in this instance basely betrayed), the old men talking over the case at the village blacksmith's forge.

The Name of the Tree

There is a very curious story, found in places as far apart as Corisco Bay in the north and Transvaal in the south, in which the tortoise, as a rule, plays the principal part, though this is sometimes given to the hare. It may have a mytho-

---

[1] From a manuscript taken down by me at Blantyre in 1893.

logical background now partly or completely forgotten : this
is suggested by the fact that God (Leza, Maweza) is introduced in some versions as the owner of the mysterious
tree.

On occasions it opens with the statement that there was
a famine in the land. The animals, searching for food (or
sometimes accidentally, while hunting), come across a tree
previously unknown to them, full of ripe and tempting fruit.
They send messenger after messenger to the tree's owner,
in order to ask its name, or sometimes, simply, " what sort
of a tree it is, that we may know whether the fruit can be
eaten or not." But the exact name is so often insisted on
that it would seem to have some magical significance. The
"owner of the tree" is in two cases (Subiya, Bena Kanioka[1])
said to be 'God'; the Bapedi and Baila speak of " an old
woman "; the Basuto say, " The owner of the tree is called
Koko." As this word means 'grandmother,' it would seem
as if the old woman were the tribal ancestress. Other versions
do not specify the owner more particularly, or call him, or
her, simply " the chief."

The messengers (in some instances a whole series is
enumerated; in others, after the first, only " all the rest of
the animals " are mentioned) invariably forget the name on
the way back. At last an insignificant and despised member
of the community—usually the tortoise, but sometimes the
hare, and in one case the gazelle—is successful. Here the
story should end, and does so in, I think, the best versions,
with the triumph of the tortoise. But in some the animals
turn on their benefactor and refuse him a share in the fruit.
The Bapedi make him revenge himself by a trick which
properly belongs to the hare, and several subsequent incidents are identical with those in a Ronga hare story, in
which that of the tree follows on one of an entirely different
character. This, like the Suto and Pedi versions of our
tortoise story, makes it an essential point that the fruit on
the topmost branch is not to be touched, but left for the
chief. The Ronga hare gets at the fruit and eats it out of

---

[1] On the Upper Sankuru, in the Belgian Congo.

mere mischief (afterwards putting the blame on the elephant);
the tortoise to revenge himself for ill-usage.

Here follows the Lamba tale : [1]

In a time of famine all the animals gathered near a tree
full of wonderful fruit, which could not be gathered unless
the right name of the tree was mentioned, and built their
huts there. When the fruit ripened Ŵakalulu (" Mr Little
Hare ") went to the chief of the tree and asked him its name.
The chief answered, " When you arrive just stand still and
say *Uŵungelema*." The hare started on his way back, but
when he had reached the outskirts of his village he tripped,[2]
and the name went out of his head. Trying to recover it, he
kept saying to himself, "*Uŵungelenyense, Uŵuntuluntumba,
Uŵu*—what?"

When he arrived the animals asked, " What is the name,
Little Hare, of these things?" But he could only stammer
the wrong words, and not a fruit fell. Next morning two
buffaloes arose and tried their luck—it seems to have been
considered safer to send two—but on their return both
tripped and forgot the word. In answer to their eager
questioners they said, " He said, *Uŵumbilakanwa, Uŵuntuluntumba*, or what?"—which, of course, could not help
matters.

Then two elands were sent, with the same result.

Then the lion went, and, though he took care to repeat
the word over and over again on the way home, he too
tripped against the obstacle and forgot it. " Then all the
animals, the roans and the sables, and the mungooses,[3] all
came to an end going there. They all just returned in
vain."

---

[1] Doke, *Lamba Folklore*, p. 61.

[2] Some versions have it that the messengers, one after another, stumbled against
an ant-hill in the path. The Benga makes them go to the chief's place by sea,
and forget the name when the canoe is upset. (Also the successful one is warned
not to eat or drink while on the water, and is careful to observe this.) In the
Luba story they forget the name if they look back ; and with the Bena Kanioka
Maweza gives the tortoise a little bell, which reminds him of the name by ringing.

[3] It may be worth noting that the two kinds of antelope mentioned have in the
original the honorific prefix Ŵa. The mungooses (*mapulu*) are presumably
considered too insignificant.

"The Tortoise had a Smoke"
Photo Dr Clement M. Doke

LEGENDS OF THE TORTOISE

Then the tortoise went to the chief and asked for the name. He had it repeated more than once, to make sure, and then set out on his slow and cautious journey.

> He travelled a great distance and then said, "*Uẁungelema.*" Again he reached the outskirts of the village, again he said, "*Uẁungelema.*" Then he arrived in the village and reached his house and had a smoke. When he had finished smoking, the people arrived and said, " What is it, Tortoise ? " Mr Tortoise went out and said, "*Uẁungelema!*" The fruit pelted down. The people just covered the place, all the animals picking up. They sat down again : in the morning they said, " Go to Mr Tortoise." And Mr Tortoise came out and said, "*Uẁungelema!*" Again numberless fruits pelted down. Then they began praising Mr Tortoise, saying, " Mr Tortoise is chief, because he knows the name of these fruits."

This happened again and again, till the fruit came to an end, and the animals dispersed, to seek subsistence elsewhere.

So in the Benga country the grateful beasts proclaimed Kudu, the tortoise, as their second chief, the python, Mbama, having been their sole ruler hitherto. " We shall have two kings, Kudu and Mbama, each at his end of the country. For the one, with his wisdom, told what was fit to be eaten, and the other, with his skill, brought the news."

The Luba Version [1]

This has an entirely different opening. The animals, discussing who was to be their chief, decided to settle the point by seeing who could throw a lump of earth across the river. One after another tried, but their missiles all fell short, till it came to the turn of the little ' gazelle ' (*kabuluku*), who was thereupon unanimously elected.[2]

Some time after this the animals, wearied out with hunting,

---

[1] De Clercq, "Vingt-deux Contes," No. 9.

[2] Sir Harry Johnston said that there are no true gazelles in the Congo region, unless in the far north. I do not know the proper designation of the *kabuluku*, translated ' gazelle ' by P. De Clercq ; it may possibly be the water chevrotain, *Dorcatherium*. The Luba country is on the upper reaches of the Kasai.

came across a tree bearing large fruits, of which they did not know the name. They sent the elephant to *Mvidi Mukulu*, the High God, who told him it was *Mpumpunya-mampumpu*, but he must never look behind him on the way back or he would be sure to forget it. He did look behind him, and had to confess his failure, at which the animals were greatly annoyed, and told him he was no good. (In the original *udi chintuntu*, which P. De Clercq translates: " *Tu es un homme méprisable!* ")

Then the buffalo was sent, but did no better; then all the other animals, except the gazelle, and they also failed.

The gazelle kept her instructions in mind, never looked back, and returned successfully with the name. The ovation with which they received her is described by saying that " they all stood up, and the gazelle skipped about on their backs "—one supposes that they carried her in triumph.

Some Further Variations

The Bena Kanioka version, while beginning in much the same way, ends very differently. After the various animals have failed in their quest the tortoise comes to Maweza, who tells him the name of the tree and gives him a little bell, saying, " If you forget the name the bell will put you in mind of it." (It is not said why none of the other animals had been thus favoured.) The tortoise did, in fact, forget the name on the way, but the bell, ringing in his ear, recalled it to him. He reached the tree in safety, and told the name to the animals, who joyfully climbed the tree and ate the fruit, but refused to give him a share of it. When they had eaten their fill they killed him. But the little ants took his body away, and sang:

> " Knead the sand and mould the clay
> Till he comes whom God has made."

It is not explained who this person is or how he appeared, but the ants handed over the dead tortoise to him, and he restored him to life. The animals killed him again, smash-
284

A ZULU PLAYING UPON THE UMQANGALA

Photo A. M. Duggan-Cronin. By permission of the McGregor Museum, Kimberley

ing his shell to pieces;[1] the ants put the pieces together, and he again revived. As soon as he had regained his strength he uprooted the tree, with all the animals in its branches, and they perished in its fall.

The Pedi version, which is, I think, mixed with a hare story, contains one or two points not found elsewhere: the old woman, when telling the name (which, by the by, has not been asked for: they only say, " May we eat of this tree? "), adds, " You may eat, but leave the great branch of the chief's kraal alone! " (Elsewhere one gathers that this is the topmost branch of the tree.) The tortoise, deprived of his share in the fruit and shut up in a hut (a variant says buried by order of the chief), gets out during the night and eats all the fruit off the forbidden bough. Before returning to his prison he disposes the kernels about the body of the sleeping elephant. This and the sequel, with which we need not concern ourselves, do not, as already pointed out, belong to the tortoise.

Another incidental touch is that the tortoise—no doubt as an aid to memory—kept playing on his *umqangala* while crooning over his message to himself—strangely enough, if he is correctly reported, not the old woman's words, but the following song:

> " They say they bumped
> On the way back.
> There is an obstacle in the way."

The nature of the obstacle is not specified, but what appears to be the same story (told to Jacottet by a girl at Morija[2]) mentions an ant-hill. In this story the lion is said to be the chief of the animals who sends the messengers to Koko, and then goes himself. Angered that so insignificant a creature as the tortoise should have succeeded where he failed he has a pit dug, and orders the tortoise to be

---

[1] A point of contact with numerous stories which profess to explain the formation of the tortoise's shell. See, *e.g.*, *ante*, p. 255.

[2] *Contes populaires*, p. 42. Probably from North Transvaal. None of the Basuto seemed to be acquainted with it. Jacottet obtained another version from a Transvaal native, but this appears to be very imperfect.

buried in it. The tortoise burrows his way out in the night, eats the fruit on the top branch, and returns to the hole. The animals, of course, when questioned, deny all knowledge of the theft. The tortoise is then dug up, and asks, " How could I have eaten the fruit when you had buried me so well? "

This ends the story.

The name of the fruit is in every case different; usually it seems to be a nonsense-word (or perhaps an old forgotten one), of which no one knows the meaning. But in Pedi it is *Matlatladiane*, which the aged guardian of the tree explains to mean: " He will come presently." It is not stated who will come—perhaps the successful messenger.

In some stories in which children escape from an ogre it is the tortoise who saves them by swallowing and afterwards producing them uninjured. The Ronga version [1] of this tale, however, makes the deliverer a frog.

How the Leopard got his Spots

Another incident showing the tortoise in a kindly aspect comes from the Tumbuka,[2] in Northern Nyasaland. The hyena, for no apparent reason beyond ingrained ill-nature, put the tortoise up into the fork of a tree, where he could not get down. A leopard passed by and saw him: " Do you also climb trees, Tortoise? " " The hyena is the person who put me there, and now I can't get down if I try." The leopard remarked, " Hyena is a bad lot," and took the tortoise out of the tree.

We are not told what the leopard looked like at this time, but he would seem to have been ' self-coloured,' for the tortoise, offering out of gratitude for his rescue to " make him beautiful," did so by painting him with spots, saying, as he worked, " Where your neighbour is all right, be you also all right [*makora*]." The leopard, when he went off, met a zebra, who admired him so much that he wanted to know " who had made him beautiful," and himself went to

---

[1] " L'Homme-au-Grand-Coutelas "; see *ante*, p. 221.
[2] Cullen Young, *Tumbuka-Kamanga Peoples*, p. 229.

the tortoise. In this way he got his stripes. This "Just-so" story accounts not only for the markings of the leopard and the zebra, but for their being creatures of the wild, for when the people, hoeing their gardens, saw them they exclaimed, " Oh, the big beauty ! Catch it and let us domesticate it ! " or words to that effect, so both of them fled into the bush, where they have remained ever since. The hyena too met with his deserts, as follows.

" The zebra met a hyena, who asked, 'Who beautified you?' He said, 'It was the tortoise.' So the hyena said, 'Let him beautify me too,' and went away to the tortoise with the words, 'Make me beautiful!' 'Come,' said the tortoise, and began [the work], saying, 'Where your neighbour is a bad lot [*uhene*], be you too a bad lot!' and then said, 'Go to the place where the people are hoeing.' But at the sight 'That's an evil thing!' said they. 'Kill! kill! kill!' And the hyena turned tail and fled, dashing into the bushes, *kweche!* and saying, 'I will smash him to-day where I find the little beast! Previously I only stuck him up in a tree-fork.' And he burst out upon the spot, but found no sign of the tortoise, who had gone down a hole."

The old man who told the story added this moral for the benefit of the young : " So nowadays they laugh at a hyena in the villages. You see that one evil follows upon another."

The Great Tortoise of the Zulus

The Zulus have a rather vague tradition about a Great Tortoise (*Ufudu olukulu*), who has nothing to do with our friend of the adventures related above, but seems to be a mythical being, possibly akin to the kraken, who may not, after all, be entirely mythical. Perhaps it is not out of place, when mentioning the kraken, to relate, in passing, the experience—whether we take it as fact or as folklore— of an East African native who had served as a fireman on British ships in many waters. Somewhere between Australia and New Zealand the steamer's anchor-chain was seized by a giant octopus (*pweza:* "The *pweza* is an evil person," [1] say the Swahili). The body of the creature was out of sight, but the tentacle which held the chain was—so Ali declared—the width of the table at which we were seated—say, three to four feet. The ship's company stabbed the tentacle with a boathook till it let go, and the *pweza* sank and was seen no more. Otherwise, one was given to understand, the vessel would have gone down with all on board.

As to the Great Tortoise, Umpondo Kambule told Bishop Callaway [2] that it had taken his grandmother as she, with her three daughters, was crossing the river Umtshezi. It was " as big as the skin of an ox "—not merely " as an ox," being equal to the diameter of the spread-out skin. At any rate, it was big enough to dam up the current: " the river filled, because it had obstructed the water." The three younger women crossed in safety: the grandmother lost her footing, was seized by the tortoise, and dragged into deep water. Her children—the rest of them hastened to the spot on the alarm being given—just caught sight of her as she was raised for a moment above the surface; then she sank, and was never seen again.

The monster seemingly came out sometimes to sun itself, and on one occasion was seen by some herd-boys, who took it for a rock and played about on it, not heeding the warning of a little brother, who declared that " this rock has eyes." Nothing happened that time, but on another day the tortoise turned over with the boys who were on it and drowned them.

The Fatal Magic of the Waters

In another aspect this Great Tortoise recalls the European nixies, who entice people into the depths of rivers and pools. This is explained by Umpengula Mbanda as follows:

It is said there is a beast in the water which can seize the shadow of a man; when he looks into the water, it takes his shadow; the

---

[1] *Mtu (muntu)* properly speaking means a human being, but one often hears animals referred to as *watu*. " There are bad people in the sea," said Muhamadi Kijuma of Lamu, meaning, no doubt, sharks and such.
[2] *Nursery Tales*, p. 339.

A Luba wearing Charms
Photo Rev. W. F. P. Burton

man no longer wishes to turn back, but has a great wish to enter the pool; it seems to him that there is not death in the water; it is as if he were going to real happiness[1] where there is no harm; and he dies through being eaten by the beast, which was not seen at first, but is seen when it catches hold of him. . . . And people are forbidden to lean over and look into a dark pool, it being feared that their shadow should be taken away.[2]

This is given by way of comment on a story told by the bishop's other informant, about a boy who threw a stone into a pool (it is not said that he looked at his reflection, but this must surely be understood), and, on going home, refused his food and could not be kept from returning to the place. His father followed him, but was only in time to see the boy's head in the middle of the pool, though he did not actually sink till after sunset. Just as he disappeared he cried out, " I am held by the foot." His father, who had been forcibly restrained from throwing himself into the pool, had offered a reward to anyone who should save his son; but it seems to have been accepted as a fact that nothing could be done: " the child is already dead." And after he had sunk they said, " He has been devoured by the tortoise."

The rivers of Africa, not to mention lakes and pools, merit a chapter to themselves, which cannot here be given. The subject has scarcely been touched: we have only a few scattered hints from Zulu and Xosa sources. There is Tikoloshe,[3] or Hili, the water-sprite, who comes out to make unlawful love to women, and Isitshakamana, who scares fishermen to death, and when on land ' hirsels ' about in a sitting position (though provided with legs), like Kitunusi of the Pokomo.

Some of the stories (*e.g.*, that of Tangalimlibo, included

---

[1] *Du stiegst hinunter wie du bist,*
Und würdest erst gesund !

GOETHE, *Der Fischer*

[2] Callaway, *Nursery Tales*, p. 342.

[3] Or Tokolotshe. I have never heard what this being looks like, beyond the fact that a Natal Zulu, on my showing him the picture of a chimpanzee in Lydekker's *Natural History*, exclaimed, unexpectedly, "Tokolotshe !"

in several collections) describe cattle being driven into a river in the hope of saving the drowning, by inducing the water-spirits to accept life for life.[1] And it is said that the Umsunduzi (which rises in the Natal Table Mountain—Umkambati—near Pietermaritzburg) claims a human life every year—like the Tweed (the Till takes three and the Lancashire Ribble one every seventh year)—unless some other living creature is sacrificed. But this is to digress too far from our subject.

[1] See Theal, *People of Africa*, p. 192.

CHAPTER XIX: STORIES OF SOME OTHER ANIMALS

THE stories about the more important animals, the lion, the elephant, the antelopes, and the hyena, usually introduce the hare as the principal character; the rhinoceros, the hippopotamus, the python, and the zebra are less often found in conjunction with him. This chapter will contain a few in which he does not figure.

The first is that of " The Horned Animals and the Hyena." A great beer-drinking was arranged, to which no animals were admitted but those having horns. Every kind of horned beast assembled at the meeting-place in the forest, and the feast went on for many days. The hyena heard of it, and wished to take part, but knew, of course, that he was disqualified. He did not, however, lose heart, but wandered about till he came across a dead buck of some kind. He detached its horns, and then searched for a deserted bees' nest, where he found a sufficient quantity of wax to stick the horns on his head. Thereupon he made his way to the meeting-place, and joined the revellers without exciting remark.

The feast had gone on all night, and the hyena arrived in the early morning, so for a time all went well. But as the sun grew hot the wax began to melt. As he felt the horns getting loose he held them on with his hands, calling on all the other animals to do the same: " Quickly! quickly! because some of us have horns which come off! " The stupid hyena seems to have thought that some of the others might be in like case with himself, and that he might escape detection along with them. But the animals were not to be taken in; they saw through the trick (which, indeed, soon became impossible to carry on): they cried, " He is cheating us," and drove him away in disgrace.[1]

Curiously enough, in at least three variants (Ila, Lamba, and Nsenga) this exploit is credited to the hare; but it seems to me to fit the hyena much better. The Ila story,

[1] Told in Swahili by C. Velten, *Märchen und Erzählungen*, p. 2.

however, has one or two additional touches which it is a pity to lose. The hare was accompanied by the ground hornbill (any sort of horn was allowed to count), who sat near the door (this beer-drinking took place under cover), while the hare imprudently (and quite out of character) chose a place near the fire. When the wax began to melt the hornbill indiscreetly (or maliciously?) announced the fact, but the guests could not hear what he said, and asked the hare, who answered, " Hornbill is asking for the sediment of the beer." But he could not keep up the deception when the hot wax ran down his face, and the story ends as above.

A story from Tete[1] containing a similar incident is not a parallel : the invitation is issued to " all creatures wearing fur or feathers," and the hare assumes a pair of horns only as a disguise, the host being his deadly enemy, the lion.

Brother Wolf and the Horned Cattle

Uncle Remus,[2] I am sure, is much nearer the true tradition, though, to be precise, the story in question is not related by him, but by Aunt Tempy. It is too delicious to be paraphrased in its entirety : some of it, at any rate, must be given in her own words.

" Hit come 'bout one time dat all de creeturs what got hawns tuck a notion dat dey got ter meet terge'er an have a confab ter see how dey gwine take keer deyself, kaze dem t'er creeturs what got tush an claw, dey wuz des a-snatchin' um fum roun' every cornder."

Accordingly, they held a meeting in the woods.

" Ole Brer Wolf, he tuck'n year 'bout de muster, an he sech a smarty dat nothin' aint gwine do but he mus' go an see what dey doin'. . . . He went out in de timber an cut 'im two crooked sticks an tie um on his head an start off ter whar de hawn creeturs meet at."

When challenged by Mr Bull he announced himself as

[1] Tete is on the Zambezi ; the language spoken there is a form of Nyanja.
[2] *Nights*, No. LXII. This is followed by the incident of the wolf feigning death and being exposed by Brer Rabbit.

292

"little sucking calf," and, though Bull was somewhat suspicious, he got in. After a while, forgetting himself, he snapped at a horse-fly, and Brer Rabbit, hiding in the bushes, burst out laughing.

"Brer Bull, he tuck'n holler out, he did:
"'Who dat laughin' an showin' der manners?'
"Nobody aint make no answer, an terreckerly Brer Rabbit holler out:

> 'O kittle-cattle, kittle-cattle, whar yo' eyes?
> Whoever see a Sook Calf snappin' at flies?'"

The assembled animals did not know what to make of this voice from the unseen, and presently another slip on the part of Mr Wolf caused Brer Rabbit to exclaim:

> "Scritchum-scratchum, lawsy, my laws!
> Look at dat Sook Calf scratchin' wid claws!"

He gave the unfortunate intruder no rest, and when at last he burst out with

> "One an one never kin make six;
> Sticks aint hawns an hawns aint sticks"

Brer Wolf turned to flee, and none too soon, for Mr Bull charged him, and would have "natally tore him in two" if he had not "des scooted away from dar."

The Wart-hog's Wife comes to the Rescue

A lion story, in which the hare does not figure, is based on the same general idea as that of the man whose wife was caught in his trap and claimed as his share by the lion. In this story the case is decided by a different animal, and the details are so divergent that it seems quite worth while to reproduce it here.[1]

A lion, while hunting, got caught by the leg in the noose of a spring-trap.[2] The more he struggled the more tightly,

---

[1] Doke, *Lamba Folklore*, p. 99. The wart-hog is *ngidi* in Lamba, *njiri* in Nyanja.

[2] In the original *mwando*, which means 'a rope'; the particular kind of trap meant appears to be called *ichinsala*. A rope, with a noose at the end, is laid along the path and carefully covered up; this is connected with a strong, flexible pole, of which one end is planted firmly in the ground and the other bent over. An animal stepping on the noose releases the pole, and the jerk tightens the cord round its foot.

of course, he was held, and so he remained for some days, till quite famished and like to die. Then, as it befell, there passed by a wart-hog—that strangely ugly beast, so grotesque in his ugliness that he might well be called "jist bonnie wi' ill-fauredness." He was accompanied by his wife and his numerous family, the children trotting behind him in single file along the path. As they were searching for food they came upon the trap, and saw the lion fast in it, a mere bag of bones. He called out, "My dear Mr Wart-hog [*Mwe ŵame Ŵangidi*], loose me, your friend! I'm in trouble! I'm dying!" The good-natured wart-hog loosened the rope and freed the lion, saying, "All right. Let us be off!" As they were going away the lion happened to turn round, and, catching sight of the procession of little pigs, said, "Friend Wart-hog, what a crowd of children are yours! Do give me one of your children to eat! See how thin I have got with hunger!" The wart-hog answered, "Would you eat a child of mine? And it was I who loosed you to save you!" The lion still insisted, but now the wart-hog's wife interposed, saying—while at the same time conveying some private hint to her husband—"Listen, husband. We have loosed a wild beast on us, and he is demanding one of our children. There is nothing for it but to give way." So they ostensibly gave way (literally, "were weak towards him"), and promised that he should have one when they arrived "where we are going." But "first let us return to that thing that caught you and see what it is like." The lion agreed, and they went back to the trap. They asked, "How did it catch you? Where was it?" and the lion answered, "It was like this. Just take hold of it and bend it down." The couple did so, and, holding the end of the pole close to the ground, asked, "But how did it catch you in this way, sir?" The lion, as always, absurdly confiding, put his foot in, the wart-hogs let go, and he was caught once more. The family scattered in all directions, the lion piteously calling after them, "O my dear Wart-hog, are you going? Won't you undo me?" The parents hardened their hearts, and called back, "No! We, your friends, loosed you, and

294

then you begged a child of us ! You are a beast : stay where you are, and free yourself as best you can ! "

So he had to stay there in torment till he died. And consequently there is enmity between lions and wart-hogs to this day. " If they meet," says the narrator, " Mr Lion at once eats Mr Wart-hog." Yet one fancies in such a case the latter would be quite able to give a good account of himself.

The Wart-hog and the Elephant

The Baila make out a relationship between the wart-hog and the elephant, grounding it on the fact that both have tusks which are white (though differing in size) and " hair which is alike "—a less obvious resemblance. But originally, it would seem, the wart-hog had the large tusks and the elephant the small ones. The two were supposed to be uncle and nephew, and at one time had a serious quarrel, because, as the wart-hog said to his relative, " One day you said you would destroy things for me "—to supply him with food, no doubt—" but you broke your word." However, they made it up, the elephant's real motive being his desire to get hold of the wart-hog's tusks. He began by admiring them, and then proposed that they should exchange for a short time, so that he could show himself creditably turned out at a dance.[1] He promised to return them on a certain day ; but that day came and passed, and the wart-hog waited in vain. At last he went to look for the elephant, and demanded his tusks, only to be told that the exchange was a permanent one, and not a temporary loan. Finding his expostulations all in vain, he said, " From to-day I am going to sleep in a burrow ; as for you, you shall travel about the whole day and go far ; we shall not be friends again, because you have deceived me so." He then went to consult the ant-bear, feeling so unclothed and disreputable without his great tusks that there was nothing for it but to take refuge underground. The ant-bear

[1] This is not expressly stated in the text (Smith and Dale, *The Ila-speaking Peoples*, vol. ii, p. 365), but must be assumed as the reason for ' dressing up.'

received him hospitably, and therefore, to this day, "Ant-bear's custom is to dig burrows, and Wart-hog enters one and sleeps. When he has had enough of one he looks out for another. On his arrival he enters the burrow dug by Ant-bear."

The exchange of tusks in this "Just-so" story recalls one told by the Swahili to account for the fact that the snake has no legs and the millepede (popularly supposed to be blind) an excessive number. The snake borrowed the mille-pede's eyes, so that he could look on at a wedding dance, and lent his legs in return; but he afterwards refused to restore the eyes to their owner, and has kept them ever since.

The Varanus in the Tree

The monitor lizard [1] has already been met with in a tortoise story, but also occurs in other connexions—for instance, in the story of Hlakanyana, whose whistle is borrowed—and kept—by an *uxamu*,[2] and also in a good many tales from Nyasaland.

One of these is very curious, and seems to be widely distributed. I follow, in the main, a Swahili version, contributed by Mateo Vundala bin Tendwa to *Mambo Leo*[3] for January 1927. I have seen at least two others in manu-script (Nyanja), and Mr Cullen Young gives a Tumbuka one in the work from which I have already quoted.[4]

Once upon a time there was a man who had a beautiful daughter and looked after her very carefully. One day there arrived a young man who wanted to marry her; her father did not refuse, but told him to wait five days and come back on the sixth. When he returned at the appointed time he was told: "Go away and come again to-morrow."

---

[1] Nyanja *ng'anzi*, Tumbuka *kaŵaŵa*, Swahili *kenge*, Zulu *uxamu*. I am not certain whether the Nyanja *gondwa* is the same or another species.

[2] See *ante*, p. 164.

[3] The Swahili monthly, published at Dar-es-Salaam. It is unfortunate that the writer gives no indication as to the part of Tanganyika Territory where the story was obtained. It is entitled "The Story of a Man and a Youth and a Kenge."

[4] *Tumbuka-Kamanga Peoples*, p. 217.

Next morning the girl went to the well [1] with her water-jar as usual, and when she got there saw a *kenge* drinking. As soon as it saw her it darted off and ran up a tree. She stood gazing at it for some time, never having seen such a creature before, and then filled her jar and hastened home, calling out to her father on arriving, " Father, I've seen a beast with a long tail which ran away up a tree!" He answered, " Let us go, so that I can look at it." They went together, and he recognized it at once, but it had gone up to the topmost branches, where no human climber could reach it. The father reflected for a while, and then made up his mind that when the young wooer came back he would say to him, " If you want to marry my daughter you must go and catch that *kenge* on the top of the tree."

It is not stated why he wanted it caught, but it seems, from other sources, that it is considered good eating—at any rate, by some people. The chief in the Tumbuka version of the story " was extremely fond of eating the flesh of the monitor lizard in preference to all other meats."

The young man was somewhat startled by this declaration, but only asked to be shown the tree. When he had looked at it he was filled with despair, and went away sorrowful.

When he reached the village the girl's father asked him, " Well, have you brought the *kenge*?" He answered, " I am beaten as to climbing that tree!" The father said to him, " Well, then, you cannot marry my daughter." So the young man started for his own village " full of grief."

When he arrived he found some men sitting in the *baraza*, and one ancient asked him, " Is it all settled about your wedding?" The young man answered, " Much trouble over there! Much trouble over there!" " What sort of trouble is there yonder?" asked the old man. The youth told his story, and the old man called him aside and gave him this advice: " Go and get hold of a goat; also

---

[1] *Kisima* does not necessarily mean a well in the sense of a deep pit into which buckets have to be lowered, but may be a water-hole or reservoir where animals can drink at the edge.

catch a dog; then take a bowl of porridge and a bundle of grass and go back. When you get to the foot of the tree tie up the goat on one side and the dog on the other; then give the porridge to the goat and the grass to the dog and sit down, and you will see the *kenge* come down at once."

He did as the old man had told him, and went back to the tree. Having tied up the goat and the dog as directed, he sought out the girl's father and told him that he was going to try again. The man said, " You were beaten the first time; the second time you will succeed, so go on and try again ! "

The young man went once more to the tree, and held out the porridge to the goat and the grass to the dog. No sooner had he done so than he heard a laugh up in the tree, and the lizard spoke with a human voice, " Young man, you have no sense ! How is it you are giving porridge to the goat and grass to the dog ? " The young man answered, " Come down and show me the right way ! Please do come down and show me the right way ! " Then the *kenge* came down, and the young man at once seized it and ran off to the village, and the people, when they caught sight of him, even before he arrived, raised cries of rejoicing. And the girl's father hurried out to meet him and carried off his *kenge* in triumph. The wedding took place on the same day, and, of course, " they lived happy ever after."

It may be of interest to give, in Mr Cullen Young's translation, the conclusion of the Tumbuka story. In this after the lizard had called out to the young man he paid no heed, but did the same as before. Then :

> The monitor said, " Oh ! what a fool that so-called human is ! Goodness me ! Take the porridge and give it to the dog, and take the grass and give it to the goat. Listen, can't you ? and keep your ears open ! " But still porridge to the goat and grass to the dog. Down came the lizard. " I tell you, take the porridge and give it to the dog ! take the grass and give it to the goat, and you'll see they'll eat ! Stand back and watch me ! " Then, while the lizard was stretching out its arm to take the porridge-basket, the young fellow snatched his axe and hit the

lizard on the head twice and killed it. When he had killed it, he went with it into the presence of the chief, where . . . he marvelled, saying, " You are a lad of parts, young fellow ! That beast defeated a lot of people with their plans." And then he began to summon all his people and said, " It is he who is second in the chiefship; anyone making light of him as good as makes light of me."

Mateo Vundala does not say what was done with the *kenge* which the young man brought in alive. I have never heard of their being kept as pets.

The incident of " porridge for the goat and grass for the dog " is found in a Lamba story (Doke, *Lamba Folklore*, p. 151: " The Chief and his Councillors "), the opening of which is nearly identical with that of the Tumbuka " The Children and their Parents" (Cullen Young, *The Tumbuka-Kamanga Peoples*, p. 243). All the young men of a certain tribe were ordered by the chief to kill their parents, but one disobeyed and hid his father and mother in a cave. The land was ravaged by an ogre who swallowed people and then retreated to an inaccessible chasm. When this had gone on for some time the chief called the young men together and, as no one had anything helpful to suggest, said, " Friends, who has his father here, that he may give me advice?" They answered, " No, sir, we have none, because you said, ' All of you bring your fathers and let us kill them.' " But at last the youth who had saved his parents brought forward his father ; and the old man enticed the ogre out of his lair in the way already described. The monster was immediately killed by the people, who then, following the directions of the Kawandami lizard, got out of him those already swallowed. In the Tumbuka story the rescued parents help the chief in another kind of difficulty.

It is somewhat remarkable that the same number of *Mambo Leo* in which Mateo's story appears contains a report of what purports to be an actual occurrence, sent in by a correspondent from the Kilwa district. This man states that on October 23, 1926, he went to wash some

clothes in the river, and was warned by two boys whom he
met " to be careful in spreading out washing there, because
there is a large lizard which carries off people's clothes."
He did not believe them, and, having finished his work and
spread the things out to dry, went to bathe, when he heard
a rustling in the grass, and was startled to see a *kenge*
making off with one of the sheets just washed. His shouts
brought some men to his help, and by throwing stones at
the reptile they induced it to drop the sheet.

Whether this be taken as fact or as fiction, it is at any
rate sufficiently curious.

Frogs and Snakes

Frogs of various kinds abound in Africa, from the large
bullfrog, whose voice is so often heard in the land, to the
little *shinana*,[1] which figures conspicuously in the folklore
of the Baronga. It rivals the hare in astuteness; in fact,
some of its exploits are those elsewhere attributed to him,
and in one Ronga version of the well story it is the *shinana*,
and not the tortoise, who traps the hare at last. Wonderful
to relate, it is this same little frog who rescues the girls
enticed by the honey-guide into the ogre's hut, in the story
already alluded to.[2]

In a Lamba tale the great water-snake (*funkwe*) is said to
have changed himself into a man and married a woman
from a certain village. In accordance with the usual
custom, he settled there and worked in the gardens, but he
would never eat porridge. He would go to the river in the
early morning, and there, unseen by the people, assume his
proper form and feed on fish. After some time he told his
wife that he wished to go home, and they set out, accompanied by her brother. On the second day they reached
an enclosure which he said was his home. The wife was
surprised to see no people about, and asked where were his
relations. Though he had previously said that they were

---

[1] *Breviceps mossambicus*, called *kaswenene* at Blantyre. It is not much larger
than a shilling, but can blow itself out to twice the size.
[2] See *ante*, pp. 221 and 286.

"farther on," he now merely remarked, "No, I am left alone." He departed, saying he would go to the river and fetch water, and when out of sight changed into a water-snake and ate fish and frogs as usual, returning at night. This happened every day, and at last the brother grew suspicious, followed him to the river, and found out the truth. He came back and told his sister, and she said, "At night you kill him!" which he did by heating a knife red-hot in the fire and cutting off the snake-man's head.

Then they saw multitudes of snakes, and the snakes said, "Let us kill these people." Mr Black-mamba refused, saying, "No, first let the chief come." All the time many snakes kept coming.

During this interval a frog arrived, and asked the man and woman, "If I save you, what will you give me?" They answered, "We are your slaves!" Then he swallowed them, and immediately after took a great drink of water. The snakes did not see him do it, but presently missed the people and asked where they were. The frog said, "They have gone to drink water," and set off for their village. On the way he met many snakes, who noticed that he seemed unusually corpulent, and asked, "What are you filled with?" He said, "Water that I have just drunk." They were suspicious, however, and would not be satisfied till he had brought up some water to prove the truth of his words. This happened more than once, but he reached his destination in safety, and the people exclaimed, "What a huge frog!" He said, "I am not a frog; I am a man.[1] Did not some people leave here?" Explanations followed, and the woman's mother began to cry. The frog said, "If I bring your children, what will you give me?" She offered him slaves, but he said he did not want them. "What do you want, then?" "I want beans." So they gave him two granaries full. And,

---

[1] This is not a usual touch. More commonly animals are simply taken for granted as being what they appear to be. But the man transformed by witchcraft into the shape of a beast (usually a snake) appears in several Zulu stories, and is disenchanted (like Tamlane) by fearless true love.

making a great effort, he produced the brother and sister safe and sound.[1]

The Frog and his Wife

Another story about a frog, heard in Nyasaland, was at first extremely puzzling; but with the help of parallel versions it becomes quite coherent.

A frog who had some difficulty in finding a wife at last carved the trunk of a tree into the shape of a woman, and fixed a *mpande* shell[2] in the place where her heart should be. This, we are to understand, brought her to life; he then married her. Her name was Njali, and she was very beautiful. They lived happily enough in his hut in the depths of the forest, till one day in his absence some of the chief's men happened to pass by and saw her sitting outside. They asked for fire and water, which she gave them, and on their return told the chief about her. He shortly afterwards sent the men back to the same place, and they, finding the husband again absent, carried her off. She cried out, " Mother! I am being taken away! " but there was none to hear, and when the husband came back he found her gone.

Here the tale, as I took it down, becomes difficult to follow, and there is evidently a gap, but the variants (in some ways hard to reconcile with this and with each other) suggest that he made ineffectual efforts to get her back. When these had failed he sent a pigeon, and told her to bring back the *mpande* shell, but she could not get it. He sent the pigeon again, and this time she brought it back; but as soon as it was taken out the wife died and was

[1] Doke, *Lamba Folklore*, p. 247. The Mpongwe tortoise (Nassau, *Where Animals Talk*, p. 33) swallows his wife and servants to save them from the leopard, and eats some mushrooms after them.

[2] A disk cut from the base of a particular kind of white spiral shell. It is highly valued by many tribes, and in some is the emblem of chieftainship, or (as among the Pokomo) the badge worn by the highest order of elders. Father Torrend, who gives the Mukuni (Lenje) version of this story, says " he put a *cowry* on the head of his block of wood," but the word in his original text is *mpande*. See a note by Major Orde-Browne in the *Journal of the African Society* for April 1930, p. 285.

A POKOMO FISHERMAN

Photo Alice Werner

changed back to a block of wood. In Father Torrend's version [1] the husband takes the shell off her head, and

> she is already transformed into a simple block of wood, no, she has become but a bush standing at the door. . . . Then the little husband comes home humming his own tune, while the king and those who had seized the woman remain there with their shame.

Late Developments of this Story

Both this and a Swahili version recorded by Velten [2] make the husband a human being—indeed, the Swahili title is " The Carpenter and the Amulet." Father Torrend comments in a note: " Another version, in which the hero is a hare, has been published by Jacottet in 'Textes Louyi,' pp. 8–11. The substitution of a hare for a man seems hardly to improve the story." But it appears to me that the learned writer has entirely missed the point in supposing that the hare has been substituted for the man. Surely both hare and frog belong to the more primitive form.

The Luyi variant is interesting, but, as we have already had sufficient hare stories, I have preferred the frog for this chapter. The Lenje and Swahili ones, not being in any sense animal stories, are hardly in place here; but it may be noted that the Lenje husband, instead of sending the pigeon, carves himself some drums and goes about beating them and singing, till he finds the place where his wife is detained. Both here and in the Nyanja version it seems to be implied that in the end (though at first carried off against her will) she was unwilling to come back to him.

The Bird Messengers

Among birds introduced into folk-tales the cock, the fish-eagle, the guinea-fowl, and doves or pigeons are perhaps the most frequently mentioned, apart from the unnamed birds which reveal the secret of a murder. A favourite incident is the sending of birds with messages, as the pigeon was sent by the frog in the story just given. It will be remembered that Murile, when about to return home from

---

[1] *Bantu Folklore*, p. 44.   [2] *Märchen und Erzählungen*, p. 149.

the Moon country, sent the mocking-bird to announce his coming, after questioning several other birds and finding their replies unsatisfactory.[1]

Gutmann [2] gives the same story with less detail, mentioning of birds only the eagle (whose cry of *Kurui! Kurui!* is nearly the same as that attributed in Raum's version to the raven), the raven (who here says *Na! Na!*), and the mocking-bird, though " all the birds " are said to have been called upon. The mocking-bird's note is rendered as *Chirī! Chirī!* which she amplifies into a song of ten or twelve lines.

So, too, Mlilua, in the Iramba [3] story, called the birds. " Crow, if I send you to my mother's, what will you say? " "*Gwe! Gwe!* " The crow was rejected. None of the birds he called up pleased him, till at last came one known as the *shunta*. " If I send you home, what will you go and say? " " We shall say, *Chetu! Chetu!* I have seen Mlilua and his cattle."

La Sagesse des Petits

It will have been noticed how important is the part assigned in these stories to small and insignificant creatures, such as the hare, the tortoise, the frog, the chameleon,[4] mice, and others. I do not think this fact is fully accounted for by McCall Theal,[5] who writes :

> There was nothing that led to elevation of thought in any of these stories, though one idea, that might easily be mistaken on a first view for a good one, pervaded many of them : the superiority of brain power to physical force. But on looking deeper the brain power was always interpreted as low cunning : it was wiliness, not greatness of mind, that won in the strife against the stupid strong.

To my mind, it is nearer the mark to say that much of African folklore is inspired by sympathy with the underdog,

---

[1] *Ante*, p. 74.   [2] *Volksbuch*, p. 155.

[3] Johnson, *Kiniramba*, p. 343.

[4] The chameleon, quite apart from the legend related in Chapter II, often plays a part resembling that of the hare. The Pokomo, for instance, tell how he beat the dog in a race, by holding on to his tail and getting carried to the goal.

[5] *People of Africa*, p. 275.

STORIES OF OTHER ANIMALS

arising from a true, if crude and confused, feeling that
" the weak things of the world " have been chosen " to
confound the things which are mighty."

M. Junod expresses much the same thought : [1]

> Why does this theme of the triumph of wisdom over strength
> reappear so frequently and under so many aspects in this popu-
> lar literature ? Doubtless because the thought is natural and
> eminently satisfying to the mind of man.

It is also brought out very fully in the chapter of his
earlier work which is entitled " La Sagesse des Petits."

The Shrew-mouse helps the Man

The idea is well illustrated by a little story from the
northern part of Nyasaland,[2] which may fitly conclude this
chapter. Incidentally, it shows a curious coincidence of
thought between primitive Africa and rural England, in
the belief that a shrew must die if it crosses a road.

A Namwanga man one day went hunting with his dogs,
and came upon a shrew (*umulumba*) by the roadside. It
said to him, " Master, help me across this swollen stream "
(*i.e.*, the path, which for him was just as impassable). He
refused, and was going on, but the little creature entreated
him again : " Do help me across this swollen stream, and
I will help you across yours." The man turned back,
picked it up, and carried it across, " very reluctantly."
(Why? Is there a feeling against touching a shrew, as
Africans certainly shrink from touching a chameleon or
some kinds of lizards ?) It then disappeared from his sight,
and he went on with his dogs and killed some guinea-fowl.
Then, as it came on to rain, he took refuge in one of the
little watch-huts put up in the gardens for those whose
business it is to drive away monkeys by day and wild pigs
by night. The shrew, which had followed him unseen,
was hidden in the thatch.

Presently a lion came along, and thus addressed the

---

[1] *Life of a South African Tribe*, vol. ii, p. 223 ; *Chants et contes*, p. 143.
[2] *Chinamwanga Stories*, p. 19.

hunter: " Give your guinea-fowl to the dogs, let them eat them, you eat the dogs, and then I'll eat you ! "

The man was terrified, and could neither speak nor move. The lion roared out the same words a second time. Then came a little voice out of the thatch.

" Just so. Give the guinea-fowl to the dogs, let them eat them, you eat the dogs, the lion will eat you, and I'll eat the lion."

The lion ran away without looking behind him.

The Lamba have a somewhat similar story, in which the hunter is saved from two ogres by a lizard in the wall of the house and the white ants. They seem to have acted out of pure good-nature, as there is no hint of his having rendered them a service.[1]

[1] Doke, *Lamba Folklore*, p. 143: " The Story of the Man, the Lizard, and the Termites." Compare, outside the Bantu area, the story of the caterpillar who frightened away all the animals except the frog, who in the end "called his bluff" (Hollis, *The Masai*, p. 184).

CHAPTER XX: SOME STORIES WHICH HAVE TRAVELLED

I HAVE, more than once, in previous chapters expressed my inability to accept in its entirety what is known as the Diffusionist hypothesis. I see no reason to suppose that the stories about the hare, for instance, were imported from India, even though some of them are almost exactly the same as those told of Mahdeo and the jackal, or that the tribes of the Amazon valley borrowed their tales of the Jabuti tortoise and his wiles from the imported Negroes.

But this is not to say that there are no stories which can be traced as having been introduced from outside, and we may conclude with a few of the most interesting specimens. Those chosen for the purpose must have come in long ago, so long as to have taken on a distinctly African colouring, even more thoroughly than Uncle Remus's stories have become American. I am leaving out of account such recent introductions as Æsop's fables, which circulate extensively in vernacular translations, or stories manifestly taken from Grimm or similar European collections. In a manuscript collection written by a Nyanja native I found not long ago, among a great deal of genuine local folklore, " The Story of the King's Daughter and the Frog," which the writer must have read or heard, probably in English. Again, in *Kibaraka* we find " The Story of Siyalela and her Sisters," which the compiler either failed to recognize as Cinderella, or thought sufficiently naturalized to pass muster with the rest. Contributors to *Mambo Leo* have even begun translating " Uncle Remus " into Swahili, and, though he is, in a way, only coming back to the country of his origin, there may be a danger of confusing these tales with the genuine local growth. In any case, considering the spread of reading and the circulation of extraneous matter, it behoves all interested in folklore to rescue the aboriginal stories as far as possible before it is too late.

From Assam to Nyasaland

In Captain Rattray's little book [1] " The Blind Man and the Hunchback " at once strikes one as having a distinctive character of its own; in fact, when I first read it I could recall no African parallel.   Since then I find in Mr Posselt's *Fables of the Veld* (p. 6) a version—to my mind not nearly so good—entitled " The Man and his Blind Brother." And, more recently, it is included in the manuscript collection of Walters Saukila.

Many years after the publication of Captain Rattray's book I was surprised by coming across the identical story in volume xxxi of *Folk-Lore* (1920), with, of course, considerable differences of local colouring.   It was told to J. D. Anderson by a Kachari in Assam.   This is such a far cry from Central Angoniland, where the people were, at the beginning of this century, comparatively untouched by European influence, that there might seem to be difficulties in the way of supposing this to be a case of transference.   But, though I have so far been unable to hear of an Indian or Persian analogue, it may be orally current among those populations of India whose folklore is as yet but imperfectly recorded.   Indian traders have frequented the East African coast from very early times,[2] and a tale like this, told to the coast-dwellers and speedily becoming popular, would be passed on from tribe to tribe along with the trade-goods which in this way reached the far interior.   The differences between the Kachari and the Nyanja versions are sufficient to show that it must have been a long time on the way.

The Nyanja version begins by saying that a certain village was plagued by a pair of man-eating lions (this passage is entirely wanting in the other), and the chief, by the advice of his people, opened negotiations with them: " Why are you seizing people every day?"   The lions answered, " We say, if you give us your two daughters whom you love we will not come again to seize people."   So the chief took his two daughters and built a grass hut for them on the hill where the lions were wont to show themselves.

<hr>

[1] *Chinyanja Folklore*, p. 149.   [2] See Ingrams, *Zanzibar*, p. 33.

Now, in another country there were two men, one was blind and the other humpbacked, and they set out for this chief's village. On the way the hunchback saw a tortoise on the path, and told the blind man, who said, "Pick it up." He refused, but his companion said, "Just pick it up for me," and he did so, and the blind man put it into his bag. A little farther on they came to a dead porcupine, and the blind man asked his friend to pick up one quill, which, again, he did, after refusing at first. Some time later they came upon a dead elephant, and the man who had shot it was also lying dead, with his gun beside him. The blind man, again with some difficulty, persuaded the other to pick up the gun and one tusk, and they went on their way.

When it was growing dark they climbed a hill, and the hunchback saw smoke rising from a hut on the top. They went up to it, and, finding two girls there, said that, as they had been overtaken by night, they wanted a place to sleep in. The girls said, "You cannot sleep here; our father has built this house for us, so that the lions may come and eat us." But they would not listen, and said, "This is where we are going to sleep." While they were still speaking the lions arrived; they heard them roaring, and one of the lions asked, "Who is talking in the house? Whoever you are, we are going to eat you along with the rest."

The blind man said, "You can't eat us; we are only strangers seeking shelter for the night." The lion said, "I am going to throw one of my lice at you, and see if that won't frighten you!" The girls and the hunchback fainted with terror, but the blind man kept his head, and when the lion threw his louse he groped about till he caught it, and said, "That tiny little thing! Look at that now! I'm going to throw it into the fire!" And he did so, and it burst with a loud crack. Then he said, "Now I'm going to throw my louse," and he threw the tortoise. The lion picked it up and looked at it in astonishment, but, not to be beaten, he said, "I am not afraid of you. I shall throw you one of my hairs," and he pulled one from his mane and threw it. The blind man retaliated by throwing the

309

porcupine's quill. Then the lion threw one of his teeth, and the blind man answered with the elephant's tusk, whereat the lion was so startled that he jumped and said, "Ha! Truly this person has a terrible tooth!" But he was not prepared to give in. "Now I am going to let you hear my voice," and he gave a tremendous roar. And the blind man, who had been loading his gun and getting it into position, said, "Let another of you roar, that I may hear his voice also." The other lion having done so, he said, "I have heard you. Now come close that you may hear mine." When they had done so: "Where are you?" "We are here." "Stick your heads close together." And he fired and killed them both. When the echo had died away he asked, "Have you heard my voice?" but all was silence, and he set to work to revive his companions. They would not believe his news, but he persuaded them to open the door, and they went out and found the lion and lioness both dead.

When morning dawned the grateful girls picked up their two deliverers and carried them on their backs to their father's village. When he saw them he was very angry with them for deserting their post and, as he supposed, endangering the whole village; but they soon placated him: "These men have killed those wild beasts." He was incredulous, but they swore most solemnly that it was true, and he sent some young men to see. These soon found the lions and cut off their tails. When they came back with the trophies the chief asked the people, "Now, as to these men who have killed the lions, what shall we do for them?" They replied that he ought to give them his daughters in marriage, which he did on the spot, and showed them where to build their village. He also gave them six *mpande* shells, to be divided equally between them. But the hunchback tried to cheat his friend, saying they had received only five, and giving him two. In the resulting quarrel the hunchback hit the blind man over the eyes, and the blind man struck him with a stick. And, behold! the one recovered his sight and the other was able to stand up straight. So they were reconciled.

310

In the Kachari story the men pass the night in a granary, used by a gang of robbers as a storehouse for their plunder; and, instead of the lions, a " terrible, man-eating demon " comes after them, and is scared away much after the manner described. Mr Posselt's version omits the girls; the brothers take shelter in a cave which is the lions' den, and the quarrel takes place over the sale of the lions' skins.

The Washerman's Donkey and the Pardoner's Tale

The Buddhist *Jâtakas*, which, I understand, are really folk-tales fitted into a religious framework by being represented as the adventures of the Buddha in his various incarnations, might appear to be quite remote from our theme; but some of them, in one form or another, have certainly reached the African coast. One of the best known among these is " The Washerman's Donkey,"[1] which is really the *Sumsumara Jâtaka*, and is also found in the Sanskrit collection of stories called *Panchatantra*, under the title of " The Monkey and the Porpoise." The Swahili title is only indirectly applicable to the story, or, rather, belongs to a story within the story, told by the monkey to the shark; " The Monkey who left his Heart in a Tree " describes it much better.

Another *Jâtaka* (the *Vedabbha*) has had the strangest fortunes, finally coming down to us in the shape of Chaucer's " Pardoner's Tale." It was probably brought back from the East by some returned pilgrim or crusading soldier, and embodied in that queer compilation the *Gesta Romanorum*. The Swahili version, entitled " The Heaps of Gold,"[2] would seem to have come through Persia, perhaps subjected to Christian influence on the way. This, however, is doubtful, as Moslem literature abounds in elements taken from the Apocryphal Gospels or the floating traditions which furnished the materials for these.

The story opens by saying that Christ (here called Isa, as always by Moslems) while on a journey was joined by a

[1] Steere, *Swahili Tales*, p. 1.   [2] *Kibaraka*, p. 89.

man, who, though not encouraged to do so, insisted on accompanying him.[1] When they were approaching a town Isa gave the man some money and told him to buy three loaves, " one for thee, one for me, and the third we will keep in reserve." He did so, and they sat down to rest. When they had eaten, each his loaf, they went on, the man carrying the third loaf. When they had gone some distance, thinking himself unobserved, he ate it. Next day they came to a spring and sat down there. When asked to produce the loaf the man said it had been stolen. Isa said nothing at the time, and they went on. They walked till they were both weary, and sat down to rest in a place where there was much sand. Isa made three heaps of sand, and at his prayer they were changed into gold. Then he said, " Friend, take one of these heaps to thyself, one is for me, and the third is for him who stole the loaf." The man, forgetting all else in his greed, exclaimed, " It was I who stole the loaf—I who am here ! " The Master told him to take them all, and left him there.

The wretched man could neither carry the gold nor bring himself to leave it, so remained on the spot till three horsemen came by, who, seeing the treasure, stopped and murdered him. Two of them stayed to guard it, while the third rode on to the town to buy provisions. On the way it occurred to him that he might have the gold all to himself, so he poisoned the wine which he meant to give the other two. This part of the story is so well known that it is scarcely necessary to add that the two killed him on his return, and shortly died of the poison. " So all these four men died, because of that sand which had been changed into gold."

Not long afterwards Christ passed that way with his disciples, and they marvelled at seeing the heaps of gold and the four dead men. Then he told them the story, and said, " This is not gold, but sand," and at their request he prayed to God, and what had been gold then became sand once more.

[1] This opening does not come into the " Pardoner's Tale."

STORIES WHICH HAVE TRAVELLED

The Ingratitude of Man

Another story in the *Gesta Romanorum*, which must originally have come from India, is extant in at least three Swahili versions, all of which have the same moral, equivalent to the Latin of the *Gesta* : *Quod omnium viventium in mundo de beneficiis acceptis est ingratissimus homo :* " Of all things living in the world man is the most ungrateful for benefits received."

This story should be well known to all students of Swahili, as it is contained in the elementary reader generally used (a selection reprinted from *Kibaraka*). This version, though much shorter than that given by Dr Velten,[1] contains several important points omitted by the latter. The following is an attempt to combine the two.

A king's son who wished to see the world set out alone on his travels. In course of time he found himself in a vast desert, in the midst of which he spied one solitary tree, to which, when he had reached it, he tied his horse, leaving his weapons on the ground beside it. Not far off was a well, and, being very thirsty, he hastened to let down the bucket which he found there. On drawing it up he saw that, instead of being filled with water, it contained a snake. He was about to kill it, but it said, " Don't kill me ; some day I may be able to help you." So he spared it, and let down the bucket again, drawing it up with difficulty, as it was very heavy. When he got it to the top he found in it a lion, who addressed him in the same way as the snake, and both added this warning : " Never do good to any child of Adam : the son of Adam, if you do good to him, will only repay you evil." Then they thanked him and took themselves off.

The youth let down the bucket a third time, and brought up a man, who, so far from behaving like the snake and the lion, knocked him down, tied him up with the well-rope, took his weapons, and rode off on his horse. The lion, however, who had not gone far, came back and released him. He took him along to his den, and provided him

[1] *Märchen und Erzählungen,* p. 144.

313

with food by lying up near the path to a village and, when he saw a man passing with a load of rice or beans, frightening him, so that he dropped it.

One day the lion ventured as far as the town, and, seeing the sultan's daughter walking in the garden attended by her slaves, sprang over the fence and seized her. The slave-girls scattered in terror, and the lion brought the princess back to the young man, saying, " Take her jewels, but give me the girl, that I may eat her." He answered, " If you want to give me anything give me the girl as well." So he took her for his wife, and built a hut for her in the forest, and they lived there happily for a time. One day the snake appeared, and handed the young man two of his teeth, saying, " If ever you get into trouble take a stone and beat these teeth with it, and I will come to you at once."

Now the man who had been rescued from the well had come to this very town and, by making himself very agreeable, had so got into favour with the sultan that, in the end, he became his vizier. And it happened on a day that, going out with a hunting-party, he was separated from the rest of the company, and, wandering by himself in the forest, came to the little hut, where he saw the sultan's daughter. At once he hastened back to the town to give the alarm; soldiers were sent out, and the couple were speedily brought before the sultan. Then the vizier came forward, accused the young man, not only of carrying off the princess, but of turning himself into a lion in order to do so, and advised his being shut up in a dungeon without food or room to lie down, so that he might be induced to disclose his secret arts.

This was done, but he did not quite starve, for a compassionate slave-woman fed him secretly with scraps of bread. And then he suddenly remembered the snake's teeth, and beat them with a stone. The snake appeared at once, and told him, " To-day when the sultan goes to bathe I shall bite him, and nothing can cure him except these teeth of mine." So he went and coiled himself on the ledge of the tank in the palace bathroom, and when the sultan took up the ladle to pour the water over his head struck him on the lip, and he fell down. All possible remedies were tried, but to no purpose, till at last an old woman came forward who said she had heard that the only man who knew of a cure was the one chained in the prison. He was sent for, and ground the snake's teeth to powder, which was applied to the snake-bite and soon effected a cure. The sultan made inquiries, heard the whole story, and ordered the treacherous vizier to be sewn up in a sack and cast into the sea. His daughter's wedding was celebrated in proper fashion, and the pair lived happily to the end of their days.

This clearly belongs to the " Grateful Beasts " class of stories, of which numerous examples, variations on this and other themes, are well known in Europe. The third Swahili version must be derived from the same original as the other two, but varies so considerably that this is not at first sight obvious. An ape is introduced as well as the lion and the snake, and a poor youth finds them, not in a well, but in the traps which he has set to catch game. There are other important differences, which, however, need not detain us.

Part of this—the providing of the only effectual remedy by a despised stranger—is to be found in a Persian story: "The Colt Qéytās," [1] but this is much nearer to "Kibaraka," the tale which gives its title to the collection already mentioned more than once.

The Composite Tale of Kibaraka

This is made up of various elements. The opening I have not so far traced. The sultan's son and the vizier's son, born on the same day, go for a walk together, and the former treacherously forsakes his companion, who loses his way and wanders about till he comes to a house inhabited by a *zimwi*. This being receives him kindly, to all appearance, but soon departs to call his friends to a cannibal feast. Here comes in the well-known *motif* of the Forbidden

[1] D. L. R. and E. O. Lorimer, *Persian Tales*, pp. 38–42.

Chamber.[1] The *zimwi* tells him he may go into every room but one. In the fifth, which is the forbidden one, he finds a gigantic horse, who speaks and tells him the true character of his host. The horse himself is being kept only till fat enough ; then he and every other living thing in the house will be eaten by the ogre and his friends, who are due to arrive in two days' time. He directs the youth to let out all the animals shut up in the various apartments (a lion, a leopard, a donkey, and an ox) and to take out of a great chest seven bottles—containing the obstacles of the well-known " Magic Flight." The horse then swallows all the animals and a quantity of the ogre's treasure, directs the youth to saddle and mount him, and they escape in the usual way, throwing down the seven bottles, one after another, to produce thorns, fire, sea, and so on. This part comes into far too many stories to be repeated here ; the flight, with much the same obstacles, is found, for instance, in the Persian " Orange and Citron Princess." [2]

They then build a house in the forest (one must understand that the horse produces it by magical means, but this is not stated in the Swahili), and Kibaraka ("Little Blessing" —this appears to be a name assumed for the occasion, though it has not hitherto been mentioned) strolls into the town, by the horse's advice, in the guise of a beggar. Here, one day, proclamation is made that the sultan is going to arrange the weddings of his seven daughters. All the people are ordered to assemble, and each girl is to throw a lime at the man of her choice. The eldest manages to hit the Grand Vizier's son, to the general satisfaction. Then the rest make their choice among the young nobles, up to the sixth ; but the youngest aims her lime at the beggar-lad and hits him. This incident and similar ones are found in Persian and other stories—for instance, in " The Colt

---

[1] See *The Folk-lore Journal*, vol. iii (1885), pp. 193–242. The incident is found in several Swahili stories, in very different settings : *e.g.*, " Hasseebu Kareem ed Din " and " The Spirit and the Sultan's Son," in Steere (*Swahili Tales*, pp. 353 and 379), and " Sultani Zuwera," in *Kibaraka*, p. 5.

[2] D. L. R. and E. O. Lorimer, *Persian Tales*, p. 135.

Qéytās," of which the beginning is quite different. The conclusion of this is much the same as the end of "Kibaraka," with minor variations : the sultan is ill, and can only be cured, in one case by the flesh of a certain bird, in the other by leopard's milk. The six sons-in-law try in vain to procure the remedy : the seventh, who has been despised and kept at a distance, succeeds. For a time he allows the others to take the credit, on condition of letting him brand them as his slaves. But Kibaraka has previously, in disguise (or, rather, in his own proper form and riding on the magic horse), distinguished himself in battle and routed the sultan's enemies. This does not appear in the Persian tale, though it does elsewhere. Whatever the origin of this story, the hero's words when he finally reveals himself show whence it passed to the Swahili coast: " I am not Kibaraka : I am Hamed, the son of the Wazir in the land of Basra "— the last thirteen words being Arabic.

Parts of this story seem to have spread wherever the Arabs have carried their language and their traditions. The lime-throwing incident occurs both in Somali and in Fulfulde (the language of the Fulani, in West Africa). The Somali story of " Lame Habiyu " begins like " The Colt Qéytās," and goes on very much as " Kibaraka."

The Merry Jests of Abu Nuwâs

There was, in the reign of Harun-er-Rashid (765–809), a certain poet at Bagdad, named Abu Nuwâs, whose work is highly praised by the best judges (it has been translated into German, if not into English), and whose name, twisted in various ways, is known up and down the Swahili coast— but not for his poems. Whether or not any of the stories told of him are true, his legend has attracted to itself all the jests and practical jokes current before or during his time, or invented since. He has got mixed up with the hare, one of whose names in Swahili is Kibanawasi, which might be punningly turned into Kibwana wasi, " Little Master of Shifts." He is always being set impossible tasks by the caliph (sometimes Harun is mentioned by name), and always cleverly turns the tables on him. When told to build a house in the air he sends up a kite hung with little bells (" Don't you hear the carpenters at work? "), and then calls on the caliph to send up stones and lime, which, of course, he is unable to do. Some of his exploits have reached Delagoa Bay, where M. Junod, misled by the local colouring they had acquired by that time, concluded that " Bonawasi " was a corruption of the Portuguese Bonifacio. One of the most popular, here as elsewhere (it has been heard from Egyptian story-tellers), is the order to the whole population to produce eggs, by which it is hoped to entrap Abu Nuwâs. The charming illustration on p. 298 of *Chants et contes des Baronga* shows the Governor of Mozambique presiding at the performance in full uniform.

The Portuguese, who at one time made their name so much dreaded on the coast (even now " Proud as a Portuguese " and " Violent as a Portuguese " are current sayings in Pate), are represented as being pitiably duped by Abu Nuwâs. He burned his house down, loaded a ship with sacks full of the ashes, and put to sea. Meeting seven Portuguese vessels loaded with silver, he pretended that he was taking a cargo of treasure as a present to his sultan, and was so ostentatiously reluctant to part with it that they determined to buy it, and finally did so for a shipload of silver. Abu Nuwâs returned with this, and went to the sultan, asking him for some men, to unload his cargo of silver. This, of course, led to inquiries, which caused the sultan to burn down the whole town and load a fleet with the ashes. Result : a collision with the Portuguese at sea, in which ships were sunk and many of the sultan's men killed. Abu Nuwâs was sought for, but escaped as usual, and played further pranks in a fresh place.

The Three Words

There seem to be endless variations of the story in which a man received three pieces of advice from his father, or spent all the money left him by his father on three pieces of advice from a wise man. These are, in one case : " If you

318

see a thing do not speak of it; if you speak of it something [unpleasant] will happen to you."[1] Secondly, "If the sun sets while you are on the road stay where you are till you can see where you are going." Thirdly, "If a friendly person hails you in passing never refuse to stop." Or, as sometimes found, if called three times you must turn aside, having returned a civil answer to the first and second summons. Other pieces of advice are: "Never tell a secret to a woman"; "A man does not betray one who trusts him"; "What is in your purse is your possession; what is in the field or in the box is no use to you." Some of these, in shortened form, are current as well-known proverbs and are frequently quoted.

The second of those enumerated above enables the hero to escape from robbers, while his companions, who insist on pressing on after dark, are attacked and murdered. The third saves him from a treacherous plot: he is sent by an enemy with a message intended to ensure his murder, but delays on the road when asked to stop—in one case by an old friend of his father's. This incident, or one very like it, is found in the *Gesta Romanorum*, as well as in some old French *fabliaux*, and was made use of by Schiller for his ballad *Der Gang nach dem Eisenhammer*. It also occurs, out of its proper setting, in a Swahili story called "The Judge and the Boy,"[2] where it is combined with parts of several other stories, imperfectly told.

There is a Persian story,[3] "The Man who bought Three Pieces of Advice," where the "three words" are of a somewhat different character, and the hero—or, rather, his wife—comes to grief through disregarding the third, though they are enabled to escape from their troubles by following the second. These counsels are:

"Don't go out when there are clouds in the sky in winter-time."

---

[1] This is much neater in the original, owing to the fact that *neno* means both 'word' and 'something,' 'anything.' Literally, "If you see something don't say anything ; if you say anything something will get you."

[2] *Kibaraka*, p. 35 : "Kadhi na Mtoto."

[3] D. L. R. and E. O. Lorimer, *Persian Tales*, p. 269.

. " Whenever you see a pigeon, a hound, and a cat for sale, buy them, whatever the price, and keep them with you and take good care of them."

" Never tell to anyone the advice you have got, and never let an outside woman enter your house."

In the old Cornish folk-tale " John of Chyanorth " [1] the three pieces of advice (or, in the original, " points of wit ") are : " Take care that thou dost not leave the old road for the new road "; " Take care that thou dost not lodge in a house where may be an old man married to a young woman "; " Be thou struck twice ere strike once "—or, as it stands in another part of the text, " Be advised twice ere strike once."

The Magic Mirror, the Magic Carpet, and the Elixir of Life

Another story imported from the East—whether from Arabia, Persia, or India I am unable to say—is that published by M. Junod [2] under the title of " Les Trois Vaisseaux." It is found in the most unexpected places, even on the Congo and the Ivory Coast, though some of these Western versions may be of independent origin. Three brothers go on a trading expedition, and acquire a magic mirror, a magic carpet (usually described as a mat or basket), and a medicine for restoring the dead to life. These enable them to see the young woman with whom all three are in love dying, if not already dead, to reach her before she is buried, and to administer the medicine. The question now arises : who has done the most towards saving her and shall consequently marry her? It is variously decided. Sometimes, as in the Congo version,[3] the narrator stops short at this point, and leaves the decision to the audience.

Portuguese Influence

Some of the stories in Chatelain's *Folk-tales of Angola* must certainly have come from Portugal, while others are

---

[1] See J. Morton Nance, *Cornish for All* (Lanham, St Ives, n.d.), pp. 38–48. I am indebted to Mr Henry Jenner, of Bospowes, Hayle, for directing my attention to this book.

[2] *Chants et contes*, p. 304.　　　[3] Dennett, *Folk-Lore of the Fjort*, No. III.

The 'Temple,' Zimbabwe

unmistakably of African growth, the latter being by far the more numerous. An interesting case of importation is the story of Fenda Madia [1]—one of the " False Bride " class. She sets out to disenchant Fele Milanda (Felix Miranda) by weeping twelve jugs full of tears, but is cheated when just in sight of success by a slave-girl, who takes her place and marries him. Here, too, a part is played by a magic mirror—a distinctly non-African element. The story is current both in Portugal and in Italy, but in all probability originated farther east. Parts of it resemble the latter portion of the Persian "Orange and Citron Princess." [2]

A magic mirror—which might as well be a ring or any other object, since its function is not to reveal what is happening at a distance, but to procure for the possessor whatever he wishes—figures in a story collected by Father Torrend at Quilimane.[3] Here the African and European elements are curiously mixed. A childless couple are told by a diviner to eat a pair of small fish ; in due course they have a son, who, when grown, goes to cut wood in the forest. He befriends a python in difficulties, and is rewarded by the gift of a mirror which gives him everything he wants, and enables him to marry the governor's daughter.

M. Junod [4] describes "La Fille du Roi" as a Portuguese story. It was told him by a Ronga woman, who had heard it from some young persons of her own tribe employed by Europeans in the town of Lourenço Marques. The first part is much the same as Grimm's " The Shoes that were danced to Pieces," except that there is only one princess, instead of twelve, and the place where she goes to dance is called " Satan's house." The rest of the story is quite unlike anything in Grimm, neither is it distinctively African. I have, so far, been unable to trace this part.

In conclusion I may mention, in passing, the curious fact that a story substantially the same as that of *The Merchant of Venice* was written out for me in Swahili by a native

---

[1] *Folk-tales of Angola*, pp. 29 and 43.   [2] See *ante*, p. 316.
[3] Seidel, in *Zeitschrift für afrikanische und ozeanische Sprachen*, vol. i, p. 247.
[4] *Chants et contes*, p. 317.

teacher at Ngao, who said he had heard it from an Indian at Kipini. The Indian, he supposed, " had got it out of some book of his." He may, of course, have read Shakespeare's play, or seen it acted, but it is quite possible that he had derived it from his own country. The story is found in the *Gesta Romanorum*, and can therefore, in all probability, be traced to an Oriental source.

It is sometimes said that " all the stories have been told " —also that there are only about a dozen plots in the whole world. But the old stories are perpetually fresh to the new generations who have not yet heard them, and the dozen plots—if that is the number—are susceptible of such infinite variation that neither the novelist nor the collector of folk-tales need be unduly discouraged.

The more fully the subject is studied the more clearly will it appear that the folklore of Bantu-speaking Africans is not inferior in variety and interest to that of Asia, Polynesia, or America—if differing from them in character.

There is much that still remains to be known, and of what has already been recorded I have been forced to leave a large amount untouched. I trust the specimens here given will be sufficient to show that the notion of Africa as a continent without history, poetry, or mythology worthy of the name is wholly erroneous.

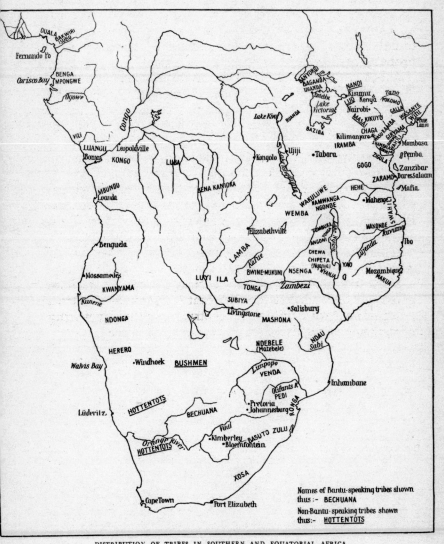

DISTRIBUTION OF TRIBES IN SOUTHERN AND EQUATORIAL AFRICA

BIBLIOGRAPHY

ABDALLAH BIN HEMED BIN ALI LIAJJEMI : *Habari ya Wakilindi* (*History of the Wakilindi*) (U.M.C.A. Press, Magila, 1895 and 1904).

ARNOUX, P.: In *Anthropos* (St Gabriel-Mödling, Vienna, 1912, 1913).

BARNES, REV. H. B., and BULLEY, M. W.: *Nyanja-English Vocabulary* (Sheldon Press, 1929).

BASKERVILLE, MRS GEORGE: *The King of the Snakes and other Folklore Stories from Uganda* (Sheldon Press, 1922).

BITTREMIEUX, LEO: *Mayombsch Idioticon* (2 vols.; Drukkerij Erasmus, Ghent, 1922).

BLEEK, W. H. I.: *A Comparative Grammar of South African Languages* (Trübner, 1862).

—— *Reynard the Fox in South Africa; or, Hottentot Fables and Tales.* Chiefly translated from original manuscripts in the library of His Excellency Sir George Grey, K.C.B. (Trübner, 1864). (Includes one or two Bantu stories.)

BRYANT, REV. A. T.: *A Zulu-English Dictionary* (Mariannhill Mission Press, Natal, 1905).

—— *Olden Times in Natal and Zululand: containing Earlier Political History of the Eastern Nguni Clans* (Longmans, 1929).

BÜTTNER, C. G.: *Anthologie der Suaheli-Litteratur* (Felber, Berlin, 1894).

CALLAWAY, HENRY: *The Religious System of the Amazulu* (Trübner, 1870; reissued by the Folk-Lore Society, 1885).

—— *Nursery Tales and Traditions of the Zulus* (Trübner, 1868).

CASALIS, EUGÈNE : *Les Bassoutos* (Meyrueis, Paris, 1859).

CHATELAIN, HÉLI: *Folk-tales of Angola* (Boston and New York; published for the American Folk-Lore Society by G. E. Stechert, 1894).

CLOUSTON, W. A.: *Popular Tales and Fictions, their Migrations and Transformations* (2 vols.; Blackwood, 1887).

COLENSO, J. W.: *Zulu-English Dictionary* (fourth authorized edition, revised and enlarged, Vause, Slatter, Pietermaritzburg, 1905).

CRASTER, J. E. E.: *Pemba, the Spice Island of Zanzibar* (Fisher Unwin, 1913).

CRIPPS, REV. A. S.: *Chaminuka* (" Little Books for Africa," No. 15) (Sheldon Press, 1928).

CRONISE, F. M., and WARD, H. W.: *Cunnie Rabbit, Mr Spider and the other Beef : West African Folk Tales* (Swan Sonnenschein, 1903).

DANNHOLZ, J. J.: *Im Banne des Geisterglaubens* (Verlag der evangelisch-lutherischen Mission, Leipzig, 1916).

DE CLERCQ, P.: " Vingt-deux Contes Luba," in *Zeitschrift für Kolonialsprachen*, vol. iv, p. 3 (Hamburg, 1914).

DENNETT, R. E.: *Notes on the Folk-lore of the Fjort* (French Congo) (Nutt, 1898).

—— *At the Back of the Black Man's Mind; or, Notes on the Kingly Office in West Africa* (Macmillan, 1906).

DEWAR, EMMELINE H.: *Chinamwanga Stories* (Livingstonia Mission Press, 1900).

DOKE, C. M.: *Lamba Folklore* (published for the American Folk-Lore Society by G. E. Stechert, 1927).

—— *The Lambas of Northern Rhodesia: A Study of their Customs and Beliefs* (Harrap, 1931).

DRIBERG, J. H.: "Yakañ," in *Journal of the Royal Anthropological Institute*, vol. lxi, 1931.

ELLENBERGER, D. F.: *History of the Basuto* (Caxton Publishing Co., 1912).

Folk-Lore Journal, vol. iii (Elliot Stock, 1885,) *Folk-Lore*, vol. xxxi (Glaisher, 1920) (quarterly journal of the Folk-Lore Society).

Folk-Lore Journal (South African Folk-Lore Society, Capetown, 1879–80).

FRASER, REV. DONALD: *Winning a Primitive People: Sixteen Years' Work among the Warlike Tribe of the Ngoni and the Senga and Tumbuka Peoples of Eastern Africa* (Seeley, Service, 1922).

FRAZER, SIR JAMES G.: *Folklore of the Old Testament* (Macmillan, 1918).

FÜLLEBORN, DR F.: *Das deutsche Njassa- und Ruwumagebiet, Land und Leute* (Reimer, Berlin, 1906).

GUTMANN, REV. DR BRUNO: *Dichten und Denken der Dschagganeger* (Verlag der evangelisch-lutherischen Mission, Leipzig, 1909).

—— *Volksbuch der Wadschagga* (Verlag der evangelisch-lutherischen Mission, Leipzig, 1914).

HARRIS, J. C.: *Uncle Remus; or, Mr Fox, Mr Rabbit, and Mr Terrapin* (Routledge, n.d.).

—— *Nights with Uncle Remus* (Routledge, n.d.).

HEWAT, DR M. L.: *Bantu Folklore* (*Medical and General*) (T. Maskew Miller, Capetown, n.d.).

HOBLEY, C. W.: *The Akamba* (Cambridge University Press, 1910).

—— *Bantu Beliefs and Magic* (Witherby, 1922).

HOFFMANN, REV. C.: In *Zeitschrift für Eingeborenensprachen*, vols. vi and xix (Hamburg, 1915–16 and 1930–31).

—— *Was der afrikanische Grossvater seinen Enkeln erzählt* (Berliner Missionsgesellschaft, 1912).

HOLLIS, A. C.: *The Masai: their Language and Folklore* (Oxford University Press, 1905).

—— *The Nandi: their Language and Folklore* (Oxford University Press, 1909).

HUREL, R. P.: *La Poésie chez les primitifs; ou, contes, fables, récits et proverbes du Rwanda* (*Lac Kivu*) (Goemaere, Brussels, 1922).

INGRAMS, W. H.: *Zanzibar, its History and its People* (Witherby, 1931).

JACOTTET, ÉMILE: *Études sur les langues du Haut Zambèze: ii Partie, "Textes Soubiya"; iii Partie, "Textes Louyi"* (Leroux, Paris, 1899 and 1901).

BIBLIOGRAPHY

JACOTTET, ÉMILE: *The Treasury of Ba-Suto Lore*, vol. i (no more published) (Kegan Paul, 1908). (Original Se-Suto texts, with a literal English translation and notes.)

—— *Contes populaires des Bassoutos* (Leroux, Paris, 1895).

JOHANSSEN, E.: *Ruanda: Kleine Anfänge—grosse Aufgaben der Evangelischen Mission im Zwischenseengebiet Deutsch-Ostafrikas* (Bethel Mission, Bielefeld, 1915).

JOHNSON, FREDERICK: "Notes on Kimakonde," in *Bulletin of the School of Oriental Studies*, vol. iii, pp. 1–32 (Luzac, 1923).

—— *Kiniramba Folk-tales: Bantu Studies*, vol. v, p. 327 (University of the Witwatersrand Press, 1931).

JUNOD, HENRI A.: *Chants et contes des Baronga* (Bridel, Lausanne, 1897).

—— *The Life of a South African Tribe* (2 vols.; 2nd ed., Macmillan, 1927).

Kibaraka: Swahili Stories (Universities Mission Press, Zanzibar, 1896).

KIDD, DUDLEY: *Savage Childhood* (Black, 1906).

—— *The Essential Kafir* (Black, 1904).

KLAMROTH, REV. M.: In *Zeitschrift für Kolonialsprachen* (Berlin and Hamburg, 1911).

LEONARD, A. G.: *The Lower Niger and its Tribes* (Macmillan, 1906).

LINDBLOM, GERHARD: *Kamba Tales of Animals* (Heffer, 1928).

LORIMER, D. L. R. and E. O.: *Persian Tales*. Written down for the first time in the original Kermānī and Bakhtiari, and translated (Macmillan, 1919).

MACDONALD, DUFF: *Africana; or, the Heart of Heathen Africa* (2 vols.; Simpkin Marshall, 1882).

MACKENZIE, REV. D. R.: *The Spirit-ridden Konde* (Seeley, Service, 1925).

Mambo Leo (monthly magazine in Swahili) (Government Press, Dar-es-Salaam).

MELLAND, F. H.: *In Witch-bound Africa* (Seeley, Service, 1923).

MELLAND, F. H., and CHOLMELEY, E. H.: *Through the Heart of Africa* (Constable, 1912).

MOFOLO, THOMAS: *Moeti oa Bochabela* (*The Traveller to the East*) (Morija Mission Press, 1912).

Nada (the Southern Rhodesia Native Affairs Department Annual) (1924).

NASSAU, R. H.: *Where Animals Talk: West African Folklore Tales* (Gorham Press, Boston, U.S.A., 1912).

—— *In an Elephant Corral, and other Tales of West African Experience* (Neale Publishing Company, New York, 1912).

NAUHAUS, K.: "Was sich die Konde in Deutsch-Ostafrika erzählen," in *Die evangelischen Missionen*, vol. v, p. 257 (Bertelsmann, Gütersloh, 1899).

ORDE-BROWNE, MAJOR G. ST J.: "An African Shell Ornament," in *Journal of the African Society*, April 1930, p. 285 (Macmillan).

POSSELT, F.: *Fables of the Veld*. With a foreword by Professor Carl Meinhof (Oxford University Press, 1929).

RATTRAY, R. S.: *Some Folklore Stories and Songs in Chinyanja* (S.P.C.K., 1907).

RAUM, REV. J.: *Versuch einer Grammatik der Dschagga-Sprache* (*Moschi-Dialekt*) (Reimer, Berlin, 1909).

REHSE, HERMANN: *Kiziba, Land und Leute* (Strecker und Schröder, Stuttgart, 1910).

ROSCOE, REV. J.: *The Baganda* (Macmillan, 1911).

—— *The Northern Bantu* (Cambridge University Press, 1915).

ROUTLEDGE, W. S. and K.: *With a Prehistoric People* (Edward Arnold, 1910).

SCHULTZE, L.: *Aus Namaland und Kalahari* (G. Fischer, Jena, 1907).

SCHUMANN, C.: "Grundriss einer Grammatik der Kondesprache," in *Mittheilungen des Seminars für orientalische Sprachen*, vol. ii, Part III (Spemann, Berlin, 1899).

SCOTT, D. C.: *Dictionary of the Mang'anja* [*Nyanja*] *Language spoken in British Central Africa* (Foreign Mission Committee of the Church of Scotland, 1892).

SEIDEL, A.: *Geschichten und Lieder der Afrikaner* (Schall und Grund, Berlin, 1896).

—— *Zeitschrift für afrikanische und ozeanische Sprachen*, vol. i (5 vols.; Reimer, Berlin, 1895).

SELOUS, F. C.: *A Hunter's Wanderings in Africa* (Rowland Ward, 1881).

—— *Travel and Adventure in South-east Africa* (Rowland Ward, 1893).

SMITH, REV. E. W., and DALE, A. M.: *The Ila-speaking Peoples of Northern Rhodesia* (2 vols.; Macmillan, 1920).

STEERE, EDWARD: *Swahili Tales* (S.P.C.K., 1871).

STOW, G. W.: *Native Races of South Africa* (Swan Sonnenschein, 1905).

TAYLOR, W. E.: *Giryama Vocabulary and Collections* (S.P.C.K., 1910).

THEAL, G. McCALL: *Kaffir Folklore* (Swan Sonnenschein, 1882).

—— *The Yellow and Dark-skinned People of Africa South of the Zambezi* (Swan Sonnenschein, 1910).

TORDAY, E., and JOYCE, T. A.: *Les Bushongo* (Publications of the Congo Museum, Brussels, 1911).

TORREND, J.: *Specimens of Bantu Folklore from Northern Rhodesia* (Kegan Paul, 1921).

TYLOR, E. B.: *Primitive Culture* (2 vols.; 6th ed., Murray, 1920).

VELTEN, C.: *Märchen und Erzählungen der Suaheli* (Spemann, Stuttgart and Berlin, 1898).

WOODWARD, H. W.: "Bondei Folk-tales," in *Folk-Lore*, vol. xxxvi (Glaisher, 1925).

WUNDT, W.: *Völkerpsychologie*, vol. v, Part II (2nd ed., Kröner, Leipzig, 1914).

YOUNG, REV. T. CULLEN: *Notes on the Customs and Folk-lore of the Tumbuka-Kamanga Peoples, in the Northern Province of Nyasaland* (Livingstonia Mission Press, 1932).

INDEX

INDEX

INDEX

INDEX